Scientific Basis of Air Conditioning

— Second Edition —

by

KEN-ICHI KIMURA

*Professor Emeritus of Architectural Science,
Waseda University, Tokyo, Japan*

INTERNATIONAL RESEARCH INSTITUTE ON HUMAN ENVIRONMENT
TOKOROZAWA, JAPAN

INTERNATIONAL RESEARCH INSTITUTE ON HUMAN ENVIRONMENT

ISBN: 978-4-9907042-3-0

Copyright © Ken-ichi Kimura

Permission is granted to copy, distribute and/or modify this document under the terms of the GNU Free Documentation License, Version 1.2 or any later version published by the Free Software Foundation; with no Invariant Sections, no Front-Cover Texts, and no Back-Cover Texts. A copy of the license is included in the section entitled "GNU Free Documentation License".

Preface to the second edition

This book was initially published by Applied Science Publishers, London in 1977 and ceased to be published in 1990s. As described in the Foreword to the Revised Edition written by Dr. S. Murakami, then Chief Executive of Building Research Institute (BRI), Japan, the revised edition with some modification in B5 size was used as the text for the international seminar under the sponsorship of Japan International Cooperation Agency (JAICA) held in 2008 – 2010. Owing to the courtesy of JAICA and BRI, this book has been open to the public domain thereafter. Several years later the contract between JACA and BRI was terminated. Then, since the entire copyright was kept by the author, another revision work was made as requested by international audience and the second edition has been determined to be published by International Research Institute on Human Environment, Tokorozawa, Japan.

The contents stay almost the same as the first edition, sticking to fundamentals in different subjects from solar radiation, various phases of heat transfer in buildings including heat from lights and stack effects to dynamic heat load calculation, simulation and computer control of air conditioning system. Although new trends have been attempted in these days, scientific basis would not change so much. Researchers and students in environmental science worldwide have used this book as a convenient reference for years. For practitioners when an unexperienced project comes in, they should not fail to refer to fundamentals for actual planning work in consultation of this book.

It would be a great pleasure for the author that this book would be used hereafter as well as in the past without being obsolete too much.

October 2016

      Ken-ichi Kimura
      Professor Emeritus, Waseda University, Tokyo, Japan
      Principal, International Research Institute on Human Environment, Tokorozawa, Japan

Foreword to the Revised Edition

This book was originally written by Professor Ken-ichi Kimura and published by Applied Science Publishers, London in 1977 as one of the Architectural Science Series edited by Late Professor Emeritus Henry J. Cowan, University of Sydney. Unfortunately the publisher decided to discontinue publication sometime in the 1990s and no more printing could not be envisaged ever since. According to the Agreement between Professor Kimura and Applied Science Publishers signed in 1974, the entire copyright of this book is now possessed by Professor Kimura.

In spite of such an unfortunate situation, revised publication of this book has long been requested worldwide by academic staffs and building scientists, as this book has been used for a long time as an advanced text book in various universities and colleges as well as practicing engineers and scientists all over the world. In fact the fundamental theories described in this book have never become obsolete.

Under such difficult circumstances, a new possibility of revival of this book has arisen. In 2009 Building Research Institute (BRI) initiated a new project of educating capable government officers of developing countries in Asia under the sponsorship of Japan International Cooperation Agency (JICA), a subsidiary organization of Ministry of International Trade and Industry. Two months course of seminar was projected for this purpose with a generous assistance by special authorities of architectural scientists. Then suitable text books written in English by Japanese scientists were sought for this course with the result that this book was selected.

As the original edition is out of print, it was decided to have the whole book electronically scanned for the seminar text. Dr. Takao Sawachi of BRI, project manager of this international seminar requested Professor Kimura to create a revised edition of this book on this occasion. Professor Kimura agreed with his proposal to have it published by BRI and worked in making some corrections, modifications and additions for this revised editions.

Without their valuable efforts this publication would not have been possible. It is hoped that this book will be widely in service again in the world for the effective use of energy in air conditioning as well as for the betterment of architectural environment in the future.

August 2010

                Shuzo Murakami
                Chief Executive, Building Research Institute,
                Tsukuba, Japan

Preface to the first edition

This book is written as an advanced text for graduate students in architectural science, building science, building engineering, architectural engineering and mechanical engineering, as well as a reference book for practising air conditioning engineers. It deals with the scientific nature of air conditioning, from the basic theories to the applied technology as it is generally accepted today. The purpose of air conditioning is to create comfortable conditions in the building environment. However, air conditioning ought to be blamed as it consumes an excessive amount of primary energy. It is therefore important to learn both the scientific basis of air conditioning and the principles of energy conservation to ensure that air conditioning is designed in the most efficient manner.

The performance of air conditioning depends on various parameters and it is related to many different aspects of science. For example, solar radiation incident on building surfaces and transmitted through windows has an important influence on the thermal environment of the occupied space, while the basic theories of solar radiation belong to physics and environmental science. Heat transfer is taught in the departments of mechanical engineering and chemical engineering; however, unsteady-state condition and non-linear heat transfer occur everywhere in a building and heat transfer in buildings entails somewhat different features from those governing heat transfer in mechanical systems. Heat conduction within the building structure, heat convection along the interior and exterior surfaces of building components, and radiation exchange between the surfaces of enclosed spaces may sometimes give rise to quite complicated problems.

In the past, teachers of air conditioning have had to collect the information applicable to air conditioning practice from different fields of science and no systematic theory seems to have been established in the realm of air conditioning. On the other hand, it is often claimed that architects do not understand environmental problems, such as air conditioning, and this is accounted for by the insufficient teaching of its scientific basis in architecture schools.

Looking at all the scientific aspects of air conditioning, it is quite difficult to organise them into a systematically routine course. The contents of this book are mainly focused on the thermal behavior of the environmental space. The first six chapters describe the basis for the heat load estimation of air conditioning, which is summarised in Chapter 7. Chapters 8 and 9 deal with engineering features and review the basic theories to be applied to engineering practice.

Part of this book is derived from a volume written by myself in Japanese entitled *Fundamental Theories of Building Services*, and I am obliged to the publisher for permission to reproduce these articles. The manuscript of this book is not a direct translation from the articles in Japanese and later developments in various research results are, of course, included.

After visiting Japan in 1972, Professor Henry J. Cowan suggested that I should write this book. Professor Cowan and his colleagues, Professor P. Smith and Dr Valerie Havyatt, were kind enough to review the first draft of the manuscript and to correct the English to a considerable extent. I would like to express my sincere thanks to them. I feel much indebted to Professor U. Inoue, Department of Architecture, Waseda University, for his advice and encouragement in writing this book and to Dr. D. G. Stephenson and Mr. G. P. Mitalas, Division of Building Research, National Research Council of Canada, for their kind guidance in the study, on which a considerable portion of this book is based, undertaken during my stay in Ottawa from 1967 to 1969. Without their valuable help this publication would not have been possible. Acknowledgements are also due to the ten graduate students in my laboratory at Waseda University for preparing the line drawings for the illustrations.

Mrach 1977

KEN-ICHI KIMURA
Waseda University, Japan

Contents

Preface ··· v

Introduction ·· 1

Chapter 1. Solar radiation ·· 4
    1.1. Solar constant and solar spectrum ··· 4
    1.2. Solar position ·· 8
    1.3. Direct solar radiation ··· 12
    1.4. Diffuse solar radiation ··· 14
    1.5. Breaking-down of global radiation into direct and diffuse
         components ··· 17
    1.6. Solar radiation on cloudy days ·· 20

Chapter 2. Unsteady State Heat Conduction through Walls and Slabs ··············· 25
    2.1. Fundamental equation of unsteady state heat conduction ···· 25
    2.2. Finite difference method ·· 27
    2.3. Periodic steady heat conduction ·· 30
    2.4. Indicial response ·· 35
    2.5. Impulse response and convolution ······································· 37
    2.6. Solution by Laplace transformation ····································· 40
    2.7. Matrix expression of surface temperature and surface heat flow ········ 44
    2.8. Response factors—definition and usage ····························· 47
    2.9. Derivation of response factors . ·· 50
    2.10. Practical application of response factors ···························· 56
    2.11. Z-transform ··· 57

Chapter 3. Radiative and Convective Heat Transfer in Buildings ····················· 61
    3.1. Film coefficient ··· 61
    3.2. Radiative heat transfer coefficient ······································· 63
    3.3. Convective heat transfer coefficient ···································· 66
    3.4. Radiation from the atmosphere ·· 68
    3.5. Heat balance at the Outside surface of buildings ················· 70
    3.6. Determination of the convective heat transfer coefficient of
         an outside surface of a building by field experiment ·········· 75
    3.7. Radiation and convection heat exchange inside the room ···· 81

Chapter 4. Solar Heat Gain from Windows ··· 85
    4.1. Absorption, reflection and transmission of solar radiation
         for sheet glass ··· 86
    4.2. Solar heat gain from glass windows of different orientation ··· 90
    4.3. Experimental determination of cooling load associated with
         solar heat gain ·· 93
    4.4. Cooling load weighting factors for solar heat gain ·············· 96
    4.5. Solar heat gain from windows with inside venetian binds ··· 102
    4.6. Experimental determination of thermal characteristics of

		venetian blinds ··· 107
	4.7.	Experimental determination of the effect of re-radiation from external shading ··· 112
	4.8.	Simplified calculation procedure of solar heat gain from glass windows with external shading using a weighting factor technique ··· 117

Chapter 5. *Effect on Air Conditioning of Heat from Lights* ································ 121
    5.1. Illumination level and heat generated by lights ······················ 121
    5.2. Integrated lighting-air conditioning system ··························· 125
    5.3. Experimental determination of heat removal efficiency of troffers with return air intake ·· 129
    5.4. Theory of cooling load caused by lights ································ 132
    5.5. Cooling load weighting factors for power input to lights ··········· 140

Chapter 6. *Infiltration and Exfiltration Caused by Wind and Stack Effects* ··············· 147
    6.1. Air leakage characteristics of openings and cracks ·················· 147
    6.2. Infiltration by wind ·· 149
    6.3. Principle of stack effect ··· 150
    6.4. Infiltration by stack effect ··· 152
    6.5. Combination of wind and stack effects ·································· 156

Chapter 7. *Heat Load of Air Conditioning* ·· 159
    7.1. Heat gain and cooling load ·· 159
    7.2. Components of space cooling load ·· 162
    7.3 Algorithm of calculating space cooling load ··························· 164
    7.4 Heat extraction and room air temperature variation ················ 169
    7.5 Preconditioning load and Preconditioning period ··················· 173

Chapter 8. *System Simulation of Air Conditioning* ·· 181
    8.1. System model of air conditioning ·· 182
    8.2. Simulation of dual duct system ·· 185
    8.3. An example of component simulation ··································· 190
    8.4. Part-load performance of air conditioning components ·········· 192
    8.5. Simulation of heat storage system ··· 196
    8.6. Simulation of heat recovery system ······································· 200
    8.7. Simulation of solar heat collector ·· 202
    8.8. Simulation of solar heating system ·· 205

Chapter 9. *Computer Control of Air Conditioning* ·· 209
    9.1. A system model for computer control of air conditioning ········ 209
    9.2. Method of optimisation in the control ··································· 211
    9.3. Control of start and stop of air conditioning components ········ 212
    9.4. Control of outside air intake ·· 213
    9.5. Prediction control ·· 215

References ··· 221
Index ·· 226

Introduction

Man's settlement on the earth's surface has become sufficiently extensive during the last hundred years to give rise to considerable changes in the natural environment. It seems that nature is being subjugated by man with his science and technology. Penetration of human activities into areas with less favourable living conditions is taking place as he learns to modify the environment to suit him with his machinery and energy. This may be seen as progress, but excessive use of fossil fuels for the purpose of seeking comfort eventually brings about thermal pollution in the urban environment as well as a shortage of fossil fuels which are in limited supply.

The urban environment in the modern society is a product of interaction between nature and man. From the viewpoint of thermal behaviour, the temperature, humidity, air movement and radiation in the inhabited area are quite different from the earlier conditions before human activities appeared.

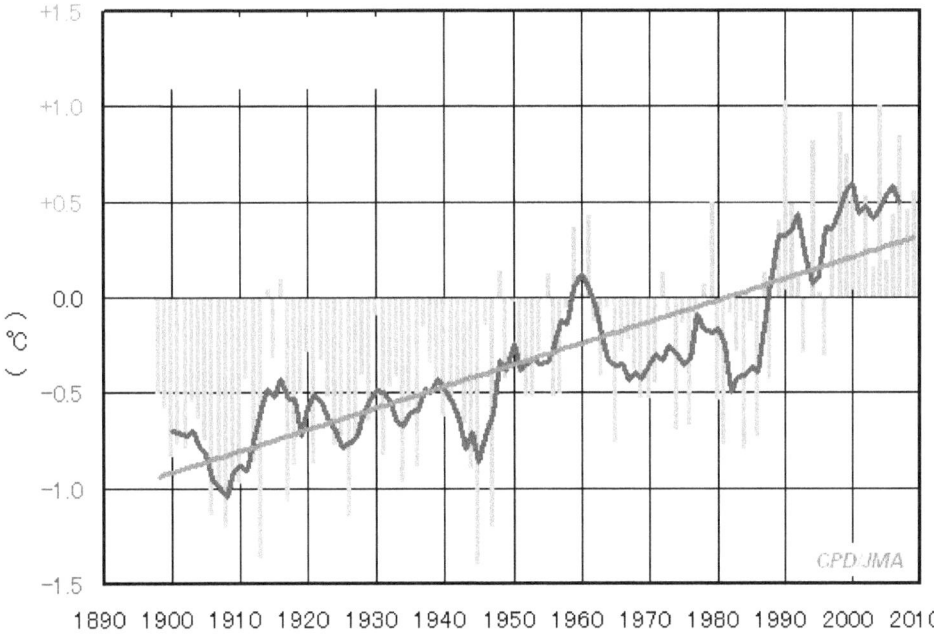

*Fig. I.*1. Annual average air temperature deviation from the mean value for 30 years from 1971 – 2000 in Japan (Source: Japan Meteorological Agency)

Fig. I.1 gives a clear evidence of this trend over the past century from the data of the average air temperature deviation in Japan. The trend of long term is shown by the straight line together with 5 years moving mean value. It can be seen that the annual air temperature in Japan is increasing at a rate of 1.13 deg. C per 100 years on the basis of long term. Especially a frequent appearance of high temperature years can be manifested since 1990.

It is necessary for architectural scientists and air conditioning engineers to understand the quality and behaviour of the urban environment if the buildings of the future are not to make a detrimental contribution. Figure I.2 shows how the air conditioning and other building services systems function in the inter-relationship between the environment that is supplied to and exhausted from these building services systems. All of the energy supplied as power, oil, gas, coal and pressurised city water is primarily taken from and returned to the environment; part of it will be thrown away without being effectively used. Consequently the natural environment cannot remain in its natural state and will be distorted as shown in the figure, with the result that we can see 'real nature' only in the distance, as yet undeveloped. On the other hand, the human activities under the artificially comfortable environment are contributing to new energy demands and to an industrialised society that in turn causes environmental disruption by the solid, liquid and gaseous wastes emerging from industrial production.

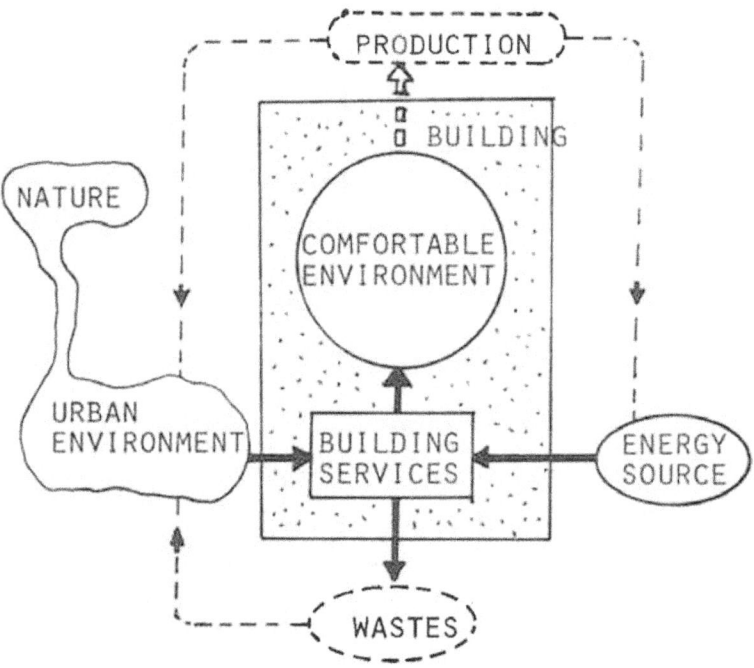

Fig. I.2. Interaction between building services and environment.

The Purpose of air conditioning is primarily to create a comfortable environment for human beings, not only in providing pleasant conditions to work or to relax, but also to give protection from unhealthy or harmful conditions. On the other hand air conditioning systems have to work in the midst of circumstances which destroy the balance of nature. In studying the scientific basis of air conditioning, one must always keep these interactions in mind and consider the role of air conditioning in creating an urban environment inevitably different from the original natural environment.

Chapter 1

Solar Radiation

Solar radiation can be regarded as the only original energy source for living creatures on the earth and all of the weather patterns that occur every day throughout the world can be attributed to the energy from the sun. From the viewpoint of air conditioning, solar radiation makes an important contribution to space heating in winter and gives rise to a considerable amount of cooling load in summer. Hence solar radiation must be treated as thermal energy in air conditioning. Subsequent consideration must be given to the spectrum characteristics of solar radiation for estimating the rate of solar radiation absorbed by or transmitted through various building materials.

In this chapter studies are to be carried out to understand how much, when and what kind of solar radiation reaches the building surface of a certain orientation and inclination at a given locality.

1.1. SOLAR CONSTANT AND SOLAR SPECTRUM

The intensity of solar radiation received by building surfaces on the earth at any time and at any location must be estimated for the heat load calculation of air conditioning. The key value for estimating the intensity of solar radiation for given conditions is the solar constant. The solar constant may be defined as the intensity of solar radiation outside or the atmosphere in the normal direction to the sun's ray when the distance between the sun and the earth is averaged over a year.

Values for the solar constant have been proposed by a number of meteorologists throughout the world based on data obtained from observations made at high altitude in the atmosphere. One of the most reliable values would be 1353 W m^{-2} proposed by Thekaekara [1.1] which is based mainly on the data obtained by aircraft, rockets and satellites under conditions almost free from the effect of the atmosphere.

Thekaekara also proposed a standard solar spectrum as shown in Fig. 1.1. The values of irradiance against wavelength are listed in Table 1.1, where the integral over the whole wavelength is equal to 1353 W m^{-2}. It is found that 99% of total solar radiation outside of the atmosphere lies in the wavelength range from 0·28µm to 5µm.

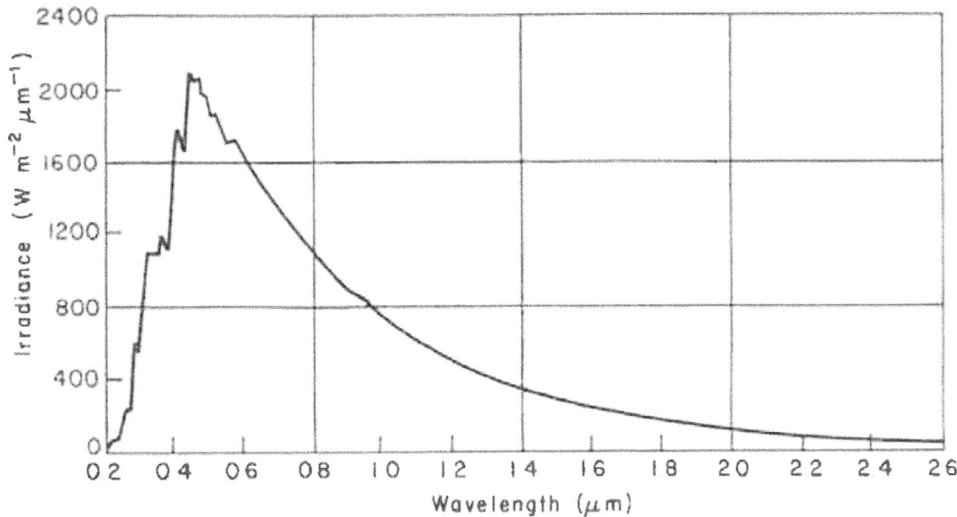

Fig. 1.1. The standard solar spectral irradiance curve (NASA), 0·2 to 2·6μm. (By permission of Thekaekara [1.1].)

The relationship between the solar constant and the spectral irradiance can be expressed by the following:

$$I_0 = \int_0^\infty E(\lambda) d\lambda \qquad (1.1)$$

where I_0 = solar constant (W m^{-2}), λ = wavelength (μm), $E(\lambda)$ = spectral irradiance averaged over small bandwidth centred at λ (W m^{-2} μm^{-1}).

Table 1.2 gives the standard values of the intensity of solar radiation outside of the atmosphere, often called the extraterrestrial solar radiation for every month, taking into account the distance between the sun and the earth.

Table 1.1
Solar spectral irradiance—standard curve (*By permission of Thekaekara* [1.1])

λ	E(λ)	E(0–λ)	D(0–λ)
0·12	0·900	0·004 8	0·000 3
0·14	0·030	0·007 3	0·000 5
0·16	0·230	0·009 3	0·000 6
0·18	1·250	0·023 0	0·001 6
0·20	10·7	0·109 8	0·008 1
0·22	57·5	0·679 8	0·050 2
0·24	63·0	1·935 6	0·143 0
0·26	130	3·651 6	0·269
0·28	222	7·636 6	0·564
0·30	514	16·381 6	1·210
0·32	830	30·021 6	2·218
0·34	1 074	50·356 6	3·721
0·36	1 068	71·936 6	5·316
0·38	1 120	94·756 6	7·003
0·40	1 429	110·054 1	8·725
0·42	1 747	151·839	11·222
0·44	1 810	185·706	13·725
0·46	2 066	225·321	16·653
0·48	2 074	266·296	19·681
0·50	1 942	305·766	22·599
0·52	1 833	343·379	25·379
0·54	1 783	379·979	28·084
0·56	1 695	414·669	30·648
0·58	1 715	448·874	33·176
0·60	1 666	482·796	35·683
0·62	1 602	515·469	38·098
0·64	1 544	546·899	40·421
0·66	1 486	577·159	42·657
0·68	1 427	606·284	44·810
0·70	1 369	634·284	46·879
0·72	1 314	661·139	48·864
0·74	1 260	686·909	50·769
0·76	1 211	711·614	52·595
0·78	1 159	735·314	54·346
0·80	1 109	757·984	56·023
0·85	990	810·434	59·899
0·90	891	857·329	63·365
0·95	837	900·509	66·556
1·00	748	940·184	69·488
1·10	593	1 007·109	74·435
1·20	485	1 060·809	78·404
1·30	397	1 104·759	81·652
1·40	337	1 141·009	84·331
1·50	288	1 172·234	86·639
1·60	245	1 198·909	88·611
1·70	202	1 221·234	90·261

Table 1.1—*contd.*

λ	E(λ)	E(0–λ)	D(0–λ)
1·80	159	1 239·259	91·593
1·90	126	1 253·484	92·644
2·00	103	1 264·909	93·489
2·5	55	1 302·809	96·290 3
3·0	31	1 323·609	97·827 7
3·5	14·6	1 334·329	98·620 0
4·0	9·5	1 340·254	99·057 9
4·5	5·92	1 344·035 1	99·337 40
5·0	3·79	1 346·399 9	99·512 19
10	0·241 0	1 352·177 4	99·939 20
15	0·048 1	1 352·752 4	99·981 70
20	0·015 200	1 352·892 0	99·992 02
30	0·002 970	1 352·968 3	99·997 65
40	0·000 942	1 352·986 0	99 998 87
50	0·000 391	1 352·992 7	99·999 46
100	0·000 025 70	1 352·999 0	99·999 92
200	0·000 001 69	1 352·999 8	99·999 99
400	0·000 000 11	1 352·999 9	99·999 99
1 000	0·000 000 00	1 353·000 0	100·000 00

λ = Wavelength (μm)

$E(\lambda)$ = Solar spectral irradiance averaged over small bandwidth centred at λ (W m^{-2}μm^{-1})

$E(0-\lambda)$ = Integrated solar irradiance in the wavelength range 0 to λ (W m^{-2})

$D(0-\lambda)$ = Percentage of solar constant associated with wavelengths shorter than λ

Solar constant = 1353 Wm^{-2}

Table 1.2
Monthly standard extraterrestrial solar radiation (W m^{-2})

Month (M)	I_0 (M)
1	1 405
2	1 394
3	1 378
4	1 353
5	1 334
6	1 316
7	1 308
8	1 315
9	1 330
10	1 350
11	1 372
12	1 392

1.2. SOLAR POSITION

It is essential to know the direction of the sun seen from a given point on the earth, generally called the solar position. The solar position is expressed by the two angles: solar altitude and solar azimuth. As shown in Fig. 1.2, solar altitude is defined as the angle of the sun's direction to the horizontal plane and solar azimuth as the angle of the horizontal projection of the sun's direction deviated from the south.

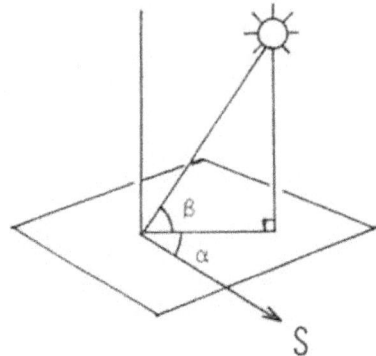

Fig. 1.2.   Solar azimuth α and solar altitude β.

These two angles are geometrically expressed by the following formulas:

$$\sin \beta = \sin\varphi \sin\delta + \cos\varphi \cos\delta \cos t \tag{1.2}$$

$$\sin\alpha = \frac{\cos\delta \sin t}{\cos\beta} \tag{1.3}$$

$$\cos\alpha = \frac{\sin\beta \sin\varphi - \sin\delta}{\cos\beta \cos\varphi} \tag{1.4}$$

where β = solar altitude (degree), α = solar azimuth (degree), φ = latitude of locality (degree), δ = declination angle (degree), t = hour angle (degree).

Declination angle varies with season, but for engineering purposes monthly average values are sufficient for any calculation in practice. Fairly good approximation is obtained by a sinusoidal function with a period of 365 days and δ = 0 for spring and autumnal equinoxes, δ = 23° 27' for summer solstice and δ = -23° 27' for winter solstice.

The hour angle may be determined from the deviation of the hour from noon, which is converted into angular measurement on the basis of 15 degrees per hour. Positive values are applied to the afternoon hours and negative to the morning hours. If the hour is expressed in local standard time, it should be converted into solar time. The equation of time is also often taken into account for determining the hour angle. In short, the following formula gives the hour angle t:

$$t = \left(t_s \pm \frac{L - L_s}{15} + \frac{e}{60} - 12 \right) \times 15 \tag{1.5}$$

where t_s = hour expressed in local standard time (h), L = longitude of the locality (degree), L_s = longitude of the standard location of solar time (degree), e = equation of time (min). The double signs indicate that (+) is applied to the eastern hemisphere and (−) to the western.

Table 1.3 shows the monthly standard values of declination angle and equation of time which may be used for practical engineering calculation with sufficient accuracy.

As the solar radiation passes through the atmosphere, part of it being absorbed by small particles such as water vapour and carbon dioxide until it reaches the ground where the intensity is substantially decreased.

Table 1.3
Monthly standard values of declination angle
δ (M) and equation of time e (M)

Month (M)	δ (M) (degrees)	e (M) (min. of time)
1	−20·280	−11·1
2	−11·723	−13·8
3	0	−7·3
4	11·723	+1·2
5	20·280	+1·7
6	23·445	−1·6
7	20·280	−6·2
8	11·723	−3·0
9	0	+6·9
10	−11·723	+15·2
11	−20·280	+14·0
12	−23·445	+1·8

The gradient of this decrease through the distance dx in the atmosphere may be regarded as proportional to the intensity itself. Taking the x-axis as shown in Fig. 1.3, this relationship is given by the following equation:

$$\frac{dI(x)}{dx} = -kI(x) \tag{1.6}$$

where $I(x)$ = intensity of solar radiation at boundary of the atmosphere (Wm^{-2}), k = constant of proportionality (m^{-1}).

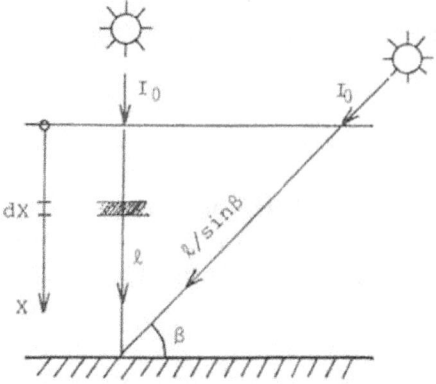

Fig. 1.3. Path length or solar beam.

Solving eqn. (1.6) for I, it gives:

$$I(x) = I_0 \exp(-kx) \quad (1.7)$$

It is clear that the larger the value of k, the quicker the intensity decreases, so the constant k is called the extinction coefficient. When the sun is at the zenith, i.e. solar radiation falls perpendicularly to the ground, the ratio of the intensity at the ground to the extraterrestrial radiation is called the atmospheric transmissivity, namely:

$$P = \frac{I(l)}{I_0} = \exp(-kl) \quad (1.8)$$

where l = length of passage in the atmosphere (m).

When the sun is not at the zenith and the solar altitude is β degrees, the length of passage is longer than l. As shown in Fig. 1.3, the length of passage becomes $l \operatorname{cosec} \beta$. The value m, known as the air mass, is usually used to describe the path length relative to the perpendicular path length through the atmosphere, because the true value of t is not known.

$$m = \frac{l \operatorname{cosec}\beta}{l} = \operatorname{cosec}\beta \quad (1.9)$$

The general expression to give the intensity of solar radiation on the surface normal to the sun's ray is

$$\begin{aligned} I_{DN} &= I(l\operatorname{cosec}\beta) \\ &= I_0 \exp(-kl\operatorname{cosec}\beta) \end{aligned} \quad (1.10)$$

where I_{DN} = direct normal solar radiation (W m^{-2}).

It follows, therefore, that

$$I_{DN} = I_0 P^{\operatorname{cosec}\beta} = I_0 P^m \tag{1.11}$$

Equation (1.11) is known as Bouguer's formula.

The atmospheric transmissivity on a clear day is different from month to month primarily because of the difference in water vapour content in the atmosphere. The monthly standard values of the atmospheric transmissivity for Tokyo area are given in Table 1.4. It is interesting, however, to see that the value of the atmospheric transmissivity still varies with time of the day when compared with actual values observed at meteorological stations.

Table 1.4
Monthly standard values of atmospheric transmissivity of clear sky for Tokyo

Month	Atmospheric transmissivity
1	0·800
2	0·785
3	0·740
4	0·740
5	0·695
6	0·655
7	0·680
8	0·685
9	0·745
10	0·760
11	0·770
12	0·775

The author has tried two approaches to express the value of P using measured values in Tokyo. One approach is to express P as a function of time deviation t (h) from solar noon in the following expression:

$$P = P_0 + at^2 \tag{1.12}$$

where P_0 and a are constant values for each month to be given in Table 1.5.

The other approach is to express P as a linear function of $\sin \beta$, viz.,

$$P = S - T . \sin \beta \tag{1.13}$$

where S and T are constant values for each month to be given also in Table 1.5.

Table 1.5
Constants for eqns. (1.12) *and* (1.13)

Month	Eqn. (1.12)		Eqn. (1.13)	
	P_0	a	S	T
1	0·800	0·005 5	0·83	0·25
2	0·785	0·005 0		
3	0·740	0·004 5	0·84	0·25
4	0·720	0·004 0		
5	0·695	0·004 0	0·85	0·35
6	0·600	0·004 0		
7	0·620	0·004 0	0·80	0·40
8	0·625	0·004 5		
9	0·700	0·004 5	0·87	0·44
10	0·760	0·004 5		
11	0·785	0·005 0	0·83	0·24
12	0·800	0·005 5		

In reducing these formulas from the measured values of global radiation, Berlage's formula to give diffuse sky radiation on a horizontal surface, which will be described later, was used.

1.3. DIRECT SOLAR RADIATION

The American Society of Heating, Refrigerating and Air Conditioning Engineers takes a different approach to give direct normal solar radiation, i.e. instead of using the real value of extraterrestrial solar radiation, a hypothetical solar constant A and hypothetical extinction coefficient B are used to give direct normal solar radiation in the expression:

$$I_{DN} = A \exp(-B \operatorname{cosec} \beta) \qquad (1.14)$$

The values A and B vary with the month but do not vary with time of the day. It must be noted, however, that this expression will give smaller values of direct normal solar radiation than actual values when cosec β is larger than 3. It is assumed that such errors would not contribute much to the air conditioning load because they appear at the lower intensity region of solar radiation.

Comparing the ASHRAE formula with Bouguer's formula, one can recognise such equivalences as:

$$A \doteqdot I_0 \quad \text{and} \quad \exp(-B) \doteqdot P \qquad (1.15)$$

In reality there are slight differences between them and it always follows that

$$A < I_0 \quad \text{and} \quad \exp(-B) > P \tag{1.16}$$

Knowing the direct normal solar radiation, direct solar radiation on a horizontal surface can be given by the equation:

$$I_{DH} = I_{DN} \sin \beta \tag{1.17}$$

Direct solar radiation on a vertical surface differs with the orientation of the vertical surface. Defining the wall solar azimuth γ as the angle between the solar azimuth α and the wall orientation ε as shown in Fig. 1.4:

$$\gamma = \alpha - \varepsilon \tag{1.18}$$

Then the direct solar radiation on a vertical surface I_{DV} is expressed as

$$I_{DV} = I_{DN} \cos \beta \cos \gamma \tag{1.19}$$

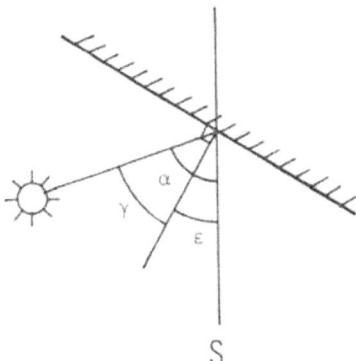

Fig. 1.4. Solar azimuth α, wall orientation ε and wall solar azimuth γ

Furthermore, direct solar radiation on a tilted surface can be given by the following expression, when the tilt angle of the surface is ψ to the horizontal, viz.,

$$I_{D\psi} = I_{DN} (\sin \beta \cos \psi + \cos \beta \cos \gamma \sin \psi) \tag{1.20}$$

and when $\phi \leq \psi$ $I_{D\psi} = 0$.

Figure 1.5 shows the two conditions where the sun is in front of the slope or behind it; ϕ is called profile angle.

The profile angle is defined by the formula:

$$\tan \phi = \frac{\tan \beta}{\cos \gamma} \tag{1.21}$$

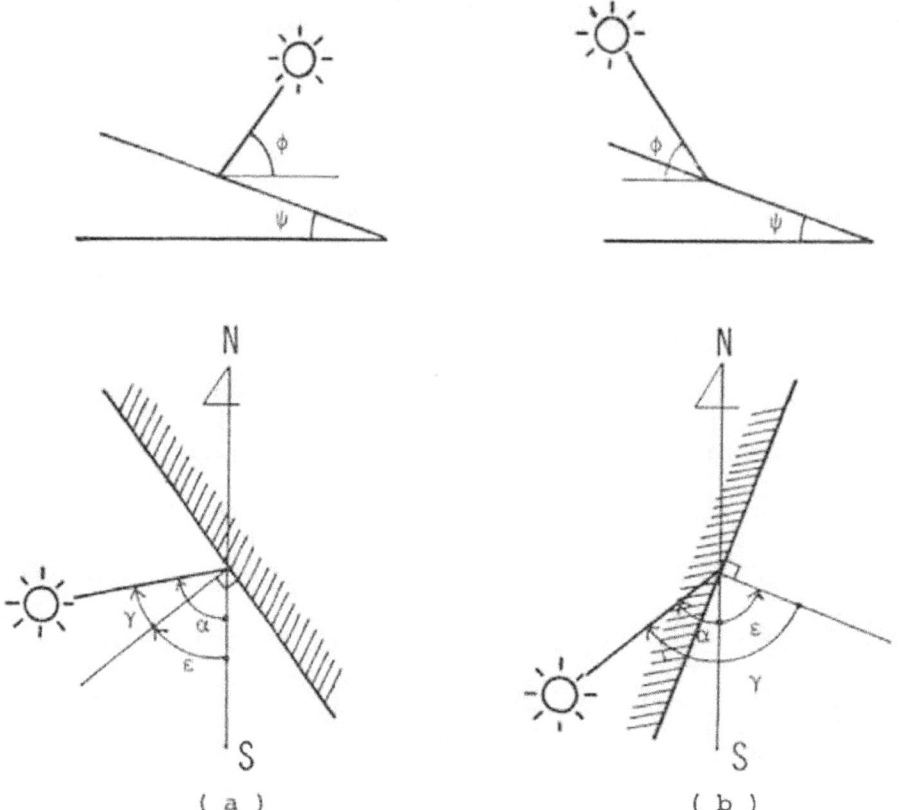

Fig. 1.5. Direct solar radiation on a tilted surface (a) $|\gamma| \leq 90°$, (b) $|\gamma| > 90°$, $\phi \geq \psi$

1.4. DIFFUSE SOLAR RADIATION

The diffuse component of solar radiation is insignificant on clear days but relatively large under turbid sky conditions. In air conditioning practice, therefore, diffuse radiation is important for estimation of annual air conditioning load calculations.

Four kinds of diffuse solar radiation come in contact with the surfaces of a building, namely:

1. Diffuse sky radiation that comes from the blue part of the sky because of the scattering of the solar radiation. Short wave length radiation is predominant.
2. Solar radiation transmitted through thin layers of cloud plus solar radiation reflected from the ground surface, then being reflected at the lower surface of cloud. These are diffuse in nature.

3. Backward radiation as a long wavelength radiation emitted mainly by the water vapour particles in the atmosphere which have absorbed radiation from the ground surface.
4. Solar radiation reflected on to the building exterior (except the roof) from the ground surface.

These are all diffuse components of solar radiation and the sum of all of these constitutes the diffuse solar radiation on the building surface concerned.

In reality the diffuse sky radiation on horizontal surfaces on clear days should be determined as a key component in order to estimate the other three components. Many investigators with different approaches have presented formulas of diffuse sky radiation on horizontal surfaces on clear days.

Among them Berlage's formula [1.2] has been generally accepted by Japanese architectural scientists and air conditioning engineers as described in the following expression:

$$I_{SH} = 0 \cdot 5 I_0 \sin\beta \frac{1 - P^{\cosec\beta}}{1 - 1 \cdot 4 \ln P} \tag{1.22}$$

This is a theoretical equation derived from the assumption that the sky vault has uniform brightness under clear sky conditions.

ASHRAE uses the empirical formula derived by Stephenson [1.3] which gives diffuse sky radiation on clear days as proportional to direct normal solar radiation as follows:

$$I_{SH} = C\, I_{DN} \tag{1.23}$$

where the value of C is varied with the months.

Nehring [1.4] introduced a simplified formula to give diffuse sky radiation on a horizontal surface as a function of direct normal solar radiation from the relationship originally proposed by Reitz.

The formula is

$$\begin{aligned} I_{SH} &= \tfrac{1}{3}(I_0 - I_{DN})\sin\beta \\ &= \tfrac{1}{3} I_0 \sin\beta (1 - P^{1/\sin\beta}) \end{aligned} \tag{1.24}$$

Nagata [1.5] proposed a formula to obtain diffuse sky radiation derived from his own theoretical background which gives nearly equal values to those by Berlage and Nehring and is expressed by:

$$I_{SH} = I_0 \sin\beta (1 - P^{1/\sin\beta})(0 \cdot 33 P + 0 \cdot 1) \tag{1.25}$$

Figure 1.6 shows a comparison of the various methods of obtaining diffuse sky radiation.

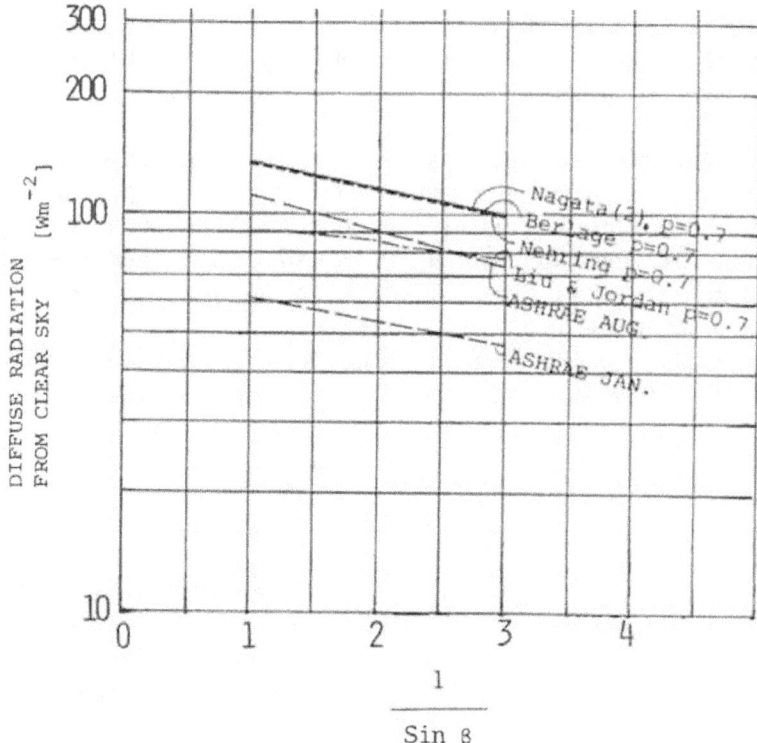

Fig. 1.6. Comparison of various equations to obtain the diffuse radiation from clear sky.

Diffuse sky radiation on tilted surfaces is given by:

$$I_{S\psi} = \cos^2 \frac{\psi}{2} I_{SH} \qquad (1.26)$$

where ψ is tilt angle of the surface to the horizontal. Making $\psi = 90°$ in the above, diffuse sky radiation on a vertical surface I_{sv} can be derived as:

$$I_{SV} = \frac{1}{2} I_{SH} \qquad (1.27)$$

When the tilted surface of a building receives reflected radiation from the ground, the radiation is considered diffuse. The amount of such diffuse radiation can be expressed by:

$$I_{R\psi} = \left(1 - \cos^2 \frac{\psi}{2}\right) \rho_G I_{TH} \qquad (1.28)$$

where ρ_G = reflectivity of the ground surface. Reflectivity of the ground covering a certain extent of area expressed in percentage is often called 'albedo', which is a term used in meteorology. Some examples of albedo are shown in Fig. 1.7.

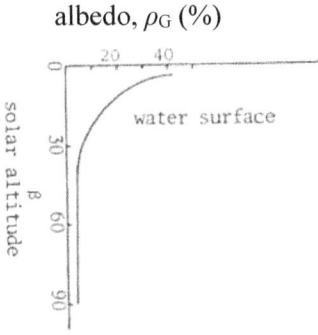

Fig. 1.7. Albedo collected from different sources.

1.5. BREAKING-DOWN OF GLOBAL RADIATION INTO DIRECT AND DIFFUSE COMPONENTS

There are very few weather stations where direct and diffuse solar radiation data are recorded and an even smaller number of stations where global radiation is observed. It is necessary, however, for air conditioning engineers to estimate direct and diffuse components of solar radiation knowing the value of global radiation, i.e. total solar radiation on horizontal surface, in order to obtain the amount of solar radiation on any building surface. This is the breaking-down procedure. Several approaches have been proposed so far to determine the two key components, namely direct normal solar radiation I_{DN} and diffuse sky radiation on horizontal surface I_{SH}, from total horizontal solar radiation I_{TH}.

The subcommittee on Standard Weather Data at the Society of Heating, Air-Conditioning and Sanitary Engineers of Japan has worked extensively on this procedure using a ten-year period of weather data taken at the weather station in Tokyo. The basic approach to carry out the breaking-down is to establish the basic equation that expresses the total horizontal solar radiation as a function of direct normal radiation as in the following:

$$I_{TH} = I_{DH} + I_{SH}$$
$$= I_{DN} \sin \beta + \tfrac{1}{2} I_0 \sin \beta \frac{1 - P^{\operatorname{cosec}\beta}}{1 - 1 \cdot 4 I_n P} \qquad (1.29)$$

It must be noted here that Berlage's formula as in eqn. (1.29) is used for any weather conditions in spite of the fact that Berlage's original theory is only valid for clear sky conditions. It was proved, however, by Matsuo that the results deduced from the above equation using actual observed data on hourly basis gave a quite good agreement with the results of separate observations of direct and diffuse solar radiation. This shows that, for engineering purposes, Berlage's formula could be applicable not only to clear sky conditions but also to cloudy sky conditions with reasonable accuracy.

Parmelee [1.6] derived a relationship to show that the proportion of direct component to the total solar radiation I_{TH} on horizontal surface increases as I_{TH} itself increases. Conversely, the more turbid the sky, the more the diffuse component prevails as shown in Fig. 1.8.

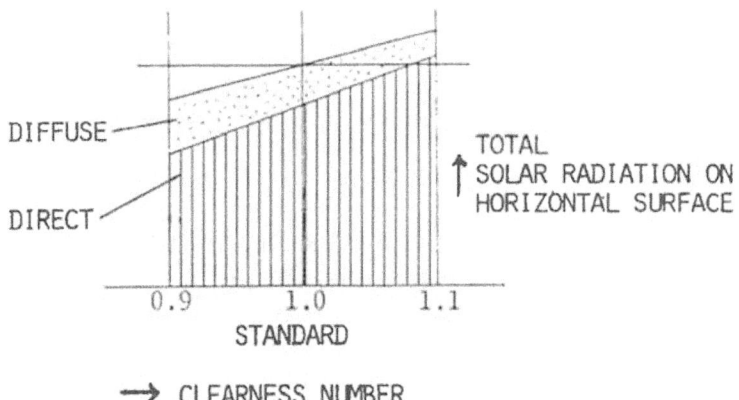

Fig. 1.8.   Direct and diffuse solar radiation with clearness number.

Parmelee's original equation is:

$$I_{SH} = X - Y \cdot I_{DH} \qquad (1.30)$$

where X and Y are functions of the solar altitude as given in Table 1.6. If the total horizontal solar radiation is P' times the total horizontal solar radiation for standard clear sky conditions, viz.,

$$I_{TH}^* = P' \cdot I_{TH} \qquad (1.31)$$

It follows that:

$$I_{TH}^* = X + (1-Y) I_{TH}^* = P'\{X + (1-Y)I_{DH}\} \qquad (1.32a)$$

$$I_{DH}^* = P' \cdot I_{DH} + \frac{(P'-1)X}{1-Y} \qquad (1.32b)$$

Then the increase of direct component due to P' larger than unity is:

$$I_{DH}^* - I_{DH} + \frac{P'-1}{1-Y} I_{TH} \qquad (1.33)$$

where Y can be approximated as:

$$Y = 0.309 - 0.137 \sin \beta + 0.394 \sin^2 \beta \qquad (1.34)$$

Table 1.6
Parmelee's constants for eqn. (1.30) (By permission of ASHRAE [1.6])

Solar altitude	X (W m^{-2})	Y (dimensionless)
10°	(63.0)	(0.295)
20°	134.7	0.314
30°	222.1	0.360
40°	284.2	0.362
50°	383.0	0.424
60°	484.5	0.492
70°	(552)	(0.520)
80°	(606)	(0.545)
90°	(625)	(0.560)

Liu and Jordan [1.7] presented a linear relationship between the diffuse horizontal solar radiation and the direct normal solar radiation as expressed by the equation:

$$\frac{I_{SH}}{I_0} = \sin\beta \left(0\cdot 2710 - 0\cdot 2913 \frac{I_{DN}}{I_0}\right) \tag{1.35}$$

Being derived from a number of actual observation data, this gives a remarkable correlation for the high intensity region. It is found, however, that considerable inaccuracy results for the low intensity region if the above linear relationship is extended to this area.

1.6. SOLAR RADIATION ON CLOUDY DAYS†

Hour by hour calculation of heating and cooling load of a space is needed for estimating annual energy requirements, and solar radiation data in direct and diffuse components on hourly basis must be prepared.

As described in the preceding section, breaking-down procedures could be applied for the locations where global radiation is observed, but there are not so many such weather stations. There are many stations, however, where total amount of cloud is observed on hourly basis. For such a location, it is necessary to develop a procedure to deduce solar radiation from cloud cover data.

The author has made this study [1.8] in collaboration with Stephenson to find correlation between the cloud cover and the ratio of the total horizontal solar radiation to the case that could appear if the sky was cloudless, using computer techniques to analyse the actual observation data in combination with theoretical formulas. Figure 1.9 shows the plots of the correlation with two ranges of solar altitude angles using recorded observation data of Ottawa, Canada (45°27′N, 75°37′W), where the ASHRAE formula was used for estimating the theoretical values of direct and diffuse solar radiation on clear days. The value of CC† in the graph is defined as the total amount of cloud recorded minus half of the amounts of cirrus, cirrostratus and cirrocumulus. This reduction of the CC values for each of these three types of cloud helped to condense the scatter of points in the graph which would have resulted if this deduction was not made. This seems quite reasonable because these types of cloud are relatively thin and transmit a certain part of solar radiation.

---

† Parts of the passages in this section are taken from the paper by Kimura and Stephenson in ASHRAE Transactions [1.8] by permission of the American Society of Heating, Refrigeration and Air-Conditioning Engineers, Inc.

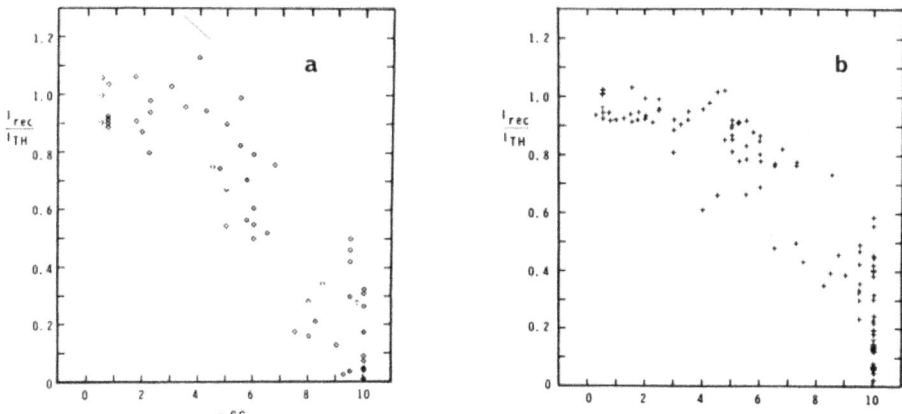

Fig. 1.9. Ratio of radiation incident on a horizontal surface to the amount calculated for cloudless day for sin β (a) 0·3-0·5, (b) 0·7-0·9, in June 1967, Ottawa. (Reprinted by permission of the American Society of Heating, Refrigeration and Air Conditioning Engineers Inc., from *ASHRAE Transactions.*)

Udagawa and the author [1.9] repeated the calculations using solar radiation and cloud cover data of Tokyo (35°41′N,139°46′E) and theoretical formulas by Bouguer and Berlage. Figure 1.10 shows the plots of the correlation similar to the ones in Fig. 1.9.

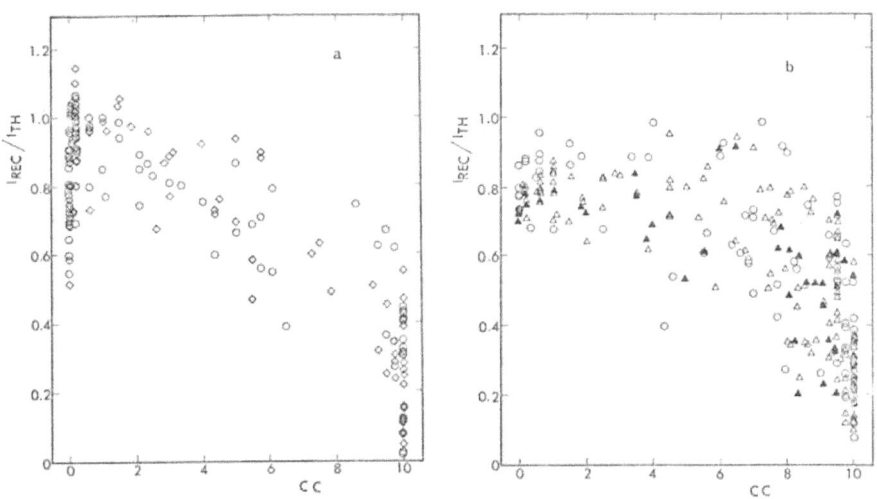

Fig. 1.10. Ratio of radiation incident on a horizontal surface to amount calculated for cloudless day versus cloud cover in (a) January 1966, Tokyo (for $0·3 < \sin \beta < 1·0$).
(b) August 1966, Tokyo (for $0·5 < \sin \beta < 10$).
Sin β: ▽, 0·0-0·1; □, 0·1-0·3; ◊, 0·3-0·5; ○, 0·5-0·7; △, 0·7-0·9; ▲, 0·9-1·0.

The correlation was not so clear for low altitude angles, probably because of the quite variable component of radiation reflected by clouds compared to the relatively small amount of global radiation.

Using the plots for higher altitude angles, standard curves to determine the cloud cover factor CCF as a function of CC† in the second order polynomial are determined as follows:

$$CCF = P + Q \cdot CC + R(CC)^2 \tag{1.36}$$

Table 1.7 (a) shows the constants P, Q and R obtained from Ottawa data for the above equation and Table 1.7 (b) from Tokyo data for 12 different months.

Table 1.7 (a)
Constants in eqn. (1.36) for Ottawa

Month	P	Q	R	Sin β
March	1·06	0·012	−0·008 4	0·5–0·9
June	0·96	0·033	−0·010 6	0·5–1·0
September	0·95	0·030	−0·010 8	0·5–0·9
December	1·14	0·003	−0·008 2	0·3–0·5

Table 1.7 (b)
Constants in eqn. (1.36) for Tokyo

Month	P	Q	R	Sin β
January	0·892	0·012 2	−0·007 20	0·3–0·7
February	0·934	0·002 5	−0·006 38	0·3–0·7
March	0·928	0·045 2	−0·011 06	0·3–0·9
April	0·895	0·032 6	−0·009 68	0·5–1·0
May	0·778	0·085 1	−0·012 76	0·5–1·0
June	0·755	0·138 0	−0·018 46	0·5–1·0
July	0·731	0·060 5	−0·010 15	0·5–1·0
August	0·740	0·050 0	−0·009 21	0·5–1·0
September	0·650	0·079 5	−0·012 14	0·3–0·9
October	0·866	0·050 7	−0·011 07	0·3–0·9
November	0·898	0·017 0	−0·007 42	0·3–0·7
December	0·835	0·000 8	−0·004 82	0·3–0·7

† CC is expressed in tenths, i.e. for complete cloud cover CC = 10

The value of CCF given by eqn. (1.36) and the data in Table 1.7 (a) were used to calculate I_{THC}, the solar intensity that could be expected with the observed cloud conditions for all the daylight hours during each month. These computed values of I_{THC} versus the actual measured values of I_{rec} are plotted. Figure 1.11 shows the plots for Tokyo.

These graphs show that all the points fall in a band centred on the 45° line. This indicates that the absolute error in the solar intensity estimated using the CCF based on the high solar altitude measurements is fairly constant regardless of the actual solar attitude.

Then the total horizontal solar radiation on cloudy days I_{THC} is given by:

$$I_{THC} = I_{TH} \cdot CCF \quad (1.37)$$

Direct and diffuse components on cloudy days I_{DHC} and I_{dHC} can be obtained by the following expression; using the theory of probability, viz.,

$$I_{DHC} = I_{DH}\left(1 - \frac{CC}{10}\right) \quad (1.38)$$

$$I_{dHC} = I_{THC} - I_{DHC} \quad (1.39)$$

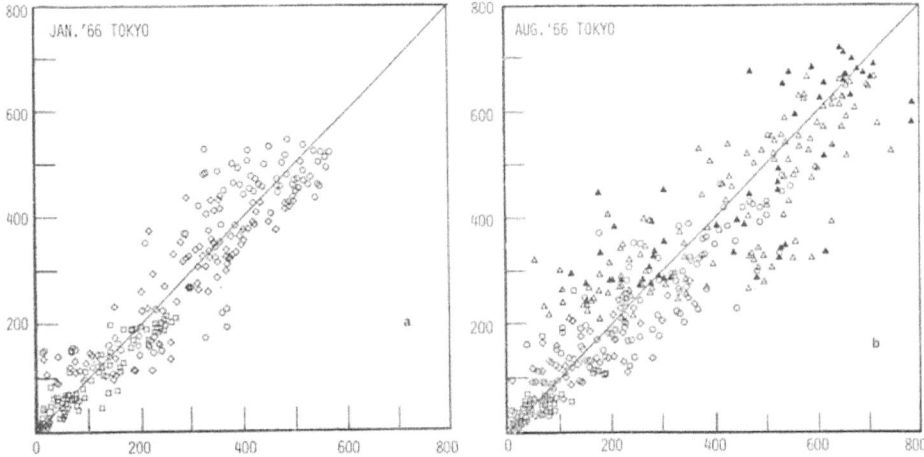

Fig. 1.11. Correlation between calculated radiation based on CCF and recorded radiation on a horizontal surface for an daylight hours in (a) January 1966, Tokyo, (b) August 1966, Tokyo. Key as for Fig. 1.11. ordinate I_{THC} (Wm^{-2}), abscissa I_{rec} (Wm^{-2}). Symbols of sinβ are the same as in Fig. 1.10.

Figure 1.12 shows the relationship generalized for cloudy conditions.

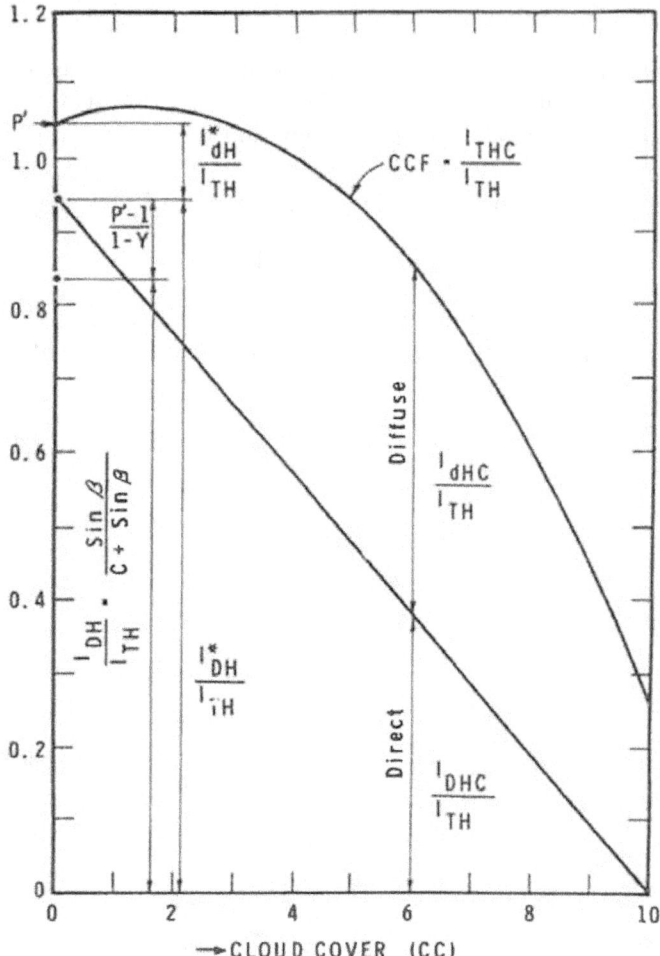

Fig. 1.12, Direct and diffuse components of cloud cover factor (CCF). (Reprinted by permission of the American Society of Heating Refrigeration and Air Conditioning Engineers) Inc., from *ASHRAE Transactions*.)

Chapter 2

Unsteady State Heat Conduction Through Walls and Slabs

One of the most important aspects of air conditioning is to supply heat or extract heat from interior spaces. The amount of heat required very much depends on the amount of heat entering into or coming out of the surfaces that enclose an occupied space. This amount of heat varies with time because all of the natural changes, both outdoor and indoor, give rise to thermal effects on a time-dependent basis. Furthermore the heat capacity of the building structure is significant. Building elements such as walls and slabs play an important role in damping and delaying the effects of heat flow. It is necessary, therefore, for air conditioning scientists and engineers to understand the behaviour of heat conduction through walls and slabs on the unsteady state basis.

The factors contributing to the unsteady state heat conduction through building structures can be classified into four major categories as follows:

1. Estimations must be made of the heat gain or heat loss through exterior walls and roofs that receive the effects of outside air temperature and solar radiation upon their outside surfaces is a primary consideration.
2. Slabs and interior walls also receive radiation upon their surfaces as well as convection heat from the inside air temperature which generally differs from their surface temperatures. The heat flow at the interior surfaces of the room enclosure is quite significant and, depending on the time of the day, often occurs in a reverse direction from the heat flow through exterior walls.
3. The surface temperatures of the building elements which form the enclosure are also important in evaluating comfort and radiation exchange between the surfaces on a time-dependent basis.
4. In order to check the water vapour condensation on the surface or inside of a wall, the temperature distribution across the wall section must be estimated on the unsteady state basis.

2.1. FUNDAMENTAL EQUATION OF UNSTEADY STATE HEAT CONDUCTION

It is well known that the heat flow through a unit area of a flat, homogeneous wall section is expressed by the equation:

$$q = -\lambda \frac{\partial \theta}{\partial x} \tag{2.1}$$

where q = rate of heat flow at position x and at time t (W m^{-2}), θ = temperature of wall at position x and at time t (°C), x = position distant from the origin at one surface of the wall, and λ = thermal conductivity of the wall material (W m^{-1} deg C^{-1}).

$\partial \theta / \partial x$ in eqn. (2.1) is the temperature gradient and the equation implies that the heat flow is proportional to the temperature gradient. It is important to recognise the minus sign in the equation, which identifies that the heat flows in the opposite direction to the direction of temperature gradient; for example when the temperature increases as x increases, the heat flows in the direction that x decreases.

Taking the difference in heat flow per unit area between at x and at $x + dx$ in reference to Fig. 2.1, it follows that:

$$-\lambda \frac{\partial \theta}{\partial x} - \left[-\lambda \frac{\partial}{\partial x}\left(\theta + \frac{\partial \theta}{\partial x} dx\right) \right] = \lambda \frac{\partial^2 \theta}{\partial x^2} \tag{2.2}$$

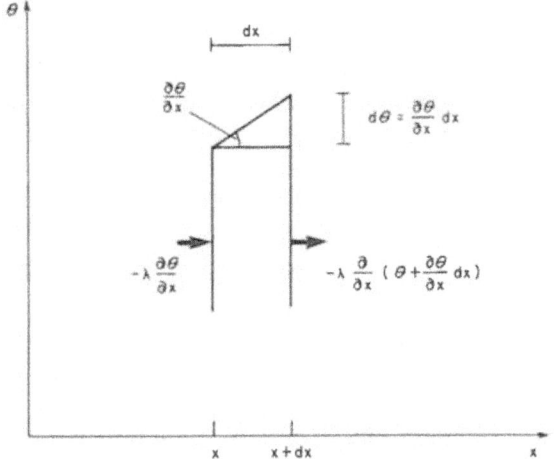

Fig. 2.1. Temperature gradient between x and $x + dx$.

This amount of heat must be accumulated in an incremental section of the wall, the volume of which is dx (m^3) as the area is 1 m^2, and contribute to the rise of the temperature of the section by $\partial \theta$ (°C).

As the amount of heat required to raise the temperature of the section by $\partial \theta$ during the period of time ∂t is $C_p \rho (\partial \theta / \partial t) dx$ where C_p is specific heat of the wall material (J kg^{-1} deg C^{-1}) and ρ is mass density (kg m^{-3}), it yields the equation:

$$\lambda \frac{\partial^2 \theta}{\partial x^2} dx = C_p \rho \frac{\partial \theta}{\partial t} dx \qquad (2.3)$$

The common expression of one-dimensional unsteady state heat conduction is given in the following form of partial differential equation:

$$\frac{\partial \theta}{\partial t} = a \frac{\partial^2 \theta}{\partial x^2} \qquad (2.4)$$

where $a = \lambda/C_p\rho$, thermal diffusivity of the material ($m^2 h^{-1}$).

The solution of eqn. (2.4) is always calculated for temperature θ as a function of x and t with values appropriate to the particular conditions.

2.2. FINITE DIFFERENCE METHOD

Any type of differential equation can be solved by the finite difference method, but this approach always gives an approximate solution. For engineering purposes there are many cases when a numerical solution could bring fast and satisfactory results. In a very complicated system, however, quite a lot of computation time may be consumed with the finite difference method.

In solving eqn. (2.4) by the finite difference method, it is necessary first to convert every variable item in the differential equation into a finite form. Defining $t = k \Delta t$ and $x = m \Delta x$ where Δt is time increment, Δx is incremental length and k and m are integers, temperature $\theta(x, t)$ is to be expressed as $_k\theta_m$. Then, the temperature gradients from $x = (m - 1) \Delta x$ to $m \Delta x$ and from $x = m\Delta x$ to $(m + 1) \Delta x$ are expressed as:

$$\frac{_k\theta_m - _k\theta_{m-1}}{\Delta x} \quad \text{and} \quad \frac{_k\theta_{m-1} - _k\theta_m}{\Delta x}$$

respectively. This is illustrated in Fig. 2.2.

The rate of change in the temperature gradient to the incremental length Δx is given by:

$$\frac{1}{\Delta x}\left(\frac{_k\theta_{m+1} - _k\theta_m}{\Delta x} - \frac{_k\theta_m - _k\theta_{m-1}}{\Delta x}\right) \qquad (2.5)$$

which is a converted form in finite difference of the right-hand side of eqn. (2.4).

On the other hand, the left-hand side of eqn. (2.4) is the temperature gradient of the thermal mass at $x = m \Delta x$ in reference to the time increment Δt, thus the converted form can be expressed as:

$$\frac{_{k+1}\theta_m - _k\theta_m}{\Delta t} \tag{2.6}$$

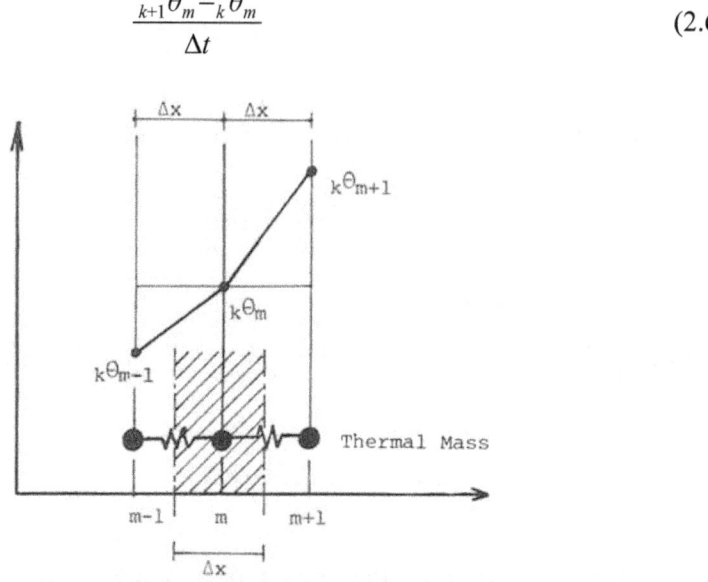

Fig. 2.2. Temperature distribution for finite difference method. Ordinate: θ. Abscissa: x.

Then by combining (2.5) and (2.6), the temperature at $x = m\,\Delta x$ and $t = (k+1)\,\Delta t$ can be derived in the form:

$$_{k+1}\theta_m = p\left[_k\theta_{m+1} + _k\theta_{m-1} - \left(2 - \frac{1}{p}\right)_k\theta_m\right] \tag{2.7}$$

where

$$p = a\frac{\Delta t}{(\Delta x)^2} \tag{2.8}$$

It is important to note that the value of Δt and Δx must be determined so that $p \leq 0 \cdot 5$. Given the initial conditions, the successive operation of calculation would yield the temperatures at every $x = m\,\Delta x$ as $t = k\,\Delta t$ increases. In the case of $p = 0 \cdot 5$, eqn. (2.7) becomes very simple:

$$_{k+1}\theta_m = \frac{1}{2}\left(_k\theta_{m+1} + _k\theta_{m-1}\right) \tag{2.9}$$

At the boundary where heat transfer takes place between the surface and the fluid, the equation to be used should be different from eqn. (2.9) in reference to Fig. 2.3. The temperature gradient at the boundary is:

$$\left(\frac{\Delta t}{\Delta x}\right)_{m=0} = \frac{{}_k\theta_0 - {}_k\theta_f}{\dfrac{\Delta x}{2} + \dfrac{\lambda}{\alpha}} \quad (2.10)$$

where ${}_k\theta_0$ = average temperature of surface layer at time k (°C), ${}_k\theta_f$ = fluid temperature at time k (°C), and α = film coefficient (W m^{-2} deg C^{-1}).

Making $m = 0$ in eqn. (2.5) and replacing the second term of eqn. (2.5) by eqn. (2.10), ${}_{k+1}\theta_0$ can be obtained by the expression:

$$_{k+1}\theta_0 = 2p\left[{}_k\theta_1 + \frac{{}_k\theta_f}{1+\dfrac{2\lambda}{\alpha\Delta x}} - {}_k\theta_0\left(1 + \dfrac{1}{1+\dfrac{2\lambda}{\alpha\Delta x}} - \dfrac{1}{p}\right)\right] \quad (2.11)$$

The above application of the finite difference method is called an explicit procedure and in practice it tends to require quite extensive computation time.

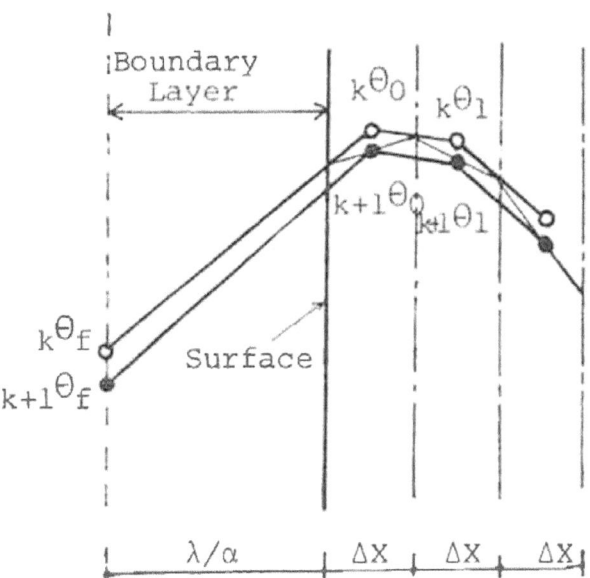

Fig. 2.3. Temperature distribution with boundary layer.

The implicit method is often used when computer calculation is applicable. In this case instead of eqn. (2.6) the temperature gradient of $({}_k\theta_m - {}_{k-1}\theta_m)/\Delta t$ is introduced. Then the basic formula corresponding to eqn. (2.7) is expressed by:

$$_{k+1}\theta_m = p\left[\left(2 + \frac{1}{p}\right){}_k\theta_m - {}_k\theta_{m+1} - {}_k\theta_{m-1}\right] \quad (2.12)$$

and at the boundary:

$$_{k-1}\theta_0 = 2p\left[_k\theta_0\left(1 + \cfrac{1}{1+\cfrac{2\lambda}{\alpha\Delta x}} + \cfrac{1}{p}\right) - _k\theta_1 - \cfrac{_k\theta_f}{1+\cfrac{2\lambda}{\alpha\Delta x}}\right] \qquad (2.13)$$

It is necessary in this case to solve for $_k\theta_m$ ($m = 0, 1, 2,...$) by simultaneous equations, but there is no requirement in the range of p. This reduces the computer time to a large extent in comparison with the explicit method.

2.3. PERIODIC STEADY HEAT CONDUCTION

A wall can be considered as a thermal system, when it receives an excitation such as change of outside air temperature or solar radiation incident on the outside surface and yields various kinds of response such as variation in the temperature distribution across it and in the heat flow through it. The excitation is quite random in the case of natural phenomena, but it can be idealised in such a way that outside air temperature varies and repeats over a period of 24h. In consequence, heat flow at the inside surface, room air temperature and all other variables should be varied over a period of 24h. Under these conditions the unsteady state heat conduction differential equation can be solved as a frequency response when the basic excitation is given in the form of cos ωt. If the actual excitation is given in the form of a Fourier series, it is easy to arrive at the actual form of response in a Fourier series.

The basic form of frequency response is expressed as $\eta \cos(\omega t + \mu)$, where η is called damping factor if excitation and response are in the same units and μ is called time lag.

Fourier's series are defined as the series consisting of a multiple number of trigonometrical functions by which any functions could be approximated. For example, a function f(x) can be expressed in the form of the following, viz.,

$$f(x) = \sum_{n=1}^{\infty} a_n \sin nx + b_0 + \sum_{n=1}^{\infty} b_n \cos nx \qquad (2.14)$$

where

$$a_1 = \frac{1}{\pi}\int_{-\pi}^{\pi} f(\xi)\sin\xi\, d\xi$$

$$a_2 = \frac{1}{\pi}\int_{-\pi}^{\pi} f(\xi)\sin 2\xi\, d\xi$$

$$\vdots$$

$$a_n = \frac{1}{\pi}\int_{-\pi}^{\pi} f(\xi)\sin n\xi\, d\xi \qquad (2.14a)$$

$$b_n = \frac{1}{\pi}\int_{-\pi}^{\pi} f(\xi)\cos n\xi\, d\xi$$

$$b_0 = \frac{1}{\pi}\int_{-\pi}^{\pi} f(\xi)\, d\xi$$

In the case when f(x) is defined within the range of $-l \leq x \leq l$,

$$f(x) = \sum_{n=1}^{\infty} a_n \sin\frac{n\pi x}{l} + b_0 + \sum_{n=1}^{\infty} b_n \cos\frac{n\pi x}{l} \qquad (2.15)$$

where

$$a_1 = \frac{1}{l}\int_{-l}^{l} f(\xi)\sin\frac{n\pi\xi}{l}\, d\xi$$

$$b_n = \frac{1}{l}\int_{-l}^{l} f(\xi)\sin\frac{n\pi\xi}{l}\, d\xi \qquad (2.15a)$$

$$b_0 = \frac{1}{2l}\int_{-l}^{l} f(\xi)\, d\xi$$

The function f(x) must not be infinity and must not have an infinite number of discontinuous points within the defined range.

The principle of periodic heat conduction through a wall is the following, When the excitation function is expressed by:

$$f(t) = \sum_{n=1}^{\infty} b_n \cos(n\omega t + \mu_n) \qquad (2.16)$$

where t is time and ω is angular velocity (rad h^{-1}), the temperature or the heat flow at point x and at time t can be obtained in the expression:

$$g(t) = \sum_{n=1}^{\infty} b_n P_n \cos[n\omega t + (\gamma_n + \mu_n)] \qquad (2.17)$$

if the thermal properties of wall elements are given. The problem is to find a method to obtain P_n and γ_n. In order to do this, it is necessary only to determine the response g(t) in the form of:

$$g(t) = P\cos(\omega t + \gamma) \tag{2.18}$$

against the basic excitation expressed by:

$$f(t) = \cos \omega t \tag{2.19}$$

Here g(t) is called as frequency response of f(t).

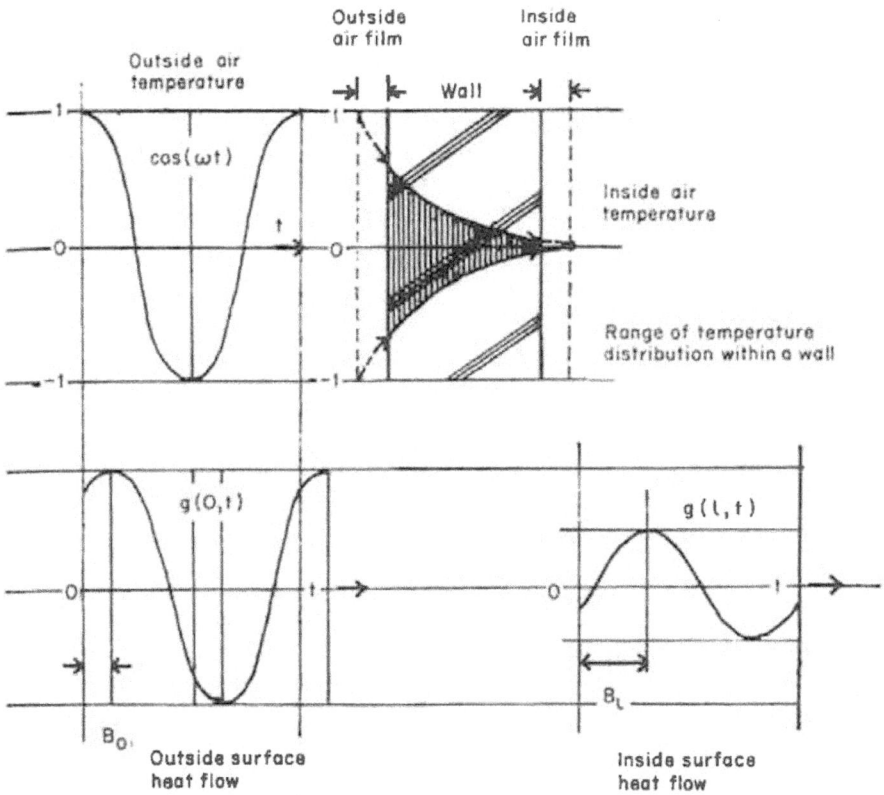

Fig. 2.4.   Periodic steady heat conduction through a wall.

Figure 2.4 shows the patterns of frequency response of heat flow at outside and inside surfaces for periodic steady heat conduction through a wall, when outside air temperature is given in periodic function and inside air temperature is kept zero.

Maeda [2.1] solved the differential equation (eqn. (2.4)) under periodic steady conditions. The Frequency response of the temperature within the walls at x and at time t for flat single layer homogeneous wall derived by Maeda is expressed in the form:

$$\theta(x, t) = P(x) \cos \{\omega t + \gamma(x)\} \quad (2.20)$$

against the conditions that:

$$\theta(0, t) = \cos \omega t$$
$$\theta(l, t) = 0 \quad (2.21)$$

where l is the wall thickness (m). $P(x)$ and $\gamma(x)$ are to be given in the following formulae, making:

$$A = \sqrt{\frac{\omega}{2a}} \quad (2.22)$$

$$P(x) = \sqrt{\frac{\cosh 2A(l-x) - \sinh 2A(2l-x)\sin Ax}{\cosh A(2l-x)\cos Ax - \cosh Ax \cos A(2l-x)}} \quad (2.23)$$

$$\gamma(x) = \tan^{-1} \frac{\sinh Ax \sin A(2l-x) - \sinh A(2l-x)\sin Ax}{\cosh A(2l-x)\cos Ax - \cosh Ax \cos A(2l-x)} \quad (2.24)$$

The heat flow at the surfaces $x = 0$ and $x = l$ is given in the following, viz.,

$$q(0,t) = \lambda A P_0 \cos(\omega t + \Gamma_0) \quad (2.25)$$

where

$$P_0 = \sqrt{\frac{2(\cosh 2Al + \cosh 2Al)}{\cosh 2Al - \cos 2Al}} \quad (2.26a)$$

$$\Gamma_0 = \frac{\sinh 2Al - \sinh 2Al}{\sinh 2Al + \sin 2Al} \quad (2.26b)$$

$$q(l,t) = \lambda A P_l \cos(\omega t + \Gamma_l) \quad (2.27)$$

where

$$P_l = \frac{2}{\sqrt{\cosh 2Al - \cos 2Al}} \quad (2.28a)$$

$$\Gamma_l = \frac{\sin Al \cos Al - \cos Al \sinh Al}{\sin Al \cos Al + \cos Al \sinh Al} \quad (2.28b)$$

Maeda presented a number of charts to give $P(x)$ and $\gamma(x)$ for different cases when the excitation was given as fluid temperature as well as surface temperature. Table 2.1 shows the values of P_0, Γ_0, P_l and Γ_l to be used for calculation of surface heat flow with eqns. (2.25) and (2.27).

Table 2.1
Values of P_0, Γ_0, P_l *and* Γ_l (Maeda [2.1])

Al	P_0	Γ_0	P_l	Γ_l	Al	P_0	Γ_0	P_l	Γ_l
0·00	∞	+0°00′	∞	−0°00′	2·5	1·420	+45°44′	0·2326	−97°52′
0·02	50·00	+0°01′	50·00	−0°00′	2·6	1·422	+45°34′	0·2106	−103°41′
0·04	25·00	+0°04′	25·00	−0°02′	2·7	1·422	+45°24′	0·1906	−109°30′
0·06	16·67	+0°08′	16·67	−0°04′	2·8	1·422	+45°16′	0·1725	−115°18′
0·08	12·50	+0°15′	12·50	−0°07′	2·9	1·422	+45°10′	0·1560	−121°05′
0·1	10·00	+0°23′	10·00	−0°11′	3·0	1·421	+45°05′	0·1412	−126°51′
0·2	5·002	+1°32′	5·000	−0°45′	3·1	1·420	+45°01′	0·1277	−132°36′
0·3	3·342	+3°26′	3·333	−1°43′	3·2	1·419	+44°59′	0·1155	−138°21′
0·4	2·520	+6°04′	2·499	−3°03′	3·3	1·418	+44°57′	0·1045	−144°06′
0·5	2·038	+9°24′	1·997	−4°46′	3·4	1·417	+44°56′	0·09449	−149°50′
0·6	1·732	+13°18′	1·662	−6°52′	3·5	1·416	+44°56′	0·08547	−155°34′
0·7	1·531	+17°38′	1·421	−9°20′	3·6	1·415	+44°56′	0·07732	−161°18′
0·8	1·398	+22°11′	1·239	−12°11′	3·7	1·415	+44°56′	0·06995	−167°02′
0·9	1·314	+26°41′	1·095	−15°23′	3·8	1·414	+44°57′	0·06328	−172°45′
1·0	1·266	+30°56′	0·9784	−18°56′	3·9	1·414	+44°57′	0·05725	−178°29′
1·1	1·242	+34°43′	0·8808	−22°50′	4·0	1·414	+44°58′	0·05180	−184°12′
1·2	1·237	+37°57′	0·7972	−27°03′	4·1	1·414	+44°58′	0·04687	−189°56′
1·3	1·245	+40°36′	0·7242	−31°33′	4·2	1·414	+44°59′	0·04241	−195°39′
1·4	1·261	+42°39′	0·6596	−36°19′	4·3	1·414	+44°59′	0·03838	−201°23′
1·5	1·281	+44°12′	0·6014	−41°20′	4·4	1·414	+44°59′	0·03473	−207°06′
1·6	1·303	+45°16′	0·5487	−46°32′	4·5	1·414	+45°00′	0·03142	−212°50′
1·7	1·326	+45°59′	0·5005	−51°56′	4·6	1·414	+45°00′	0·02843	−218°34′
1·8	1·347	+46°23′	0·4563	−57°27′	4·7	1·414	+45°00′	0·02573	−224°17′
1·9	1·365	+46°34′	0·4156	−63°06′	4·8	1·414	+45°00′	0·02328	−230°01′
2·0	1·381	+46°35′	0·3782	−68°49′	4·9	1·414	+45°00′	0·02106	−235°45′
2·1	1·394	+46°30′	0·3438	−74°35′					
2·2	1·404	+46°21′	0·3122	−80°23′					
2·3	1·411	+46°09′	0·2832	−86°12′					
2·4	1·416	+45°56′	0·2568	−92°02′					

2.4. INDICIAL RESPONSE

Taking a section of a wall as a thermal system, the response coming from the system when the excitation is in the form of a unit function is called indicial response. Unit function $U(t)$ is defined as the function of time characterised by:

$$U(t) = 0 \quad \text{for } t \leq 0$$
$$U(t) = 1 \quad \text{for } t > 0$$

Figure 2.5. shows the unit function.

Fig. 2.5.   Unit function.

The unit function is one of the basic excitation functions and the indicial response is the basic response function that characterises the system. Using the indicial response, the response to any excitation can be obtained by the convolution principle to be described later.

In the case of unsteady state heat conduction through a flat, homogeneous wall, the unit function and indicial response can be temperature or heat flow. It is always important, therefore, to specify the nature of these functions.

Let us take a unit function representing the surface temperature at $x = 0$, keeping the other surface temperature at $x = l$ to be always 0, where l is wall thickness. Then the task is to obtain the response function of temperature within the wall section. The procedure to obtain such an indicial response is to solve the partial differential equation of unsteady state heat conduction of eqn. (2.4) under the conditions that

$$\theta(0,t) = U(t)$$
$$\theta(l,t) = 0 \qquad (2.29)$$

It is known that the form of the solution equation, eqn. (2.4), is expressed by:

$$\theta(x,t) = Ax + B + \sum_{n=1}^{\infty} C_n \exp(-D_n t)\sin\frac{n\pi x}{l} \qquad (2.30)$$

A, B, C and D are the unknown constants to be determined from the boundary conditions as given by eqn. (2.29) in this case. $B = 1$ can be derived from $\theta(0, t) = U(t)$ and $Al + B = 0$ from $\theta(l, t) = 0$ that gives $A = -1/l$.

Substituting $\partial\theta/\partial t$ and $\partial^2\theta/\partial x^2$ from eqn. (2.30) into eqn. (2.4):

$$D_n = a\frac{n^2\pi^2}{l^2} \qquad (2.31)$$

can be obtained.

From the condition $\theta(x, 0) = 0$ and the above results, it follows that:

$$1 - \frac{x}{l} + \sum_{n=1}^{\infty} C_n \sin\frac{n\pi x}{l} = 0 \qquad (2.32)$$

Using the formula (2.15a) where $f(x) = -1 + x/l$, C_n can be obtained as:

$$C_n = \frac{2}{l}\int_0^l \left(-1 + \frac{\xi}{l}\right)\sin\frac{n\pi\xi}{l}d\xi = -\frac{2}{n\pi} \qquad (2.33)$$

Then the solution is expressed by the following, denoting it as $\Phi_{\theta 0}(x, t)$:

$$\Phi_{\theta 0}(x,t) = 1 - \frac{x}{l} - \frac{2}{\pi}\sum_{n=1}^{\infty}\frac{1}{n}\exp\left(-\frac{an^2\pi^2}{l^2}t\right)\sin\frac{n\pi x}{l} \qquad (2.34)$$

This is the indicial response of the temperature of the wall section against the excitation of the surface temperature at $x = 0$. The rate of heat flow is derived from eqn. (2.34) and expressed as:

$$\begin{aligned}\Phi_{q0}(x,t) &= -\lambda\frac{\partial\Phi_{\theta 0}(x,t)}{\partial x} \\ &= \lambda\left[\frac{1}{l} + \frac{2}{l}\sum_{n=1}^{\infty}\frac{1}{n}\exp\left(-\frac{an^2\pi^2}{l^2}t\right)\cos\frac{n\pi x}{l}\right]\end{aligned} \qquad (2.35a)$$

The heat flow at $x = l$, which essentially becomes a characteristic function for heat gain through walls, is given by:

$$\Phi_{q0}(l,t) = \lambda\left[\frac{1}{l} + \frac{2}{l}\sum_{n=1}^{\infty}(-1)^n\exp\left(-\frac{an^2\pi^2}{l^2}t\right)\right] \qquad (2.35b)$$

In a similar manner, the indicial response of the temperature of the wall section to the excitation of the surface temperature at $x = l$ can be obtained. It is denoted by $\Phi_{\theta l}(x, t)$ expressed as:

$$\Phi_{\theta 0}(x,t) = \frac{x}{l} + \sum_{n=1}^{\infty} \frac{2(-1)^n}{n\pi} \exp\left(-\frac{an^2\pi^2}{l^2}t\right) \sin\frac{n\pi x}{l} \qquad (2.35c)$$

2.5. Impulse Response and Convolution

Impulse response is simply a derivative of indicial response, viz.,

$$\varphi(x,t) = \frac{d\Phi(x,t)}{dt} \qquad (2.36)$$

where $\Phi(x, t)$ identifies indicial response and $\varphi(x, t)$ impulse response. Two subscripts are used for Φ and φ in this book. The first subscript identifies the temperature or heat flow and the second subscript the location where temperature excitation is given; for example $\Phi_{\theta 0}$ means the indicial response of temperature against temperature excitation at $x = 0$, and φ_{q1} means the impulse response of heat flow against temperature excitation at $x = l$.

Impulse response is often called a weighting function and is also defined as the response against the excitation given in the form of Dirac's delta function. The delta function $\delta(t)$ is again a derivative of the unit function, namely:

$$\delta(t) = \frac{dU(t)}{dt} \qquad (2.37)$$

and defined as the function of time characterized by:

$$\delta(t) = \frac{1}{\varepsilon} \quad \text{for } 0 \leq t \leq \varepsilon$$

$$\delta(t) = 0 \quad \text{for } t < 0, t > \varepsilon \qquad (2.38)$$

$$\lim_{\varepsilon \to 0} \int_0^\varepsilon \delta(t)dt = 1$$

Figure 2.6 shows the delta function. Impulse response is also a characteristic function relating excitation to response. When the actual excitation is given in the form of a function of time f(t), the actual response g(t) is expressed in the following form, using impulse response for the system $\varphi(t)$, viz.,

$$g(t) = \int_0^\infty \varphi(\tau) f(t - \tau) d\tau \qquad (2.39)$$

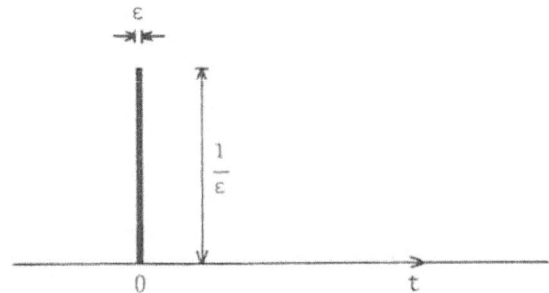

Fig. 2.6. Delta function.

This form of integral expression is called convolution or Duhamel's integral, and is a very important expression. It is always difficult for beginners to understand the real meaning of the convolution. One must bear in mind that the integral is a function of t not of τ and τ is also expressed in time domain, starting from $\tau = 0$ at time t to the reverse direction towards the past as shown in Fig. 2.7.

The product of $\varphi(\tau)f(t-\tau)d\tau$ corresponds to the shaded volume in Fig. 2.7. The excitation that appeared τ ago from the present time t brings effect at t as a part of the response at t.

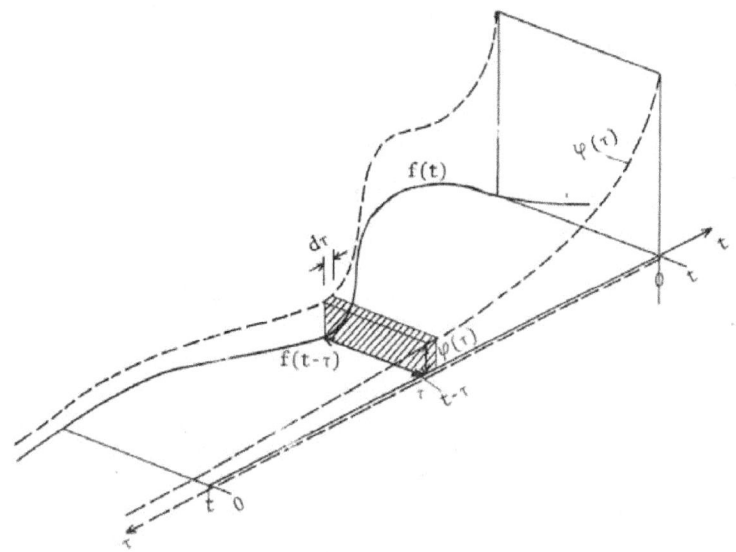

Fig. 2.7. Graphical interpretation of convolution.

So the integral is the sum of these effects of incremental responses from $\tau = 0$ to infinity, which corresponds to the total volume of Fig. 2.7, making the actual response $g(t)$ of eqn. (2.39).

The impulse response of the surface heat flow at $x = 0$ and $x = l$ against the surface temperature excitation at $x = 0$ can be obtained by differentiation from eqn. (2.35a) as follows:

$$\varphi_{q0}(0,t) = -2\lambda \sum_{n=1}^{\infty} \frac{an^2\pi^2}{l^2} \exp\left(-\frac{an^2\pi^2}{l^2}t\right) \qquad (2.40)$$

$$\varphi_{q0}(l,t) = -2\lambda \sum_{n=1}^{\infty} (-1)^n \frac{an^2\pi^2}{l^2} \exp\left(-\frac{an^2\pi^2}{l^2}t\right) \qquad (2.41)$$

Figure 2.8 shows the generalised pattern of the impulse response of the inside surface heat flow against the surface temperature excitation at $x = 0$ and $x = l$.

For example, the surface heat flow at $x = l$, $q(l, t)$, when the surface temperature excitation at $x = 0$ is given as $f(t) = -ct^2$, can be obtained from the calculation of the following convolution, viz.,

$$q(l,t) = \int_0^\infty -2\lambda \sum_{n=1}^{\infty} (-1)^n \exp\left(-\frac{an^2\pi^2}{l^2}\tau\right)\left[-c(t-\tau)^2\right]d\tau$$

$$= 2c\lambda \sum_{n=1}^{\infty} (-1)^n -\frac{an^2\pi^2}{l^2} \int_0^\infty \exp\left(-\frac{an^2\pi^2}{l^2}\tau\right)\cdot(t-\tau)^2 d\tau$$

$$= 2c\lambda \sum_{n=1}^{\infty} (-1)^n -\frac{an^2\pi^2}{l^2} I.$$

Letting

$$\frac{an^2\pi^2}{l^2} = k$$

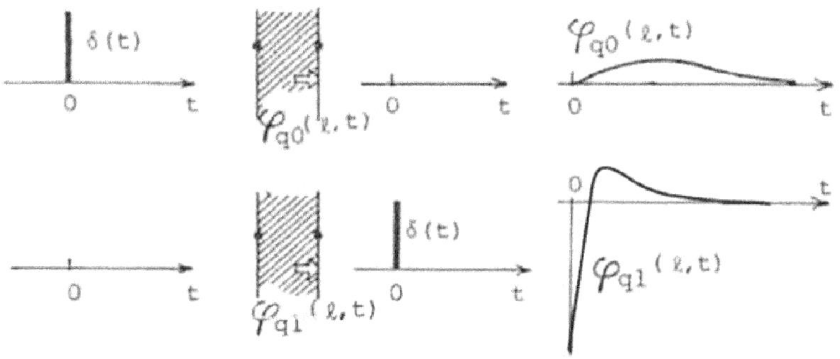

Fig. 2.8. Impulse response of inside heat flow for surface temperature excitation,

and

$$I = \int_0^\infty \exp(-k\tau)(t-\tau) d\tau$$
$$= [\exp(-k\tau)\tfrac{1}{3}(t-\tau)^3]_0^\infty - \int_0^\infty -k\exp(-k\tau)(t-\tau)^2 d\tau$$
$$= -\tfrac{1}{3}t^3 + kI$$

Therefore,

$$I = \frac{t^3}{3(k-1)} = \frac{t^3}{3\left(\dfrac{an^2\pi^2}{l^2}-1\right)}$$

and thus

$$q(l,t) = 2c\lambda \sum_{n=1}^\infty (-1)^n \cdot \frac{an^2\pi^2}{l^2} \cdot \frac{t^3}{3\left(\dfrac{an^2\pi^2}{l^2}-1\right)}$$

$$= \tfrac{2}{3}c\lambda t^3 \left[-\frac{1}{1-\dfrac{l^2}{a\pi^2}} + \frac{1}{1-\dfrac{l^2}{4a\pi^2}} - \frac{1}{1-\dfrac{l^2}{9a\pi^2}} + \cdots \right]$$

(2.42)

2.6. Solution by Laplace Transformation

Solution of the partial differential equation of unsteady state heat conduction in a flat wall by the method of Laplace transformation is described in various text books such as those by Carslaw and Jaeger [2.2] and Churchill [2.3].

The Laplace transformation is a very convenient tool for solving differential equations. The method of solution appears quite easy as if it were solved by a trick. It is made in the same way as a multiplication is performed by the operation of an addition in the imaginary space of logarithm, where 'log' is called operator. In the case of the Laplace transformation, every term in a differential equation is transformed into another form within an imaginary space according to a certain rule by the operator 'L', so that the differential equation in the original space is transformed into a simple algebraic equation in the imaginary space and can be solved quite easily. The solution in the imaginary space is then transformed back into the form of the original space by the same rule to become a solution function.

The rules for the transformation are rather simple. By definition the original function f(t) of time t, is transformed into φ(s) in the imaginary space according to the formula:

$$\varphi(s) = \int_0^\infty f(t) \exp(-st)\, dt \qquad (2.43)$$

The function φ(s) is called the Laplace transform of f(t) and may be denoted as:

$$L\{f(t)\} = \varphi(s) \qquad (2.44)$$

There are some fundamental rules of Laplace transformation as follows:

(1) $\quad L\{af_1(t) + bf_2(t)\} = a\, L\{f_1(t)\} + b L\{f_2(t)\} = a\varphi_1(s) + b\varphi_2(s)$

$$\qquad (2.45)$$

where a and b are constants.

(2) $\quad L\left\{\dfrac{\partial f(t)}{\partial t}\right\} = s\varphi(s) - f(0) \qquad (2.46)$

where f(0) is value of f(t) at $t = 0$

(3) $\quad L\left\{\dfrac{\partial^n f(t)}{\partial t^n}\right\} = s^n \varphi(s) - s^{n-1} f(0) - s^{n-2} f'(0) - \cdots - f^{(n-2)}(0) \qquad (2.47)$

(4) $\quad L\left\{\displaystyle\int_0^t f(\tau)\, d\tau\right\} = \dfrac{1}{s}\varphi(s) \qquad (2.48)$

(5) $\quad L\{t\, f(t)\} = -\varphi(s) \qquad (2.49)$

(6) $\quad L\{\exp(at) f(t)\} = \varphi(s - a) \qquad (2.50)$

(7) $\quad L\left\{\displaystyle\int_0^t f_1(t-\tau) f_2(\tau)\, d\tau\right\} = \varphi_1(s) \cdot \varphi_2(s) \qquad (2.51)$

After solving an equation for φ(s), φ(s) must be transformed back into f(t). The fundamental relationships of reverse transformation are listed in Table 2.2.

The partial differential equation of the unsteady state heat conduction as in eqn. (2.4) can be rewritten in the form of imaginary space by the rules of Laplace transformation, making $L\{\theta(x,t)\} = u(x,s)$ as in the following:

$$a\frac{\partial^2 u(x,s)}{\partial x^2} = su(x,s) \tag{2.52}$$

The solution form of this equation is

$$u(x,s) = c_1 \exp(d_1 x) + c_2 \exp(-d_2 x) \tag{2.53}$$

where c_1, c_2, d_1 and d_2 and determined by boundary conditions. When the boundary conditions are $u(0, s) = 0$ and $u(l, s) = f(s)$, it follows that:

$$d_1 = d_2 = \sqrt{\frac{s}{a}}$$

$$c_1 = \frac{f(s)}{\exp(l\sqrt{s/a}) - \exp(-l\sqrt{s/a})}$$

$$c_2 = \frac{-f(s)}{\exp(l\sqrt{s/a}) - \exp(-l\sqrt{s/a})}$$

Then the solution of eqn. (2.52) is expressed by:

$$u(x,s) = f(s)\frac{\sinh x\sqrt{s/a}}{\sinh l\sqrt{s/a}} = f(s)\varphi_{\theta 1}(x,s) \tag{2.54}$$

where

$$\tau_{\theta 1}(x,s) = \frac{\sinh x\sqrt{s/a}}{\sinh l\sqrt{s/a}} \tag{2.55}$$

$\tau_{\theta 1}(x, s)$ is the Laplace transform of the impulse response of the temperature at x against the surface temperature excitation at $x = l$ and is called the transfer function. In general, the transfer function may be defined as the Laplace transform of the impulse response. The transfer function could also be interpreted as the solution when excitation is given as a delta function in the original space, i.e. $f(s) = 1$ as one of the boundary conditions. Reverse transform of $\tau_{\theta 1}(x, s)$ gives impulse response as in the following, viz.,

$$\tau_{\theta 1}(x,s) = \frac{\sinh x\sqrt{s/a}}{\sinh l\sqrt{s/a}}$$
$$= -\frac{2\pi a}{l^2}\sum_{n=1}^{x}(-1)^n n \exp\left(-\frac{an^2\pi^2}{l^2}t\right)\sin\frac{n\pi x}{l} \tag{2.56}$$

It is obvious that this is the derivative of eqn. (2.35).

Table 2.2
Reverse transformation of simple functions

$\varphi(s)$	$f(t)$
$\dfrac{a}{s}$	a
$\dfrac{1}{s-a}$	$\exp(at)$
$\dfrac{a}{s^2+a^2}$	$\sin at$
$\dfrac{s}{s^2+a^2}$	$\cos at$
$\dfrac{a}{s^2-a^2}$	$\sinh at$
$\dfrac{s}{s^2-a^2}$	$\cosh at$
$\dfrac{1}{s(s+a)}$	$\dfrac{1}{a}[1-\exp(-at)]$
$\dfrac{1}{s^2}$	t
$\dfrac{1}{s^3}$	$\dfrac{t^2}{2}$
$\dfrac{1}{s^n}$	$\dfrac{t^{n-1}}{(n-1)!}$
1	$\delta(t)$
$\exp(-as)$	$\delta(t-a)$
$\dfrac{1}{s}$	$U(t)$
$\dfrac{\exp(-as)}{s}$	$U(t-a)$
$\dfrac{\exp(-a\sqrt{s})}{s}$	$\operatorname{erfc}\dfrac{a}{2\sqrt{t}}$

43

Table 2.2—contd.

$\varphi(s)$	$f(t)$
$\dfrac{ab}{(s^2+a^2)(s^2+b^2)}$	$\dfrac{a\sin bt - b\sin at}{a^2 - b^2}$
$\dfrac{\sinh x\sqrt{s}}{\sinh l\sqrt{s}} \ (-l < x < l)$	$-\dfrac{2\pi}{l^2}\sum_{n=1}^{\infty}(-1)^n n \sin\dfrac{n\pi x}{l}\exp\left(-\dfrac{n^2\pi^2 t}{l^2}\right)$
$\exp(-a\sqrt{s})$	$\dfrac{a}{2\sqrt{\pi t^3}}\exp\left(-\dfrac{a^2}{4t}\right)$

2.7. MATRIX EXPRESSION OF SURFACE TEMPERATURE AND SURFACE HEAT FLOW

In the air conditioning load calculation, we are interested in the temperature and heat flow particularly at both surfaces of the wall. When the temperature excitation is given on both surfaces at $x = 0$ and $x = l$ in the expression $\theta(0, t)$ and $\theta(l, t)$ simultaneously, the superposition principle yields the equations to give the heat flow at both surfaces as in the following convolution expression:

$$q(0,t) = \int_0^x \varphi_{q0}(0,\tau).\theta(0,t-\tau)\,d\tau + \int_0^x \varphi_{q1}(0,\tau).\theta(l,t-\tau)\,d\tau \tag{2.57}$$

$$q(l,t) = \int_0^x \varphi_{q0}(l,\tau).\theta(0,t-\tau)\,d\tau + \int_0^x \varphi_{q1}(l,\tau).\theta(l,t-\tau)\,d\tau \tag{2.58}$$

In converting these equations into Laplace transform, the following notations are to be used:

$$\begin{aligned}L\{\theta(x,t)\} &= u(x,s), & L\{q(x,t)\} &= h(x,s),\\ L\{\varphi_{q0}(x,t)\} &= \tau_{q0}(x,s), & L\{\varphi_{q1}(x,t)\} &= \tau_{q1}(x,s),\end{aligned} \tag{2.59}$$

Then eqns. (2.57) and (2.58) can be rewritten in the following Laplace transform applying the formula that convolution becomes a product in the imaginary space as shown in eqn. (2.51).

$$h(0,s) = \tau_{q0}(0,s)u(0,s) + \tau_{q1}(0,s)u(l,s)$$
$$h(l,s) = \tau_{q0}(l,s)u(0,s) + \tau_{q1}(l,s)u(l,s)$$
(2.60)

These can be rewritten in matrix expression as follows,

$$\begin{bmatrix} h(0,s) \\ h(l,s) \end{bmatrix} = \begin{bmatrix} \tau_{q0}(0,s) & \tau_{q1}(0,s) \\ \tau_{q0}(l,s) & \tau_{q1}(l,s) \end{bmatrix} \begin{bmatrix} u(0,s) \\ u(l,s) \end{bmatrix}$$
(2.61)

The first matrix in the right-hand side of the above expression is called transfer matrix, in the sense that it relates the temperature matrix to the heat flow matrix. This is analogous to the relationship between electric current and voltage in a system as explained by Pipes [2.4]. The four elements of the transfer matrix can be obtained from the transfer function of temperature given in eqn. (2.55). The relation between the transfer function of heat flow and the transfer function of temperature is the same as in the original space, viz.,

$$\tau_{q1}(x,s) = -\lambda \frac{\partial \tau_{\theta 1}(x,s)}{\partial x}$$
$$= -\lambda \sqrt{\frac{s}{a}} \frac{\cosh x\sqrt{s/a}}{\sinh l\sqrt{s/a}}$$

Therefore

$$\tau_{q1}(0,s) = -\frac{\lambda\sqrt{s/a}}{\sinh l\sqrt{s/a}}$$
$$\tau_{q1}(l,s) = -\lambda\sqrt{\frac{s}{a}} \frac{\cosh l\sqrt{s/a}}{\sinh l\sqrt{s/a}}$$
(2.62)

Similarly,

$$\tau_{q0}(x,s) = -\lambda \frac{\partial \tau_{\theta 0}(x,s)}{\partial x} = -\lambda \frac{\partial}{\partial x}\left(\frac{\sinh(l-x)\sqrt{s/a}}{\sinh l\sqrt{s/a}} \right)$$
$$= -\lambda \sqrt{\frac{s}{a}} \frac{\cosh(l-x)\sqrt{s/a}}{\sinh l\sqrt{s/a}}$$

Therefore,

$$\tau_{q0}(0,s) = \lambda\sqrt{\frac{s}{a}}\frac{\cosh l\sqrt{s/a}}{\sinh l\sqrt{s/a}}$$

$$\tau_{q0}(l,s) = \frac{\lambda\sqrt{s/a}}{\sinh l\sqrt{s/a}} \qquad (2.63)$$

It must be noted that:

$$\tau_{q1}(0,s) = \tau_{q0}(l,s)$$
$$\tau_{q1}(l,s) = \tau_{q0}(0,s) \qquad (2.64)$$

Furthermore eqn. (2.61) can be rewritten as

$$\begin{bmatrix} u(0,s) \\ h(0,s) \end{bmatrix} = \begin{bmatrix} A(s) & B(s) \\ C(s) & D(s) \end{bmatrix} \begin{bmatrix} u(l,s) \\ h(l,s) \end{bmatrix} \qquad (2.65)$$

where

$$A(s) = \frac{\tau_{q1}(l,s)}{\tau_{q0}(l,s)} = \cosh l\sqrt{\frac{s}{a}}$$

$$B(s) = \frac{1}{\tau_{q0}(l,s)} = \frac{\sinh l\sqrt{s/a}}{\lambda\sqrt{s/a}}$$

$$C(s) = \tau_{q1}(0,s) - \frac{\tau_{q1}(l,s)}{\tau_{q0}(l,s)}\tau_{q0}(0,s) = -\lambda\sqrt{\frac{s}{a}}\sinh l\sqrt{\frac{s}{a}} \qquad (2.66)$$

$$D(s) = \frac{\tau_{q0}(0,s)}{\tau_{q0}(l,s)} = \cosh l\sqrt{\frac{s}{a}}$$

The meaning of eqn. (2.65) is that it gives responses of temperature and of heat flow at one surface when both excitations of temperature and heat flow at the other surface affect the thermal system of a wall section as characterised by the transfer matrix.

For the wall whose thermal capacity can be neglected, i.e. $1/a = 0$, the transfer matrix in eqn. (2.65) can be reduced to the following:

$$\begin{bmatrix} A(s) & B(s) \\ C(s) & D(s) \end{bmatrix} \begin{bmatrix} 1 & R \\ 0 & 1 \end{bmatrix} \qquad (2.67)$$

Where R = thermal resistance ($m^2 degC\ W^{-1}$).

For a multi-layer wall, the transfer matrix of the whole wall is to be expressed simply by the product of the transfer matrices of every layer of the wall. Thus, using simplified notation,

$$\begin{bmatrix} u_0 \\ h_0 \end{bmatrix} = \begin{bmatrix} A_1 & B_1 \\ C_1 & D_1 \end{bmatrix} \begin{bmatrix} A_2 & B_2 \\ C_2 & D_2 \end{bmatrix} \cdots \begin{bmatrix} A_m & B_m \\ C_m & D_m \end{bmatrix} \begin{bmatrix} u_1 \\ h_1 \end{bmatrix} \qquad (2.68)$$

Having the product of these transfer matrices converted into one transfer matrix, the relationship of surface temperature and heat flow between at one surface of a multi-layer wall and at the other surface of it can be expressed in the same form as in the case of single layer wall, namely:

$$\begin{bmatrix} u_0 \\ h_0 \end{bmatrix} = \begin{bmatrix} A & B \\ C & D \end{bmatrix} \begin{bmatrix} u_1 \\ h_1 \end{bmatrix} \qquad (2.69)$$

When the boundary layer of surface film is to be taken into account, i.e. excitation and response are given in fluid temperature instead of surface temperature, the procedure is so simple that the first and the last transfer matrices need only be substituted by the matrix for the layer without thermal capacity as expressed by eqn. (2.67).

After obtaining the combined transfer matrix as expressed by eqn. (2.69), it is necessary to convert back into the original form as in eqn. (2.61) in order to have the surface heat flows expressed as responses and the surface temperatures as excitations. Thus the final form of a multi-layer wall is expressed in the following:

$$\begin{bmatrix} h_0 \\ h_1 \end{bmatrix} = \begin{bmatrix} \dfrac{D(s)}{B(s)} & \dfrac{1}{B(s)} \\ \dfrac{1}{B(s)} & \dfrac{A(s)}{B(s)} \end{bmatrix} \begin{bmatrix} u_0 \\ u_1 \end{bmatrix} \qquad (2.70)$$

The problem is then to transform the four elements in the matrix back into their original form in the original space.

2.8. RESPONSE FACTORS—DEFINITION AND USAGE

In order to make use of eqn. (2.70) to obtain surface heat flow as heat gain through a wall, temperature excitation should be given as an algebraic function which can be transformed easily into the Laplace imaginary form, although the calculation process in the convolution can still be complicated.

Mitalas and Stephenson [2.5] presented an approach which introduced a time series expression into the calculation process. Looking at the natural excitations such as outside air temperature and solar radiation, they were found to vary in a quite random fashion. It is necessary, therefore, to incorporate these natural random processes into the thermal system if a rather rigorous manipulation of theoretical process is to be made, as discussed so far.

The time series expression is very simple. For example, the variation of outside air temperature is expressed in time series by picking out hourly values of the temperature and putting them in an array in the order of time in hours. If one tried to use Fourier's series or other mathematical expressions, the real form of the function to express such a random variable would become quite complicated. In the time series expression each term of the array represents a triangle whose height is equal to the value of the term and whose base width is equal to the time span of two hours. Thus the area of triangle is equal to the value of the term as shown in Fig.2.9 and, interestingly enough, the pattern of the straight lines connecting all peak points of the triangles turns out to be an approximation of the original curve. This approximation can be considered reasonably good for air conditioning purposes and the responses can also be obtained in time series on the hourly basis.

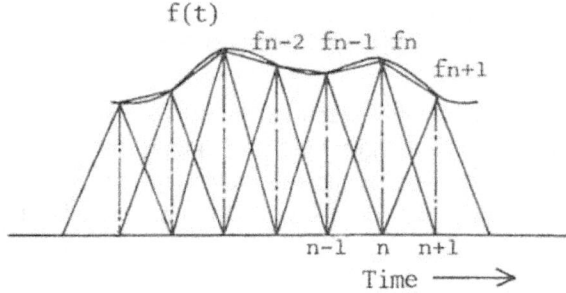

Fig. 2.9.   Superposition of triangle pulse

In Fig. 2.9 the function expressed in the curve may be replaced by the series of values of f(*t*) at a specified time interval Δt such as ..., f_{n-2}, f_{n-1}, f_n, f_{n+1}, f_{n+2}, ..., where $t = n \Delta t$. Likewise temperature and heat flow may be expressed as θ_n and q_n respectively in time series.

The surface heat flow responses against the unit triangle pulse of the surface temperature excitation whose height is unity are obtained to give the fundamental response functions. Then, taking the values of the function at the same time interval, i.e. one hour in this case, the response function of heat flow can be expressed in the form of a time series. The values for the series thus obtained are called response factors. There are four kinds of response factors in heat conduction through walls. Referring to Fig. 2.10, they are the response factors of heat flow at:
1. outside surface for outside surface temperature excitation $X(j), j = 0, 1, 2, ...,$
2. inside surface for outside surface temperature excitation $Y(j)$,
3. outside surface for inside surface temperature excitation $Y(j)$,
4. inside surface for inside surface temperature excitation $Z(j)$.

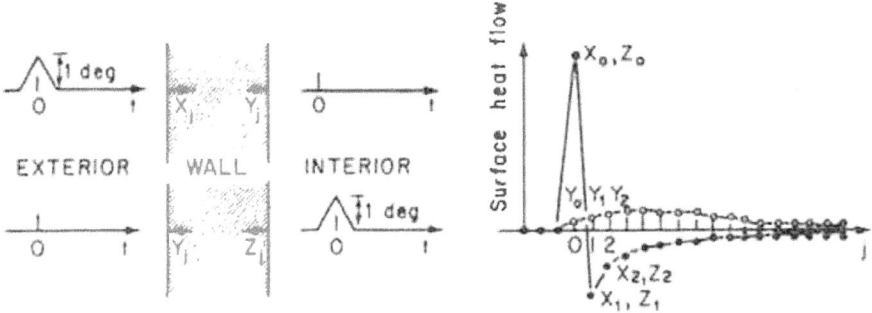

Fig. 2.10. Response factors [7.4].

These surface temperature excitations are given in the form of a unit triangular pulse. Response factors also characterise the thermal system of a wall as do the transfer function and the impulse response. The convolution expression in time series then allows for calculation of actual response of the surface heat flow as in the following.

When the surface temperature at $x = 0$ is given in time series as ..., $\theta(n-2)$, $\theta(n-1)$, $\theta(n)$, the responses of surface heat flow at time $t = n\,\Delta t$ at $x = 0$ and $x = l$ due to these temperatures can be expressed by using response factors $X(j)$ and $Y(j)$ as follows:

$$q_0(0,n) = X(0)\theta(n) + X(1)\theta(n-1) + X(2)\theta(n-2) + \cdots$$
$$= \sum_{j=0}^{\infty} X(j)\theta(n-j) \qquad (2.71)$$

$$q_0(l,n) = Y(0)\theta(n) + Y(1)\theta(n-1) + Y(2)\theta(n-2) + \cdots$$
$$= \sum_{j=0}^{\infty} Y(j)\theta(n-j) \qquad (2.72)$$

When the surface temperature at $x = l$ is given as $\theta(n)$, the responses of surface heat flow are expressed in the following, taking the direction of heat flow reversed:

$$q_1(0,n) = \sum_{j=0}^{\infty} Y(j)\theta(n-j) \qquad (2.73)$$

$$q_1(l,n) = \sum_{j=0}^{\infty} Z(j)\theta(n-j) \qquad (2.74)$$

These are the fundamental convolution forms using response factors. The real problem is then how to obtain response factors.

2.9. DERIVATION OF RESPONSE FACTORS

The core equation from which the response factors are derived is the matrix equation in the Laplace imaginary form as expressed in eqn. (2.70) for a general multi-layer wall. The response factors $X(j)$, $Y(j)$ and $Z(j)$ are expressed in time series of the function of t as the reverse transform of

$$\frac{D(s)}{B(s)} \quad \frac{1}{B(s)} \quad \text{and} \quad \frac{A(s)}{B(s)}$$

respectively, when u_0 and u_1 are given in the Laplace transform of the unit triangle surface temperature. The unit triangle pulse for a given time increment Δt as shown in Fig. 2.11 can be expressed by the superposition of three ramp functions:

$$f(t) = \frac{1}{\Delta t}(t + \Delta t) - \frac{2}{\Delta t}t + \frac{1}{\Delta t}(t - \Delta t) \tag{2.75}$$

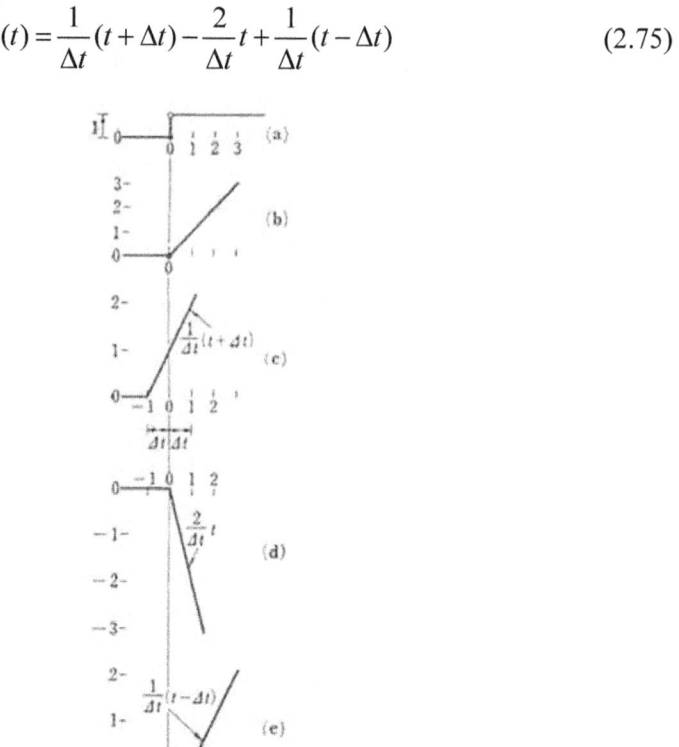

Fig. 2.11. Composition of unit triangle pulse [7.4]. (a) Unit function, (b) ramp function, (c) $(1/\Delta t)(t+\Delta t)$, (d) $-2t/\Delta t$, (e) $(1/\Delta t)(t-\Delta t)$, (f) unit triangle pulse as (c) + (d) + (e).

Figure 2.11 illustrates the composition of unit triangle pulse.

In consequence, the response function for the excitation of f(t) = t must be obtained first, namely as $L\{t\} = 1/s^2$. Then the reverse transforms of

$$\frac{D(s)}{s^2 B(s)} \quad \frac{1}{s^2 B(s)} \quad \text{and} \quad \frac{A(s)}{s^2 B(s)}$$

will be obtained next. If these reverse transforms are expressed in the function of time t, the response functions for f(t) in eqn. (2.75) can easily be obtained by superposition. Then taking the values of the response functions at $t = j \Delta t$ ($j = 0, 1, 2, \cdots$), next step to obtain the response factors $X(j)$, $Y(j)$ and $Z(j)$ must follow.

In order to obtain the reverse transforms described above, Heaviside's expansion theorem must be used. This theorem gives a general method of reverse transform when the prepared formulas for reverse transform as listed in Table 2.2 cannot be applied. In general Heaviside's expansion theorem is explained as follows.

When the function of s in the imaginary space is expressed as $\varphi(s) = p(s)/q(s)$, where both $p(s)$ and $q(s)$ are polynomials of s and the order of polynomial of $p(s)$ is lower than that of $q(s)$, the reverse transform of $\varphi(s)$ can be given by the expression:

$$f(t) = \sum_{m=1}^{\infty} \frac{p(\alpha_m)}{q(\alpha_m)} \exp(\alpha_m t) \tag{2.76}$$

where α_m, $m = 1, 2, \ldots$, are the roots of $q(s) = 0$, $|\alpha_{m+1}| > |\alpha_m|$ and there are no double roots. The term $p(\alpha_m)/q'(\alpha_m)$ is called residue and the roots of $q(s) = 0$ are called poles.

When $q(s)$ has a root $s = 0$, the reverse transform of $\varphi(s) = p(s)/sq(s)$ is:

$$f(t) = \frac{p(0)}{q(0)} + \sum_{m=1}^{\infty} \frac{p(\alpha_m)}{\alpha_m q'(\alpha_m)} \exp(\alpha_m t) \tag{2.77}$$

When $q(s)$ has double roots of $s = 0$, the reverse transform of $\varphi(s) = p(s)/sq(s)$ is:

$$f(t) = \frac{p(0)}{q(0)} t + \left\{\frac{d}{ds}\left(\frac{p(s)}{q(s)}\right)\right\}_{s=0} + \sum_{m=1}^{\infty} \frac{p(\alpha_m)}{\alpha_m^2 q'(\alpha_m)} \exp(\alpha_m t) \tag{2.78}$$

Back to the present problem, the roots of $B(s) = 0$ must be obtained first. In the case of a single homogeneous wall,

$$s^2 B(s) = s^2 \frac{\sinh l\sqrt{s/a}}{\lambda \sqrt{s/a}} \tag{2.79}$$

The roots of $\sinh l\sqrt{s/a} = 0$ are

$$\alpha_m = -\frac{m^2 \pi^2 a}{l^2} \tag{2.80}$$

This implies that all of the roots are negative real. There are also double roots of $s = 0$ from $s^2 = 0$. Then the reverse transform of $D(s)/s^2 B(s)$ can be expressed using the formula of eqn. (2.78) as in the following:

$$\xi(t) = \frac{D(0)}{B(0)} t + \left[\frac{d}{ds} \left(\frac{D(s)}{q(s)} \right) \right]_{s=0} + \sum_{m=1}^{\infty} \frac{D(\alpha_m)}{\alpha_m^2 B'(\alpha_m)} \exp(\alpha_m t) \tag{2.81}$$

The response factors $X(j)$ are then obtained as follows:

$$\begin{aligned} X(0) &= \xi(\Delta t) \\ X(1) &= \xi(2\Delta t) - 2\xi(\Delta t) \\ X(j) &= \xi[(j+1)\Delta t] - 2\xi(j\Delta t) + \xi[(j+1)\Delta t] \qquad \text{for } j \geq 2 \end{aligned} \tag{2.82}$$

Similarly $\eta(t)$ and $\zeta(t)$ can be expressed as the reverse transform of $1/s^2 B(s)$ and $A(s)/s^2 B(s)$ respectively, in the form as functions of t similar to eqn. (2.81) and the response factors $Y(j)$ and $Z(j)$ are obtained in the same way as in eqn. (2.82).

In the case of a multi-layer wall, the form of $B(s)$ is not so simple as in eqn. (2,79). The original method of finding the roots in the case of the multi-layer wall is presented by Mitalas and Arseneault [2.6].

Matsuo attempted to find the roots in a simpler way, using the Newton-Raphson method, as shown in Fig. 2.12 [2.7].

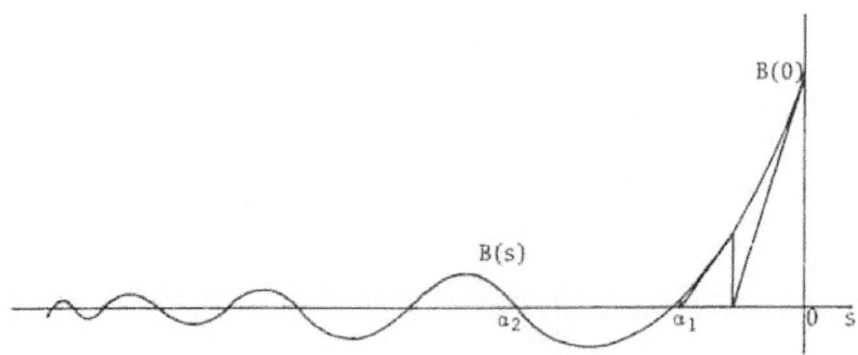

Fig. 2.12. Finding the root α_1 of $B(s) = 0$ by Matsuo.

Table 2.3
Examples of response factors

(a) Exterior Wall A

	l	λ	γ	C_p	R	Material
Layer 1	0·010 0	1·180 0	2 100	0·172 0	0·0	mortar
Layer 2	0·150 0	1·204 0	2 200	0·180 6	0·0	concrete
Layer 3	0·050 0	0·032 7	180	0·102 0	0·0	rock wool
Layer 4	0·006 0	0·103 2	700	0·172 0	0·0	hard tex

Response factors j	$X(j)$	$Y(j)$	$Z(j)$
0	24·283 013 83	0·003 788 73	1·605 057.83
1	−14·159 094 82	0·075 358 63	−0·993 800 32
2	−2·783 108 02	0·122 851 23	−0·008 744 82
3	−1·809 295 01	0·099 618 39	−0·005 731 84
4	−1·312 670 54	0·073 944 10	−0·004 183 78
5	−0·963 689 20	0·054 410 61	−0·003 073 43
6	−0·708 334 27	0·040 002 33	−0·002 259 18
7	−0·520 705 08	0·029 406 88	−0·001 660 76
8	−0·382 781 22	0·021 617 66	−0·001 220 86
Common ratio		0·73512196	

(b) Exterior Wall B

	l	λ	γ	C_p	R	Material
Layer 1	0·015 0	0·653 6	1 830	0·172 0	0·0	tile
Layer 2	0·015 0	1·118 0	2 100	0·172 0	0·0	mortar
Layer 3	0·150 0	1·204 0	2 200	0·180 6	0·0	concrete
Layer 4	0·0	0·0	0	0·0	0·244 2	air space
Layer 5	0·010 0	0·094 6	300	0·430 0	0·0	wood board
Layer 6	0·013 0	0·074 8	200	0·172 0	0·0	tex

Response factors j	$X(j)$	$Y(j)$	$Z(j)$
0	19·666 339 51	0·005 091 72	2·583 601 33
1	−10·034 132 73	0·122 811 77	−0·851 411 60
2	−2·193 832 34	0·245 855 43	−0·065 274 75
3	−1·363 268 12	0·229 722 77	−0·045 673 14
4	−1·013 929 43	0·185 570 54	−0·035 070 36
5	−0·785 252 35	0·146 058 56	−0·027 336 27
6	−0·613 099 79	0·114 395 34	−0·021 370 09
7	−0·479 444 57	0·089 511 42	−0·016 715 49
8	−0·375 040 60	0·070 027 59	−0·013 076 14
9	−0·293 388 99	0·054 782 84	−0·010 229 37
10	−0·229 516 71	0·042 856 52	−0·008 002 40
Common ratio		0·782 297 02	

Table 2.3—*contd.*

(c) Interior Wall

	l	λ	γ	C_p	R	Material
Layer 1	0·007 0	0·447 2	1 940	0·215 0	0·0	plaster
Layer 2	0·096 0	0·627 8	2 100	0·172 0	0·0	concrete block
Layer 3	0·007 0	0·447 2	1 940	0·215 0	0·0	plaster

Response factors j	$X(j)$	$Y(j)$	$Z(j)$
0	16·445 622 73	0·821 125 52	16·445 622 73
1	−9·330 643 13	2·943 619 97	−9·330 643 13
2	−1·222 898 12	1·199 841 27	−1·222 898 12
3	−0·335 427 14	0·335 294 41	−0·335 427 14
4	−0·092 843 66	0·092 842 89	−0·092 843 66
5	−0·025 703 29	0·025 703 28	−0·025 703 29
6	−0·007 115 85	0·007 115 85	−0·007 115 85
Common ratio		0·276 845 96	

(d) Roof

	l	λ	γ	C_p	R	Material
Layer 1	0·030 0	1·118 0	2 100	0·172 0	0·0	mortar
Layer 2	0·050 0	0·627 8	2 000	0·172 0	0·0	cinder concrete
Layer 3	0·010 0	0·541 8	2 120	0·189 2	0·0	asphalt
Layer 4	0·030 0	1·118 0	2 100	0·172 0	0·0	mortar
Layer 5	0·120 0	1·204 0	2 200	0·172 0	0·0	concrete
Layer 6	0·0	0·0	0	0·0	0·163 4	air space
Layer 7	0·050 0	0·032 7	200	0·172 0	0·0	glass wool
Layer 8	0·001 0	0·154 8	1 250	0·215 0	0·0	gypsum board

Response factors j	$X(j)$	$Y(j)$	$Z(j)$
0	20·498 261 54	0·000 006 35	1·465 722 62
1	−13·090 826 05	0·002 649 16	−0·870 785 49
2	−1·561 051 02	0·019 247 44	−0·026 323 95
3	−0·770 072 87	0·036 031 90	−0·007 384 52
4	−0·531 324 74	0·041 178 57	−0·005 252 71
5	−0·428 657 91	0·040 119 32	−0·004 476 46
6	−0·369 956 79	0·037 088 54	−0·003 957 56
7	−0·327 768 90	0·033 678 84	−0·003 538 06
8	−0·293 202 57	0·030 392 59	−0·003 175 27
9	−0·263 191 40	0·027 366 87	−0·002 853 58
10	−0·236 543 84	0·024 623 26	−0·002 565 72
11	−0·212 687 55	0·022 148 60	−0·002 307 29
12	−0·191 267 02	0·019 920 71	−0·002 075 03

Table 2.3—contd.

Response factors j	X(j)	Y(j)	Z(j)
13	−0·172 013 33	0·0179 163 0	−0·001 866 18
14	−0·154 700 82	0·0161 133 7	−0·001 678 37
15	−0·139 131 72	0·0144 918 1	−0·001 509 46
Common ratio		0·899 363 38	

l thickness of layer(m),
λ thermal conductivity (Wm^{-1} deg C^{-1}),
γ mass density (kg m^{-3}),
C_p specific heat (J kg^{-1} deg C^{-1}),
R thermal resistance (m^2 deg CW^{-1}),
$X(j), Y(j), Z(j)$ response factors (Wm^{-2} deg C^{-1}),
Common ratio (−).

In order to find the first root α_1 of $B(s) = 0$ by the Newton-Raphson method, a tangent line is drawn from the point $B(0)$ to intersect the zero line, then another tangent line is drawn from the point $B(s_1)$ and so on until $\varepsilon = s_m - s_{m+1}$ becomes small enough.

In order to find the second root α_2 of $B(s) = 0$, letting $B_1(s) = B(s)(s-\alpha_1) = 0$, the same procedure as used in finding α_1 can be applied to $B_1(s) = 0$. Subsequent roots also can be obtained in the same way. It would be difficult to miss a root in the solving process.

An example of the response factors for a multi-layer wall is shown in Table 2.3. It can be seen that $X(j)$, $Y(j)$ and $Z(j)$ are shown up to $j = 9$ for $j = 9$ for exterior wall A. This means that the response factors for $j > 9$ can be calculated simply by

$$X(j) = c \cdot X(j-1) \tag{2.83}$$

where c is called common ratio. The reason why this procedure is valid is that, as j increases, exp $(\alpha_m j)$ becomes negligible except for exp $(\alpha_1 j)$ and the values of response factors decrease at a constant rate to be equal to the common ratio c. It follows that

$$C = \exp(\alpha_1) \tag{2.84}$$

It is clear that the value of the common ratio is common to $X(j)$, $Y(j)$ and $Z(j)$, as the roots of $B(s)$ are common.

2.10 PRACTICAL APPLICATION OF RESPONSE FACTORS

The theoretical formula to obtain the response of surface heat flow $g(n)$ from the excitation of surface temperature $f(n)$ using response factors is expressed by definition as:

$$g(n) = \sum_{j=0}^{\infty} Y(j) \cdot f(n-j) \qquad (2.85)$$

In practice, however, the summation must be limited up to a certain large number instead of infinity. Even if the sum of 50 products of Y and f are made, a truncation error still possibly exists. Moreover, this summation of products requires quite a lot of computation time.

There is a method to avoid making the summation of as many products of Y and f without losing accuracy. Using the common ratio c of $Y(j)$, eqn. (2.85) may be rewritten as:

$$g(n) = Y(0)f(n) + Y(1)f(n-1) + \cdots + Y(k)f(n-k)$$
$$+ cY(k)f(n-k-1) + c^2 Y(k)f(n-k-2) + \cdots$$
$$= \sum_{j=0}^{k} Y(j)f(n-j) + Y(k)\sum_{j=1}^{\infty} c^j f(n-k-j) \qquad (2.86)$$

Substituting $n - 1$ into n of eqn. (2.86), it gives:

$$g(n-1) = \sum_{j=0}^{k} Y(j)f(n-1-j) + Y(k)\sum_{j=1}^{\infty} c^j f(n-1-k-j) \qquad (2.87)$$

Making a subtraction $g(n) - c\, g(n-1)$, it follows that:

$$g(n) = c\, g(n-1) + Y(0)f(n) + \sum_{j=1}^{k} \{Y(j) - Y(j-1)\} f(n-j) \qquad (2.88)$$

Thus it is evident that eqn. (2.88) represents the practical formula to obtain $g(n)$, the response at time n, from the limited small number of convolutions by making use of $g(n-1)$; the response at time $n-1$, which is naturally considered to be a known value as the calculation of eqn. (2.88) should proceed with time. In other words, it can be understood that the previous response involves the convolution for $j > k$. This is the reason why operation of computation with eqn. (2.88) contributes a substantial reduction in computer time for practical use.

Further simplification may be conceivable from eqn. (2.88) in the following way. Letting:

$$Y'(j) = Y(j) - cY(j-1) \qquad \text{for } j \geq 1$$
$$Y'(0) = Y(0) \qquad (2.89)$$
$$g'(n) = g(n) - cg(n-1)$$

eqn. (2.88) may be rewritten as:

$$g'(n) = \sum_{j=0}^{k} Y'(j) f(n-j) \qquad (2.90)$$

Taking a common ratio of $Y'(j)$ as c',

$$g'(n) = c'g'(n-1) + Y'(0)f(n) + \sum_{j=1}^{k'} [Y'(j) - c'Y'(j-1)] f(n-j) \qquad (2.91)$$

This is entirely the same form as eqn. (2.88) but $k' < k$ and the total operation of multiplication to obtain $g(n)$ is consequently shorter than the case if eqn. (2.88) was used. In a similar manner further modification may be considered by making:

$$Y''(j) = Y'(j) - c'Y'(j-1) \qquad (2.92)$$

It can thus be modified further on.

Experiences have shown, however, that the use of eqn. (2.88) is adequate enough for calculation of cooling load of buildings, where there are not such thick walls. The latter procedure may well be applicable to the case when a large mass comes into the thermal system.

2.11. Z-TRANSFORM

The advanced way of convolution is represented by so-called Z-transform, which is often used in the numerical control in random process. The basic formula of Z-transform to relate the output time series $g(n)$ to the input time series $f(n)$ is expressed by the following, viz.,

$$a_0 f(n) + a_1 f(n-1) + a_2 f(n-2) + \cdots$$
$$= b_0 g(n) + b_1 g(n-1) + b_2 g(n-2) + \cdots \qquad (2.93)$$

where a and b are the coefficients characterising the thermal system. Then the output $g(n)$ can be given by:

$$b_0 g(n) = a_0 f(n) + a_1 f(n-1) + a_2 f(n-2) + \cdots - [b_1 g(n-1) + b_2 g(n-2) + \cdots] \qquad (2.94)$$

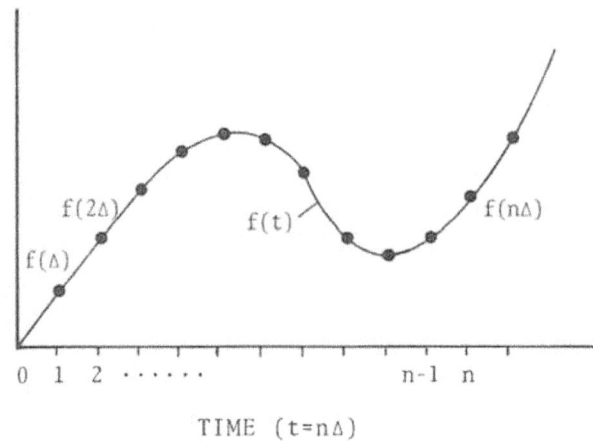

Fig. 2.13. Sample values of f(t) taken at time interval of Δ.

Equation (2.94) means that the output at time *n* can be obtained by knowing the output history. It can be derived from the following concept.

In general, the Laplace transform of f(t), a function of time *t*, is expressed by definition as:

$$\varphi(s) = \int_0^\infty f(t) \exp(-st) dt \qquad (2.95)$$

Letting f(0), f(Δ), f(2Δ), ... be the values of f(t) sampled at every Δ hours as shown in Fig. 2.13, the Laplace transform of f(n) can be given by

$$\varphi(s) = f(0) + f(\Delta)\exp(-\Delta s) + f(2\Delta)\exp(-2\Delta s) + \cdots$$
$$+ f(n\Delta)\exp(-n\Delta s) \qquad (2.96)$$

Then the following expression with a function of *z*, when exp (Δs) = z in eqn. (2,96), is defined as the Z-transform of f(t), taking Δ = 1, viz.,

$$F(z) = f(0) + f(1)z^{-1} + f(2)z^{-2} + \cdots + f(n)z^{-n} \qquad (2.97)$$

If f(t) is the input function to a system given by eqn. (2.97) and g(t) is the output function given by:

$$G(z) = g(0) + g(1)z^{-1} + g(2)z^{-2} + \cdots + g(n)z^{-n} \qquad (2.98)$$

the relationship between F(z) and G(z) is expressed as:

$$\frac{G(z)}{F(z)} = K(z) \qquad (2.99)$$

where $K(z)$ is called a Z-transfer function given by:

$$K(z) = \frac{a_0 + a_1 z^{-1} + a_2 z^{-2}}{b_0 + b_1 z^{-1} + b_2 z^{-2}} \tag{2.100}$$

When the system characteristics are known, the relationship between input time series $f(n)$ and output time series $g(n)$ can be expressed by substituting eqns. (2.97), (2.98) and (2.100) into eqn. (2.99) as follows:

$$[f(0) + f(1)z^{-1} + \cdots + f(n-1)z^{-(n-1)} + f(n)z^{-n}][a_0 + a_1 z^{-1} + \cdots]$$
$$= [g(0) + g(1)z^{-1} + \cdots + g(n-1)z^{-(n-1)} + g(n)z^{-n}]$$
$$\times [b_0 + b_1 z^{-1} + \cdots] \tag{2.101}$$

Equating the coefficients of z^{-n} on both sides of eqn. (2.101), it follows that:

$$a_0 f(n) + a_1 f(n-1) + a_2 f(n-2) + \cdots$$
$$= b_0 g(n) + b_1 g(n-1) + b_2 g(n-2) + \cdots \tag{2.102}$$

Then the output at time n, $g(n)$, can be obtained from eqn. (2.102) as expressed in eqn. (2.94). Note that $b_0 = 1$ always.

The coefficients $a(j)$, $b(j)$ are called Z-transfer factors and can be obtained directly from the formula for any type of multi-layer walls as described by Stephenson and Mitalas [2.9]. A computer program to obtain Z-transfer factors has been prepared by Mitalas and Arseneault [2.10]. The nature of the Z-transfer factors can be understood as described below, as they are related to the response factors.

Corresponding to the response factors $X(j)$, $Y(j)$ and $Z(j)$ of a multi-layer wall, Z-transfer factors of $A(j)$, $B(j)$, $C(j)$ and $D(j)$ can be expressed by the following relationships:

$$A(j) = \sum_{i=0}^{j} X(i)D(j-i) \tag{2.103}$$

$$B(j) = \sum_{i=0}^{j} Y(i)D(j-i) \tag{2.104}$$

$$C(j) = \sum_{i=0}^{j} Z(i)D(j-i) \tag{2.105}$$

where $i = 1, 2, \ldots, M$.

$D(j)$ can be obtained from the following:

$$1 + D(1)z^{-1} + D(2)z^{-2} + \cdots = \prod_{n=1}^{\infty} [1 - z^{-1} \exp(-\alpha_n \Delta)] \qquad (2.106)$$

Where α_n are the roots of $B(s)$ which appear in the inverse transform process for calculating response factors as discussed in the preceding section.

The Z-transfer factors can be used to calculate an output time series knowing an input time series. If the outside surface temperature is given by $\theta(n)$ in time series, the heat flow at the inside surface $q(n)$ can be obtained from the following expression, viz.,

$$q(n) = \sum_{j=0}^{M} B(j)\theta(n-j) - \sum_{j=1}^{N} D(j) \cdot q(n-j) \qquad (2.107)$$

It is important to note that the number of summations of the products is limited in the above expression instead of being infinite as in the case of response factors. This allows for a more precise computation with a shorter convolution operation.

Donald G. Stephenson
(1927-2009)

Dr. Stephenson is a native Canadian building physicist, well known for originator of response factors in building heat transfer. He received Ph.D. from University of Toronto. He devoted his whole life in heat transfer in buildings as Head of Building Services Section at Division of Building Research (DBR-IRC), National Research Council in Ottawa, where the author spent two years from 1967 as a postdoctorate fellow under his supervision. He wrote Chapter on Heat Load Calculation of ASHRAE Handbook of Fundamentals. ASHRAE Fellow. Father of five children.

Chapter 3

Radiative and Convective Heat Transfer in Buildings

A mixture of conduction, radiation and convection is taking place all over the thermal system of buildings. Wherever a solid surface exists, the convection between the surface and the fluid adjacent to it and the radiation between the surface and the other surfaces take place at the same time. When one can be neglected compared with the other of the two modes of heat transfer, it is quite easy to estimate the heat flow with reasonable accuracy. But when one is comparable to the other in magnitude, the problem must be solved taking account of both radiation and convection simultaneously. In this chapter the combination of radiative heat transfer and convective heat transfer that occurs on the outside and the inside surfaces is discussed.

3.1. FILM COEFFICIENT

In the calculation of heat gain or heat loss through exterior walls, a film coefficient is used in the determination of thermal transmittance of walls. The value of the film coefficient is usually higher for the outside surface of the wall than for the inside, because air movement along the surface is different. It is usually implied that both outside and inside film coefficients include the effects of radiation and convection at the surfaces. Hence the value of the film coefficient is the sum of the values of radiative heat transfer coefficient and convective heat transfer coefficient and in this sense the film coefficient is often called the combined surface heat transfer coefficient. The method of handling the radiative and convective heat transfer as a combined effect is convenient in heat transfer calculation, but this tends to lead to misunderstanding. It sometimes happens that the surface receives heat from the fluid by convection and discharges heat to the surroundings by radiation. Failure to recognise real conditions may lead to erroneous results.

The outside film coefficient is primarily related to the wind speed and it is often quoted that surface roughness contributes to its value to a considerable degree. The larger the value of the film coefficient, the larger the heat loss or heat gain through walls and in practice higher values are likely to be selected. However, in considering surfaces irradiated by the sun, the heat gain due to solar radiation on the outside surface is greater when wind speed is lower and consequently the film coefficient is lower. It is obvious that the sol-air temperature is higher when the film coefficient is lower, viz.,

$$\theta_e = \frac{a_s I}{\alpha_o} + \theta_a \qquad (3.1)$$

where θ_e = sol-air temperature (°C), a_s = absorptivity of the surface, I = solar radiation upon the surface (W m^{-2}), θ_a = outside air temperature (°C) and α_o = outside film coefficient (W m^{-2}degC^{-1}).

Table 3.1
Values of outside film coefficient used for heat load calculation in different countries (α_o(W m^{-2} deg C^{-1}))

Country	Source		Winter			Summer
USA	ASHRAE	U = 6.7 m/s	35			23
Canada	Guide 1972	U = 3.3 m/s	23			17
	Handbook of Fundamentals					
Germany	DIN 4701		23			17
United Kingdom	IHVE Guide		sheltered	normal	severe	
		Wall S	8	10	14	
		Wall WSW, SE	10	14	19	23
		Wall NW	14	19	32	
		Wall NNE, E	14	19	83	
		Roof	15	23	58	
France	Guide AICVF		U = 4 m/s	U = 8 m/s		
		Wall, roof	23	39		
		Glass	25	42		14
		Metal panel	27	44		
		Floor sofit	17	28		
Japan	SHASE Handbook 1975		23			17

U = wind velocity

Table 3.1 shows the diversity in application of the outside film coefficient as presented in the air conditioning guidebooks of different countries. It is clear that the wind effects are taken into account to a considerable extent and that summer values are relatively lower because of the reasons stated above. On the other hand, the effects of radiation are not regarded as significant in general, except for the lower values in the case of the lower surface of the slab facing the outside quoted from the French guidebook.

The inside film conductance is quite variable due to a number of different causes. It is generally assumed for winter conditions that the combined coefficient values are in the range of 7–13 Wm^{-2}degC^{-1} depending on the direction of heat flow, i.e.

horizontal, downward or upward flow. It must be remembered, however, that this could be applied only to the inside surface of exterior walls or roofs when the temperatures of other interior surfaces of walls, ceiling and floor are equal to the room air temperature. In fact, they are all different. In the case of intermittent air conditioning, the temperature of interior surfaces is quite different from the room air temperature and the effect of radiation and convection at the surface of exterior walls varies accordingly. The real problem occurs when one tries to calculate the heat flow from the interior surface to room air of vice versa, because no one knows the real value of the combined film coefficient for such cases. It is important to note that radiation takes place between one surface and the other and convection between surface and fluid as shown in Fig. 3.1.

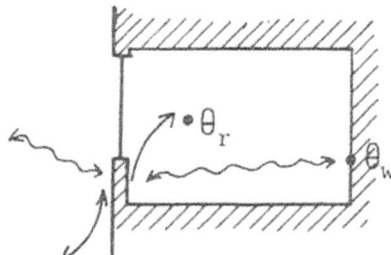

Fig. 3.1. Heat flow of exterior wall. θ_r: room air temperature, θ_w: interior wall surface temperature.

3.2. RADIATIVE HEAT TRANSFER COEFFICIENT

From the practical point of view it is very convenient that the rate of radiative heat transfer from one surface to the other is expressed in the form:

$$H_{r12} = \alpha_r (\theta_1 - \theta_2) A_1 \tag{3.2}$$

where θ_1 and θ_2 = temperatures of surface 1 and surface 2 respectively (°C), α_r = radiative heat transfer coefficient, H_{r12} = rate of radiative heat transfer from surface 1 to surface 2 (W), A_1 = area of surface 1.

It is well known, however, that the radiative heat transfer is proportional to the difference of the absolute temperature to the fourth power of the two surfaces. The configuration of two surfaces relative to each other is also important. It is well known that the radiation emitted by a black body is proportional to the absolute temperature of the surface to the fourth power according to Stefan-Boltzmann's Law which states:

$$R_b = \sigma T^4 \tag{3.3}$$

where R_b = radiation emitted by the perfect black surface that absorbs all radiation of any wavelength (Wm^{-2}), σ = black body constant (= $5 \cdot 67 \times 10^{-8}$Wm^{-2}K^{-4}) and T = absolute temperature of the black surface (K).

The radiation emitted by a general surface is expressed by:

$$R = \varepsilon R_b = \varepsilon \sigma T^4 \tag{3.4}$$

where ε is the emissivity of the surface. Kirchhoff's Law states that emissivity is equal to absorptivity for a specified temperature of the surface. The fundamental equation of radiative heat transfer between two surfaces is expressed in the following:

$$H_{r12} = \varepsilon_1 \varepsilon_2 A_1 F_{12} \sigma (T_1^4 - T_2^4) \tag{3.5}$$

where T_1 and T_2 = absolute temperatures of surface 1 and 2 respectively (K), ε_1 and ε_2 = emissivity of surface 1 and 2 respectively, F_{12} = form factor for surface 2 viewed from surface 1.

Equation (3.5) is valid only when ε_1 and ε_2 are close to unity but this is often used because most building materials have an emissivity of around $0 \cdot 9$.

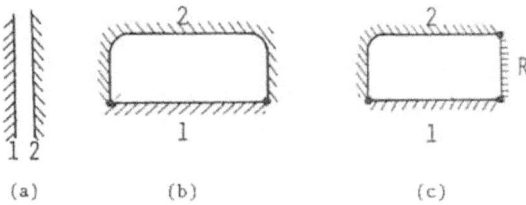

Fig. 3.2. Various configurations of two surfaces. Surface 1 is (a) parallel to surface 2, (b) enclosed with surface 2, (c) enclosed with surface 2 and a reflective surface R.

In general, the effective radiation constant combining the black body constant, the emmissivity of two surfaces and the form factor is introduced into the equation, viz.

$$H_{r12} = A_1 \sigma_{12} (T_1^4 - T_2^4) \tag{3.6}$$

where σ_{12} is the effective radiation constant (Wm^{-2}K^{-4}). For special cases of configuration, σ_{12} can be expressed as follows as shown in Fig. 3.2:

(a) Two surfaces are parallel. (Fig. 3.2(a)):

$$\sigma_{12} = \frac{1}{\frac{1}{\varepsilon_1} + \frac{1}{\varepsilon_2} - 1} \sigma \tag{3.7}$$

(b) Surface 1 is completely enclosed with surface 2. (Fig. 3.2(b)):

$$\sigma_{12} = \frac{1}{\frac{1}{\varepsilon_1} + \frac{A_1}{A_2}\left(\frac{1}{\varepsilon_2} - 1\right)} \sigma \quad (3.8)$$

(c) There is a reflective surface other than surface 1 and surface 2. (Fig. 3.2(c)):

$$\sigma_{12} = \frac{1}{\frac{1}{F'_{12}} + \left(\frac{1}{\varepsilon_1} - 1\right) + \frac{A_1}{A_2}\left(\frac{1}{\varepsilon_2} - 1\right)} \sigma \quad (3.9)$$

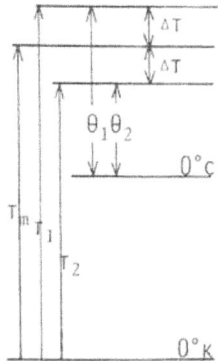

Fig. 3.3. Mean temperature of two surfaces.

where F'_{12} is F_{12} plus the fraction of the radiation reaching surface 2 after repetition of reflection by the reflecting surface R to be expressed as:

$$F'_{12} = F_{12} + \frac{F_{1R} F_{R2}}{F_{R1} + F_{R2}} \quad (3.10)$$

where F_{1R}, F_{R1} and F_{R2} are form factors from the surface of the left subscript to see the surface of the right subscript.

Equating the eqns. (3.2) and (3.5) α_r can be derived on an approximate basis. From the relationship as shown in Fig. 3.3, when ΔT is taken as:

$$T_1 = T_m + \Delta T \qquad T_2 = T_m - \Delta T$$

where T_m is average temperature of T_1 and T_2, eqn. (3.6) may be rewritten as:

$$H_{r12} = A_1 \sigma_{12}[(T_m + \Delta T)^4 - (T_m - \Delta T)^4]$$

$$\doteq A_1\sigma_{12}\cdot 8\Delta T\cdot T_m^3$$
$$= 4A_1\sigma_{12}T_m^3(\theta_1-\theta_2)$$

Hence

$$\alpha_r \doteq 4\sigma_{12}T_m^3 \qquad (3.11)$$

For example, in the case of eqn. (3.7), where $\varepsilon_1 = \varepsilon_2 = 0\cdot 9$ and $T_m = 300$ K, it follows that:

$$\alpha_r = 4\times 0\cdot 833\times 5\cdot 67\times 10^{-8}\times 300^3 = 5\cdot 1 \text{Wm}^{-2}\text{ deg C}^{-1}$$

The radiative heat transfer coefficient α_r thus derived is often used in the approximate estimation of radiation exchange between two surfaces.

3.3. CONVECTIVE HEAT TRANSFER COEFFICIENT

The convective heat transfer coefficient is also a useful invention whereby the heat transfer by convection between the solid surface and the fluid in the vicinity of the surface can easily be estimated by a simple formula:

$$q_c = \alpha_c(\theta_0 - \theta_a) \qquad (3.12)$$

where q_c = the rate of convective heat transfer (Wm^{-2}), α_c = convective heat transfer coefficient (Wm^{-2}degC^{-1}), θ_0 = solid surface temperature (°C), and θ_a = ambient fluid temperature (°C).

Because of the complexity in the mechanism of convective heat transfer, the value of α_c is dependent upon many different factors such as (1) configuration, (2) velocity of fluid flow, (3) temperature difference between surface and fluid and (4) physical properties of the fluid such as thermal conductivity, kinematic viscosity, specific weight, specific heat, thermal diffusivity, viscosity and volumetric expansion coefficient.

In expressing the convective heat transfer coefficient for such a great number of factors, the method known as dimensional analysis is normally used. The idea of the dimensional analysis is to decrease the number of variables associated with the convective heat transfer coefficient through the theoretical and experimental determination of the exponents of those dimensionless numbers for which a specific relationship can be established. The following is a list of the dimensionless numbers often used in air conditioning.

Table 3.2
Constants used for equations of convective heat transfer

Configuration	State of flow		Representative length	Applicable region	Constants for eqn. (3.14)					Simplified formulas for convection by air around room air temperature (W m^{-2} °C^{-1})
					k	a	b	c	d	
flat plate vertical	forced convection	laminar flow	length	Re < 5 × 10^5	0.664	0.5	0	0.333	0	$\alpha_c = 3.86\sqrt{u/d}$
		turbulent flow	length	Re > 5 × 10^5	0.037	0.8	0	0.333	0	$\alpha_c = 5.94u^{0.8}d^{-0.2}$
flat plate vertical	natural convection	laminar flow	height	GrPr < 10^9	0.56	0	0.25	0.25	0	$\alpha_c = 1.42(\Delta\theta/d)^{1/4}$
		turbulent flow	height	GrPr > 10^9	0.13	0	0.333	0.333	0	$\alpha_c = 1.31\Delta\theta^{1/3}$
flat plate horizontal square	natural convection	heat flow upward	side length	GrPr < 2 × 10^7	0.54	0	0.25	0.25	0	$\alpha_c = 2.64(\Delta\theta/d)^{1/4}$
		heat flow upward	side length	GrPr > 2 × 10^7	0.14	0	0.333	0.333	0	$\alpha_c = 0.966\Delta\theta^{1/3}$
flat plate		heat flow downward	side length	—	0.27	0	0.25	0.25	0	$\alpha_c = 1.31(\Delta\theta/d)^{1/4}$
inside pipe	laminar flow	fully developed flow	inside diameter l_e > 0.288 Red	Re < 2100	1.75	0	0	0	0.333	—
		entrance-flow region	inside diameter l_e < 0.288 Red		0.664	0.5	0.333	0	0	—
	turbulent flow	fully developed flow	inside diameter l_e > 0.693 Re$^{1/4}$d	Re > 2300	0.023	0.8	0.4	0	0	$\alpha_c = 0.0047(G/A)^{0.8}/d^{0.2}$
		entrance-flow region	inside diameter l_e < 0.693 Re$^{1/4}$d	40 < Re < 4000	0.0255$(d/l_e)^{0.22}$	0.855	0.4	0	0	—
outside pipe	forced convection		outside diameter		0.615	0.466	0	0	0	—
outside pipe	natural convection	laminar flow	outside diameter	GrPr < 10^9	0.53	0	0.25	0.25	0	$\alpha_c = 1.33(\Delta\theta/d)^{1/4}$
		turbulent flow	outside diameter	GrPr > 10^9	0.13	0	0.333	0.333	0	$\alpha_c = 1.24\Delta\theta^{1/3}$

l_e entrance length (m)
G flow rate (kg/h)
A sectional area (m^2)

Nusselt number	Nu	$= \alpha_c d / \lambda$
Reynolds number	Re	$= ud/v$
Prandtl number	Pr	$= v/a$	(3.13)
Grashof number	Gr	$= g\beta\Delta\theta d^3 / v^2$
Graetz number	Gz	$= \pi d^2 u C_p \gamma / 4\lambda l$

It is important to note that the convective heat transfer coefficient occurs in the Nusselt number. Thus the relationship among the dimensionless numbers can be expressed in general as:

$$\text{Nu} = k \cdot \text{Re}^a \text{Pr}^b \text{Gr}^c \text{Gz}^d \tag{3.14}$$

where k, a, b, c and d are constants determined by the different conditions as shown in Table 3.2.

It must be remembered that the relationship discussed in the mechanical engineering field is valid only when the fluid flows uniformly along the surface. For example, the relationship for laminar flow of forced convection along a flat plate surface is expressed by the relationship of three dimensionless numbers, namely:

$$\text{Nu} = 0 \cdot 664 \, \text{Re}^{0.5} \cdot \text{Pr}^{0.333} \tag{3.14a}$$

Six variables such as α_c, d, λ, u, v and a are involved in the dimensionless numbers given by eqn. (3.14a).

3.4. Radiation from the Atmosphere

Any surface on the earth emits radiation to the sky according to the surface temperature and at the same time receives radiation from the atmosphere, the balance being called the effective radiation. Since this amounts to as high as 100 Wm^{-2} during clear nights, this is often called nocturnal radiation. This high amount occurs because the atmosphere emits much less radiation than the black solid surface having the same temperature as the ambient air.

Brunt found out that the long-wave radiation falling on the earth is essentially dependent on the water vapour content in the atmosphere and presented the following formula, viz.,

$$\text{Br} = a + b\sqrt{e} \tag{3.15}$$

where e = water vapour pressure (mb), a and b = constants. Br is called the emissivity of atmosphere, meaning the ratio of radiation from the atmosphere to the radiation from a black hemisphere whose temperature is equal to the ambient air temperature. The constants a and b have been obtained by a number of meteorologists and the values proposed by Yamamoto are introduced here [3.1], viz.,

$$a = 0\cdot 51 \quad \text{and} \quad b = 0\cdot 066$$

In the case when the water vapour pressure of f (kPa) is used instead of e (mb), $b = 0\cdot 209$ and the amount of atmospheric radiation q_a (Wm^{-2}) is to be expressed by:

$$q_a = \sigma T_a^4 (0\cdot 51 + 0\cdot 209 \sqrt{f}) \qquad (3.16)$$

where T_a = absolute temperature of ambient air (K). In reality, the atmospheric radiation is the radiation emitted by the water vapour particles in the atmosphere. In consequence, it can be considered that the lower the water vapour content of the atmosphere, the larger the effective radiation emitted from the surface on the earth to the outer space.

It would be interesting to calculate the hypothetical temperature of the sky hemisphere if the sky vault were a black solid hemispherical surface under the conditions of, say outside air temperature $-10°C$ and relative humidity 90%.

As the saturated water vapour pressure for $-10°C$ is $0\cdot 286$ kPa, the water vapour pressure at 90% relative humidity can be obtained as $f = 0\cdot 286 \div 0\cdot 9 = 0\cdot 318$ Hence $Br = 0\cdot 51 + 0\cdot 209 \times \sqrt{0\cdot 318} = 0\cdot 629$.

The hypothetical temperature of the sky hemisphere T_x (K) can be calculated from the condition that $\sigma T_x^4 = 0\cdot 629 \sigma T_a^4$. Hence $T_x = \sqrt[4]{0\cdot 629}$ (273–10) = 234K = $-39°C$. This means that to neglect the effects of atmospheric radiation would possibly give rise to a considerable error in heat loss calculations.

Brunt's formula is based on the clear night sky. For cloudy sky the formula could be modified by using Philipps' research results [3.2]. Philipps made a comparison of the atmospheric radiation between clear and cloudy days and obtained the following results, viz., with reference to Fig. 3.4:

Fig. 3.4. Long wavelength radiation exchange at ground surface.

$$\sigma T_e^4 - R = (\sigma T_e^4 - R_o)(1 - K_c) \qquad (3.17)$$

where T_e = ground surface temperature (K), R, R_o = atmospheric radiation on cloudy and clear days respectively (Wm^{-2}), K_c = reduction factor dependent upon the height of cloud as shown in Table 3.3.

Table 3.3
K_c value

Height of cloud (km)	K_c
2	0·83
5	0·62
8	0·45

Since $R_o = \sigma T_a^4 Br$, it can be seen that the atmospheric radiation in cloudy conditions is also related to the ground surface temperature as expressed by:

$$R = \sigma T_a^4 Br(1 - K_c) + \sigma T_e^4 K_c \tag{3.18}$$

When part of the sky is overcast, the atmospheric radiation in general q_{aG} can be expressed by the following, taking cc as total cloud amount in tenths.

$$\begin{aligned} q_{aG} &= R_o(1-c_c) + Rc_c \\ &= (1-c_c K_c)\sigma T_a^4 Br + c_c K_c \sigma T_c^4 \end{aligned} \tag{3.19}$$

Where c_c is cloud cover ratio:

$$c_c = \frac{cc}{10}$$

3.5. HEAT BALANCE AT THE OUTSIDE SURFACE OF BUILDINGS

At the outside surface, of a building, there are always two components of heat, that coming into and that leaving the surface. The temperature of the surface is determined in such a way that the heat balance is to be maintained. The heat balance equation at the outside surface can be expressed as in the following in reference to Fig. 3.5.

$$q_s + q_a + q_e = q_c + q_r + q_o \tag{3.20}$$

where q_s = solar radiation absorbed by the surface (Wm^{-2}), q_a = atmospheric radiation absorbed by the surface (Wm^{-2}), q_e = radiation from ground absorbed by the surface (Wm^{-2}), q_c = convective heat transfer from the surface to the ambient air (Wm^{-2}), q_r = radiation emitted by the surface (Wm^{-2}) and q_o = heat conduction from the outside surface toward inside (Wm^{-2}).

The left-hand side of eqn. (3.20) is the heat coming into the surface (including the signs) and the right-hand side is the heat going out of the surface. The above terms can be rewritten as follows:

$$q_s = a_{sD} I_D + a_{sd} I_d \qquad (3.21)$$

Where I_D and I_d are direct and diffuse components of solar radiation upon the outside surface respectively; a_{sD} and a_{sd} are the absorptivity of the surface for I_D and I_d respectively:

$$q_a = \varepsilon_o \varphi_a \left[(1 - c_c K_c) \sigma T_a^4 Br + c_c K_c \sigma T_a^4 \right] \qquad (3.22)$$

Where ε_o = emissivity of the surface, φ_a = form factor for the amount of visible sky from the outside surface, a_c = cloud cover ratio, K_c = cloud reduction factor as shown in Table 3.3, Br = Brunt's emissivity of atmosphere, T_a = ambient air temperature (K).

$$q_e = \varepsilon_o \varepsilon_e \varphi_e \sigma T_e^4 \qquad (3.23)$$

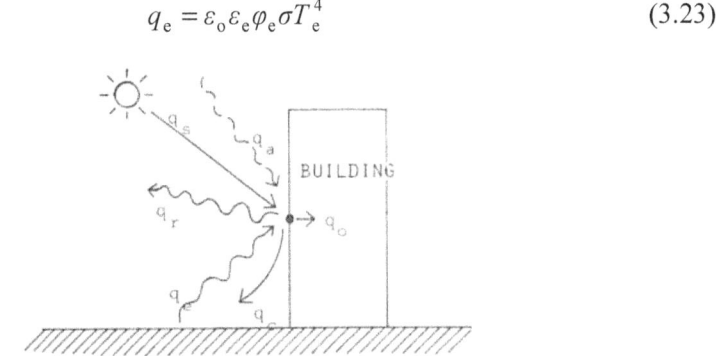

Fig. 3.5. Heat balance at outside surface of building.

where ε_e = emissivity of the ground, φ_e = form factor for the area of ground visible from the surface, T_e = temperature of ground surface (K).

$$q_c = \alpha_c (T_o - T_a) \qquad (3.24)$$

where T_o = outside surface temperature (K), α_c = convective heat transfer coefficient (Wm^{-2}degC^{-1}).

$$q_r = \varepsilon_o \sigma T_o^4 \qquad (3.25)$$

and

$$q_o = \int_0^\infty [\varphi_{q0}(0,\tau) T_o(t-\tau) + \varphi_{q1}(0,\tau) T_i(t-\tau)] d\tau \qquad (3.26)$$

where $\varphi_{q0}(0, \tau)$, $\varphi_{q1}(0, \tau)$ are impulse responses of the outside surface heat flow against the outside surface temperature and inside surface temperature respectively (Wm^{-2}deg C^{-1}), $T_i(t)$ = inside surface temperature at time t (K).

Using response factors instead of impulse response, q_o may be expressed in the form of a time series as in the following:

$$q_{o,n} = \sum_{j=0}^{\infty}(X_j \cdot T_{o,n-j} + Y_j \cdot T_{i,n-j}) \tag{3.27}$$

where X_j and Y_j are response factors of the exterior wall (Wm^{-2}degC^{-1}), $T_{o,n}$, $T_{i,n}$ are outside and inside surface temperature of the exterior wall respectively at time $t = n\Delta t$(K), $q_{o,n}$ is the heat flow at the outside surface of exterior wall at time $t = n\Delta t$.

Assuming that the instantaneous heat transfer through the exterior wall is proportional to the temperature difference across the wall, the following comes true:

$$q_o = K'(T_o - T_r) \tag{3.28}$$

where K' = overall heat transfer coefficient from the outside surface of the exterior wall to the room air (Wm^{-2}degC^{-1}), T_r = room air temperature (K).

Hence the heat balance equation can be solved for outside surface temperature applying eqn. (3.21)–(3.28) to eqn. (3.20).

The heat balance equation, assuming eqn. (3.28) is valid, can be reduced to:

$$T_o = \frac{1}{K' + \alpha_c}(A - \varepsilon_o \sigma T_o^4) \tag{3.29}$$

where

$$A = \varepsilon_o \varphi_a \sigma T_a^4 \mathrm{Br} + \varepsilon_o \varepsilon_e \varphi_e \sigma T_a^4 + a_c I + K'T_r + \alpha_c T_a \tag{3.30}$$

As this equation includes to in the right-hand side of it, iteration is necessary to arrive at the real value of T_o.

Example: Obtain heat loss from a double pane glass window under the following conditions in the winter evening of clear sky.

$K' = 3\,\mathrm{Wm}^2\,\mathrm{deg}\,\mathrm{C}^{-1}$, $\varphi_a = \varphi_e = 0 \cdot 5$, $\varepsilon_o = 0 \cdot 92$, $\varepsilon_e = 0 \cdot 9$, $a_c = 0$,

$\alpha_c = 12\,\mathrm{Wm}^2\,\mathrm{deg}\,\mathrm{C}^{-1}$, $I = 0$, $f = 4\,\mathrm{mmHg}$, $T_a = T_e = 273\mathrm{K}$

Solution:
(1)   Value A is calculated first from eqn. (3.30)

$A = 0\cdot 92 \times 0\cdot 9 \times 0\cdot 5 \times 5\cdot 67 \times 2\cdot 73^4(0\cdot 51 + 0\cdot 076\sqrt{4})$

$+ 0\cdot 9 \times 0\cdot 5 \times 5\cdot 67 \times 2\cdot 73^4 + 3 \times 293 + 12 \times 273$

$= 4383 \cdot 03$

(2) $$T_o = \frac{1}{3+12}(-0.92 \times 5.67 \times T_o^4 + 4383.03)$$

(3) Assuming $T_o = 273$, eqn. (3.29) gives

$$T_o = \frac{1}{15}(-289.75 \times 4383.03) = 272.89$$

(4) Assuming $T_o = 272.9$, it gives $T_o = 272.91$

(5) This is quite close to the assumed value. Using $T_o = 272.9$, the heat loss is:

$$q = 3(293 - 272.9) = 60.3 \quad \text{Wm}^{-2}$$

By way of comparison, if one took the value of thermal transmittance as:

$$K = \frac{1}{\frac{1}{12} + \frac{1}{3}} = 2.40$$

Neglecting the atmospheric radiation, the heat gain could be estimated as:

$$q = 2.40(293 - 272.9) = 48 \quad \text{Wm}^{-2}$$

This is smaller than the above value of 60.3 by about 20%.

The above procedure is not complicated because the iteration need not be done more than twice, even if the value in the first assumption is quite far from the true value.

When the combined radiative and convective film coefficient is used in calculation, the equivalent temperature drop for nocturnal radiation may be introduced into the heat loss calculation. It must be remembered that the radiative component in the film coefficient is defined as the radiative heat transfer coefficient between a point on the outside surface and the hypothetical black hemispherical surface surrounding the point as shown in Fig. 3.6, namely:

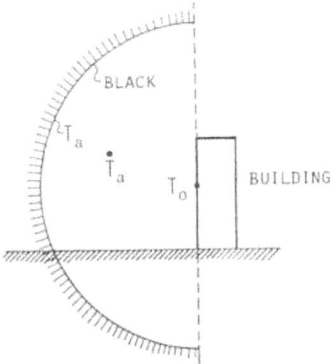

Fig. 3.6. Presumed black sky vault with air temperature.

$$\alpha_{ro}(T_o - T_a) = \varepsilon_0 \sigma T_o^4 - \sigma T_a^4 \qquad (3.31)$$

and

$$\alpha_o = \alpha_{co} + \alpha_{ro} \qquad (3.32)$$

where α_{co}, α_{ro} = outside convective and radiative heat transfer coefficients respectively (Wm^{-2}degC^{-1}).

Then the equation of heat loss from the outside surface to the ambient atmosphere is given by:

$$q_o = \alpha_o(\theta_o - \theta_a) + q_z \qquad (3.33)$$

where θ_o = outside surface temperature (°C), θ_a = ambient air temperature (°C) and:

$$q_z = \varepsilon_o \left\{ \sigma \sigma_a^4 [1 - \varphi_a(1 - a_c K_c)Br + a_c K_c] - \varphi_e \varepsilon_e \sigma T_e^4 \right\} \qquad (3.34)$$

Equation (3.33) may be expressed by applying the sol-air temperature concept to nocturnal radiation such as,

$$q_o = \alpha_o \left[\theta_o - \left(\theta_a - \frac{q_z}{\alpha_o} \right) \right] \qquad (3.35)$$

The last term in this equation q_z/α_o may be called equivalent temperature drop due to nocturnal radiation against the ambient temperature. Then the heat gain, including the effect of solar radiation, is expressed by

$$q_o = \alpha_o \left(\theta_a - \frac{q_s}{\alpha_o} - \frac{q_z}{\alpha_o} - \theta_o \right) \qquad (3.36)$$

$$= K \left(\theta_a - \frac{q_s}{\alpha_o} - \frac{q_z}{\alpha_o} - \theta_r \right) \qquad (3.37)$$

where θ_r = room air temperature (°C), K = overall heat transfer coefficient across the wall (Wm^{-2}degC^{-1}), q_s = solar radiation absorbed at the outside surface (Wm^{-2}).

The advantage of using eqn. (3.37) is that heat gain can be obtained without deriving the outside surface temperature as required for the method using eqn. (3.33). It must be noted, however, that α_r should be determined as accurately as possible by adequate assumptions.

If α_r = 5(Wm^{-2}degC^{-1}) is used in the preceding example,

$$\alpha_o = 5 + 12 = 17 \qquad \text{and} \qquad K = \frac{1}{\frac{1}{17} + \frac{1}{3}} = 2 \cdot 55$$

$$q_z = 0 \cdot 92 \times \left(5 \cdot 67 \times 2 \cdot 73^4 [(1 - 0.5(0 \cdot 51 + 0 \cdot 076\sqrt{4})] - 0.5 \times 0 \cdot 9 \times 5 \cdot 67 \times 2 \cdot 73^4 \right)$$
$$= 0 \cdot 92 \times (210 \cdot 70 - 141 \cdot 72) = 63 \cdot 46$$

$$q_o = 2 \cdot 55 \left[20 - \left(0 - \frac{63 \cdot 46}{17} \right) \right]$$

$$= 2 \cdot 55 \times 23 \cdot 73 = 60 \cdot 5 \quad \text{Wm}^{-2}$$

This turns out quite close to 60·3 which was derived from the more rigorous solution using an iteration procedure. The error could be greater for a sunlit surface when the value of α_r could not be determined accurately and for cloudy days.

3.6. Determination of the Convective Heat Transfer Coefficient of an Outside Surface of a Building by Field Experiment†

One of the most uncertain values in the heat balance equation of the outside surface of a building as expressed in eqn. (3.20) could be the value of convective heat transfer coefficient on the surface concerned. It is considered that the principal factors governing the convective heat transfer coefficient are wind speed and direction in relation to the geometry of the surface. Since the air flow along the outside surface of buildings may possibly be quite different from the natural wind speed, it is considered necessary to determine the convective heat transfer coefficient by field experiments.

The method used by Ito, Oka and Kimura [3.3, 3.4] was that of having two identical heat flow meter panels mounted side by side on the outside surface of an existing building and maintained at slightly different temperatures, so that the convective heat transfer coefficient could be obtained from the difference in heat flow measured at the two heat flow meter panels. Figure 3.7 shows a section through the panels. The relationships may be expressed by the heat balance equations at the outside surface of these two panels, viz.,

$$q_A + q_a + q_e = \varepsilon_s \sigma T_A^4 + \alpha_c (T_A - T_a) \tag{3.38}$$

$$q_B + q_a + q_e = \varepsilon_s \sigma T_B^4 + \alpha_c (T_B - T_a) \tag{3.39}$$

† Parts of the passages in this section are taken from the paper by Kimura et al. in ASHRAE Transactions [3.4] by permission of the American Society of Heating, Refrigeration and Air Conditioning Engineers, Inc.

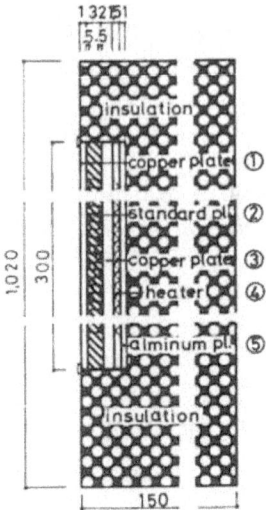

Fig. 3.7. Section of heat flow meter panel [3.3].

where q_A, q_B = rate of heat flow outward to the surface from the hot plates or panels A and B respectively (Wm^{-2}); q_a, q_e = radiation from the atmosphere and ground absorbed at the panel surfaces respectively (Wm^{-2}), ε_s = emissivity of panel surface, T_A, T_B = surface temperature of panels A and B respectively (K), T_a = ambient air temperature (K), α_c = convective heat transfer coefficient (Wm^{-2}degC^{-1}). The first term on the right side of eqns. (3.38) and (3.39) represents the radiation emitted from the surfaces of panels A and B respectively and the second term the rate of convective heat transfer from the surfaces of the panels A and B to the ambient air respectively.

As the same value of α_c can be applied to the two surfaces of slightly different temperature, elimination of q_a, q_e and T_a from eqns. (3.38) and (3.39) derives the following results:

$$\alpha_c = \frac{q_A - q_B - \varepsilon_s \sigma (T_A^4 - T_B^4)}{T_A - T_B} \qquad (3.40)$$

This shows that the convective heat transfer coefficient can be obtained if the rates of heat flow and temperature at the surface of both panels A and B are measured.

Wind speed and direction at the height of 8 m above the roof and the air flow velocity 30 cm away from the panel surface were measured and these values were read by sampling at 1 minute intervals.

Figure 3.8 shows an example of the relationship between the wind speed above the building ($\overline{U}$) and the air flow velocity near the surface ($\overline{u}$) obtained at the surface of the 6th floor level. Different symbols are used for different wind directions to the wall surface as indicated. It can be observed that $\bar{u}$ is approximately $\frac{1}{3}$ to $\frac{1}{5}$ of $\bar{U}$ when $\bar{U}$ is greater than 2m/s and the surface is windward, and that $\bar{u}$ remains around 0·5m/s when the surface is leeward or when $\bar{U}$ is less than 2m/s and the surface is windward.

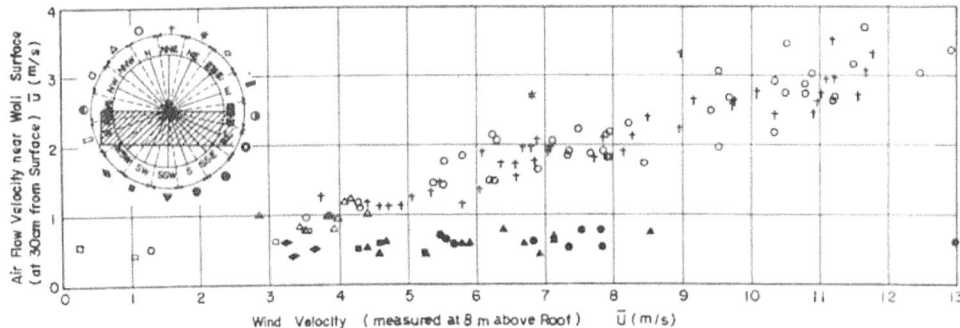

Fig. 3.8. Relationship between wind speed above building and air flow velocity near the wall surface of 6th floor level [3.3].

Figure 3.9 shows the plots of the convective heat transfer coefficient (α_c) calculated according to the above procedure against the wind speed above the building ($\bar{U}$) using the same symbols corresponding to the cases in Fig. 3.8.

It is seen that α_c increases with the increase of $\bar{U}$ when the surface is windward and α_c remains around 14 $Wm^{-2}degC^{-1}$ when the surface is leeward. Although the points are quite scattered, it is important to note that α_c can be as low as 12$Wm^{-2}degC^{-1}$.

Plots of the convective heat transfer coefficient (α_c) against the air flow velocity near the surface ($\bar{u}$) are shown in Fig. 3.10. Here the scatter of the points is less divergent than the scatter in Fig. 3.9 and this $\bar{u} - \alpha_c$ relationship is mostly independent of the relative wind direction to the surface.

This would imply that the relationship between the convective heat transfer coefficient and the wind speed and direction might possibly be broken into two relationships, $\bar{U} - \bar{u}$ relationship and $\bar{u} - \alpha_c$ relationship, using the air flow velocity near the surface as a reference parameter. It was found in additional tests that there was no significant difference in the $\bar{U} - \bar{u}$ relationship when the value of air flow velocity was measured 10 cm or 20 cm away from the surface, instead of 30cm.

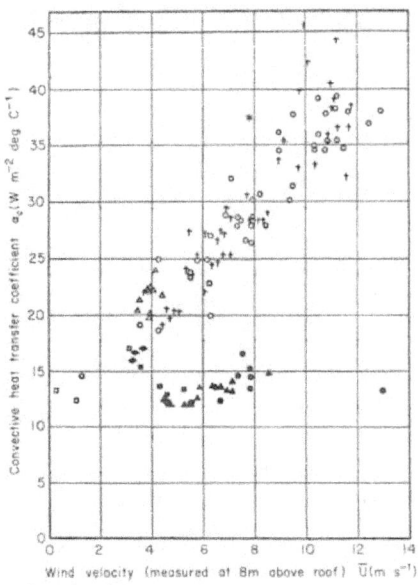

Fig. 3.9. Relationship between wind velocity (measured at 8m above roof) and convective heat transfer coefficient [3.3].

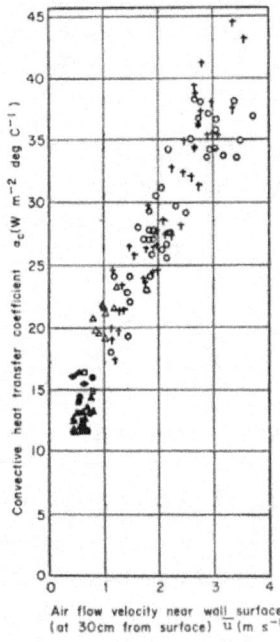

Fig. 3.10. Relationship between air flow velocity near wall surface (at 30cm from surface) and convective heat transfer coefficient at 6th floor level [3.3].

Eight sets of measurements similar to the above were made at different locations on the building surface as illustrated in Fig. 3.11.

As in the preceding example it was found again that the scatter of points in the $\overline{U} - \alpha_c$ relationship was very divergent and quite different with different cases, whereas the scatter in the $\overline{u} - \alpha_c$ relationship as shown in Fig. 3.12 was less divergent, independent of relative wind direction to the surface, and fairly consistent with different panel locations showing the patterns quite similar to that shown in Fig. 3.10.

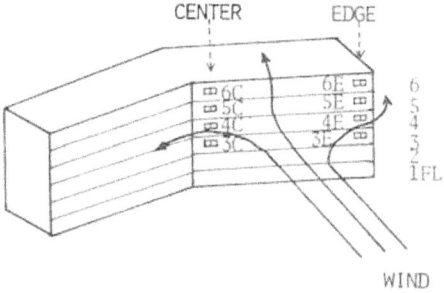

Fig. 3.11. Positions and symbols of the measurement made at the north wall surface of test building [3.3]

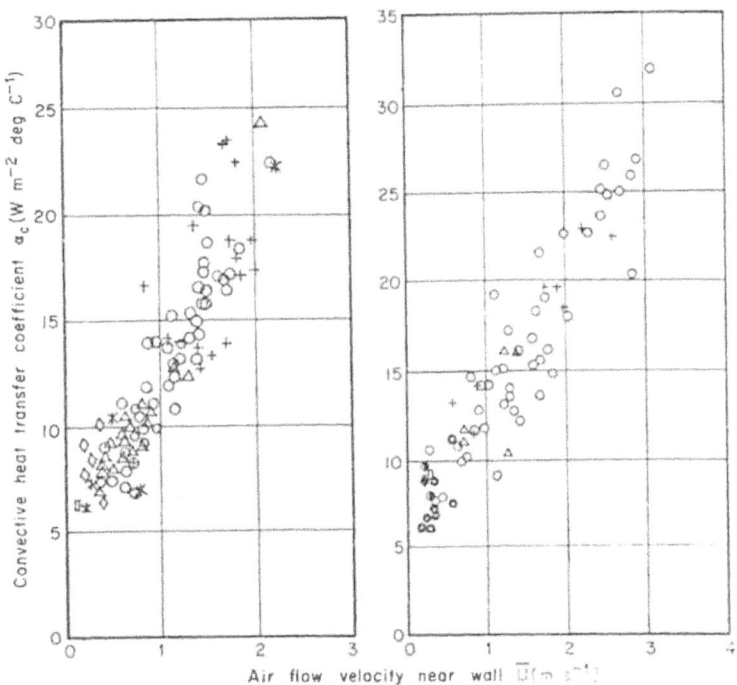

Fig. 3.12. Relationship between air flow velocity near the wall surface [3.3], (left) at the 3rd floor level, (right) at the 4th floor level.

The difference in the $\overline{U}$–α_c relationship with different locations on the building surface was apparent. A slight increase in $\overline{u}/\overline{U}$ with height for the middle part of the building and a slight increase in $\overline{u}/\overline{U}$ with distance toward the edge of the building for the 3rd and 4th floor are noticeable. This might have been to a high degree due to the configuration of surroundings as well as that of the building concerned.

In addition, it was often observed that the values were as low as $6 Wm^{-2}degC^{-1}$ on either floor under calm conditions or on the leeward surface.

It can be concluded that the test results on an actual building did not agree with the conventional relationships between convective heat transfer coefficient and air flow velocity along the surface if the wind speed was used as the air flow velocity in the formulas. This is because of the characteristic difference between convective heat transfer in the wind tunnel and in the actual building. When the building surface is leeward, the effect of wind speed is hardly observed.

It is obvious that the relationship between wind speed and the convective heat transfer coefficient can be broken down into two characteristic relationships: the relationship between wind speed and air flow velocity near the surface which is dependent upon the relative wind direction to the surface and the surface location in the building, and the relationship between convective heat transfer coefficient and the air flow velocity near the surface. The latter relationship is found to be fairly consistent and independent of either the wind direction relative to the surface or the surface location on the building. This breakdown seems necessary for the estimation of the convective heat transfer coefficient, especially when the air temperature near the surface is different from the ambient dry bulb temperature, although the experiments under summer conditions have not been carried out.

The following is an algorithm for computer calculation of the convective heat transfer coefficient on the outside surface derived from the experiments described in the above.

Input U = wind speed in general (m/s)
    θ = wind direction (angle measured clockwise from north) (degrees)
    ε = wall azimuth (positive degrees westward from south and negative eastward)

Output u = air velocity near the outside surface (m/s)
    α_c = convective heat transfer coefficient ($Wm^{-2}degC^{-1}$)

Calculation sequence
(1) Calculate wind direction relative to the wall surface γ

$$\left.\begin{array}{l}\gamma = \varepsilon + 180 - \theta \\ \text{If } |\gamma| > 180, \quad \gamma = 360 - |\gamma|\end{array}\right\} \quad (3.41)$$

If $-45 \leq \gamma \leq 45$, the surface is windward and otherwise the surface is leeward

(2) Calculate air velocity near the outside surface u

(i) If the surface is windward:

$$\text{for } U > 2 \quad u = 0 \cdot 25U$$
$$\text{for } U \leq 2 \quad u = 0 \cdot 5$$
(3.42)

(ii) If the surface is leeward:

$$u = 0 \cdot 3 + 0 \cdot 05U \qquad (3.43)$$

(3) Calculate convective heat transfer coefficient α_c

$$\alpha_c = 4 \cdot 7 + 7 \cdot 6u \qquad (3.44)$$

3.7. Radiation and Convection Heat Exchange inside the Room

Radiation and convection are always taking place in a mixed mode inside the room whether it is air-conditioned or not. Radiation occurs among the inside surfaces of the room and convection occurs between the air in the room and the surfaces of the room.

The values of the inside surface heat transfer coefficient used in the calculations of heat transfer across the wall are given in Table 3.4, where the values are different with the direction of heat flow: upward, downward or horizontally and these values include the effects of both radiation and convection. It must be remembered,

Table 3.4
Inside film coefficient α_i ($Wm^{-2}degC^{-1}$)

		Convective component	Radiative component	Combined
Vertical wall or window	In the case where there is an air conditioning outlet along window surface	7	Summer 6 Winter 4·5	13 11·5
	In the case where there is no air conditioning outlet along window surface and when air conditioning is off	3·5	Summer 6 Winter 4·5	9·5 8
Ceiling		Summer 1 Winter 4	Summer 6 Winter 4·5	7 8·5
Floor		Summer 4 Winter 1	Summer 6 Winter 4·5	10 5·5

however, that these values of α_i should be used only for the inside surfaces of exterior walls, the ceiling surfaces of roofs and surfaces of floors whose undersides are exposed to outside conditions. In a strict sense these values should be

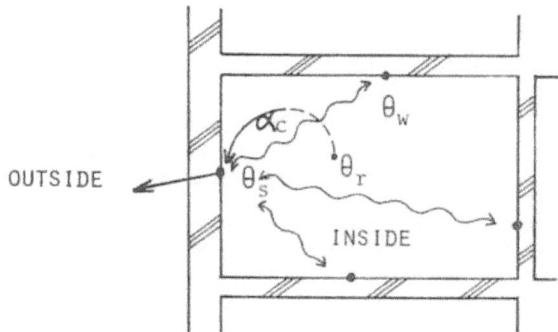

Fig. 3.13. Heat balance at the inside surface of exterior wall.

applied only to the cases where all inside surfaces of the room enclosure elements, other than that of the exterior wall concerned, stay at the same temperature as the room air, because in such a case as shown in Fig. 3.13 the following conditions can be shown to exist, viz.,

$$\alpha_i = \alpha_{ci} + \alpha_{ri} \tag{3.45}$$

where α_i = inside film coefficient (Wm^{-2}degC^{-1}), α_{ci} = inside convective heat transfer coefficient (Wm^{-2}degC^{-1}), α_{ri} = inside radiative heat transfer coefficient (Wm^{-2}degC^{-1})

$$\alpha_{ri} = \frac{\varepsilon_s \varepsilon_w \sigma (T_s^4 - T_w^4)}{T_s - T_w} \doteq \frac{\varepsilon_s \varepsilon_w \sigma (T_s^4 - T_r^4)}{T_s - T_r} \tag{3.46}$$

where T_s = inside surface temperature of exterior wall (K), T_w = inside surface temperature of interior walls (K), T_r = room air temperature (K), ε_s = emissivity of the inside surface of the exterior wall, ε_w = emissivity of the inside surface of the interior walls. Nearly equal sign in eqn. (3.46) shows that the temperature of all interior surfaces other than exterior wall surface is equal to room air temperature.

On the other hand, the heat transfer from the floor surface to the room in such a case as shown in Fig. 3.14 should be expressed as

$$\begin{aligned} q &= \alpha_c (T_f - T_r) + \varepsilon_f \varepsilon_s F_{fs} \sigma (T_f^4 - T_s^4) \\ &\doteq \alpha_c (T_f - T_r) + \alpha_r F_{fs} (T_f - T_s) \\ &\neq \alpha_i (T_f - T_r) \end{aligned} \tag{3.47}$$

where T_f = floor surface temperature (K), ε_f = emissivity of floor surface, F_{fs} = form factor from floor surface to inside surface of exterior wall. In this case, the procedure using the combined heat transfer coefficient would not be applicable.

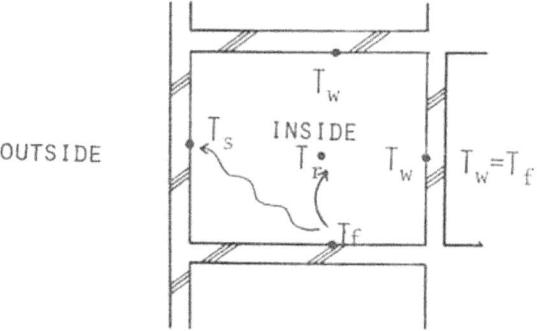

Fig. 3.14. Heat balance at the floor surface.

Here, the inside surface temperature of interior walls and slabs is different from the room air temperature and this is particularly evident during early morning hours in the case of intermittent operation of air conditioning. In reality, surface temperatures can be determined by convective heat transfer to or from the room air and radiative heat exchange between the surfaces. It is necessary, therefore, to find these temperatures by solving the simultaneous equations as given below. Using the time series notation on the unsteady state basis, the heat balance at the ith surface is

$$\alpha_{ci}(T_i - T_r) + \sum_{k=1}^{N\dagger} F_{ik}\varepsilon_i\varepsilon_k\sigma(T_i^4 - T_k^4) = q_i \qquad (3.48)$$

$\dagger$ except $i = k$

or

$$\alpha_{ci}(T_i - T_r) + \sum_{k=1}^{N\dagger} \alpha_{rik}(T_i - T_k) = q_i \qquad (3.49)$$

where T_i = temperature of ith surface (°C), N=number of surfaces and q_i can be expressed in a time series such as

$$q_i = \sum_{j=o}^{\infty} Y(j).T_{io}(n-j) - \sum_{j=o}^{\infty} Z(j).T_i(n-j) \qquad (3.50)$$

The heat balance for the room air is

$$\sum_{i=1}^{k} \alpha_{ci}(T_i - T_r)S_i = H_{ex} \qquad (3.51)$$

where $Y(j)$ and $Z(j)$ are response factors of ith wall (Wm^{-2}degC^{-1}), where $T_{i(n)}$ = temperature of ith surface at time n (°C), $T_{io(n)}$ = surface temperature of the other side of ith wall (°C), S_i = area of ith surface (m^2), H_{ex} = heat extraction from the space (W). This deals only with sensible heat and latent heat is considered separately. These simultaneous equations may be expressed in a matrix form as shown below referring to Fig. 3.15.

$$\begin{bmatrix} T_1 \\ T_2 \\ \vdots \\ T_k \\ T_r \end{bmatrix} \begin{bmatrix} \alpha_{c1}+\alpha_{r1} & -\alpha_{r12} & -\alpha_{r13} & \cdots & -\alpha_{r1k} & -\alpha_{c1} \\ -\alpha_{r21} & \alpha_{c2}+\alpha_{r2} & -\alpha_{r23} & \cdots & -\alpha_{r2k} & -\alpha_{c2} \\ \vdots & \vdots & \vdots & & \vdots & \vdots \\ -\alpha_{rk1} & -\alpha_{rk2} & -\alpha_{rk3} & \cdots & \alpha_{ck}+\alpha_{rk} & -\alpha_{ck} \\ \alpha_{c1}S_1 & \alpha_{c2}S_2 & \alpha_{c3}S_3 & \cdots & \alpha_{ck}S_k & -\alpha_{ci}\sum_{i=1}^{k} S_i \end{bmatrix} = \begin{bmatrix} q_1 \\ q_2 \\ \vdots \\ q_k \\ H_{ex} \end{bmatrix}$$

(3.52)

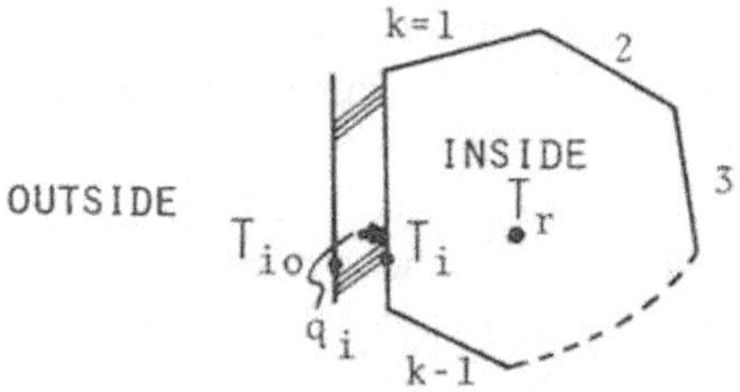

Fig. 3.15. Radiation exchange at inside surface.

where

$$\alpha_{rik} = \sum_{k=1}^{Nt} \alpha_{rik}$$

$$\alpha_{rik} = F_{ik}\varepsilon_i\varepsilon_k\sigma(T_i+T_k)^3/2$$

(3.53)

The heat flow q_i is again a function of the temperature at the other surface of the enclosure, which in most cases is unknown. Then another set of simultaneous equations must be combined with the above equations. It is necessary, therefore, to set up assumptions so that the simultaneous equations can be solved. The most general one would be that the temperature on the other side of enclosure would be assumed on a reasonably realistic basis.

It would be interesting to construct a model for the entire thermal system of a building including all boundary conditions, but this might become too complicated to yield a final solution.

Chapter 4

Solar Heat Gain from Windows

When the solar radiation falls on glass windows, most of it is transmitted through the window and ultimately appears as the cooling load of an interior space. Since the glass window area of modern buildings is comparatively large, a large part of the space cooling load is considered to be caused by solar radiation through glass windows. Various types of shading devices are being used to reduce the heat from the sun through windows and, from the standpoint of air conditioning, it is necessary to establish a method of estimating accurate values of cooling load for different kinds of glass and shading combinations. Information on this is published in reference books on air conditioning design [4.1, 4.2], but the available data are not sufficient for more precise calculations. The solar radiation that enters the space through fenestration, which is called the solar heat gain, would not be exactly equal to the required rate of heat to be removed from the space to keep the occupied zone comfortable, which is called the cooling load. Most of the solar heat gain is absorbed by and stored in the building structure, coming back into the space later on by convection. This process is important for estimating the cooling load associated with solar radiation through windows.

In this chapter, therefore, successive consideration is to be given to

1. solar radiation transmitted through unshaded windows,
2. solar radiation transmitted through windows with external shading,
3. solar heat gain from windows, with internal shading and
4. cooling load associated with solar heat gain.

4.1. ABSORPTION, REFLEXION AND TRANSMISSION OF SOLAR RADIATION FOR SHEET GLASS

A part of solar radiation incident upon the glass surface is transmitted through the glass, a part of it absorbed by the glass and the remainder reflected towards outside. The mechanism of these three components can be expressed by surface reflectance and absorption coefficient inherent to the glass concerned.

The surface reflectance is defined as the fraction of reflected radiation at the outer or inner surface of a sheet glass and given by the following expression derived from Fresnel's equation, viz.,

$$r = \frac{1}{2}\left(\frac{\tan^2(i-i')}{\tan^2(i+i')} + \frac{\sin^2(i-i')}{\sin^2(i+i')}\right) \qquad (4.1)$$

where r = surface reflectance, i = angle of incidence and i' = angle of refraction.

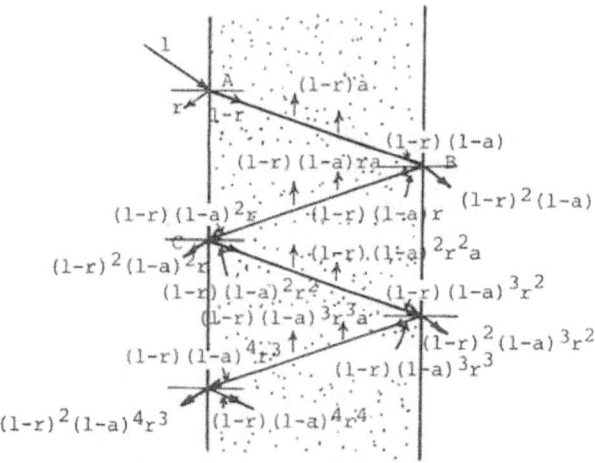

Fig. 4.1. Process of absorption within the glass by multiple reflection at surfaces.

Referring to Fig. 4.1, at point A, where unit energy is incident, r is reflected and $(1 - r)$ refracted into the substance of the sheet glass, being gradually absorbed as it proceeds. Part of the energy is absorbed within the glass until it reaches point B at the other surface. The fraction absorbed can be expressed by the following formula:

$$a = 1 - \exp\left(-\frac{kl}{\cos i'}\right) \qquad (4.2)$$

where l = thickness of the sheet glass (mm) and k = absorption coefficient (mm^{-1}). Absorption coefficient k is a characteristic of the glass and the value of it for regular sheet glass is around $0 \cdot 02$/mm. As the value of a is determined by the product kl, it is convenient to use kl for a respective sheet of glass.

Necessary information is transmissivity and absorptivity related to the angle of incidence. In most practical cases the angle of incidence is known from the problem concerned. Figure 4.2 shows the relationship between transmissivity or absorptivity and the angle of incidence for regular clear glass and grey heat absorbing glass.

The transmissivity of sheet glass also varies with different wavelengths of radiation, as shown in Fig. 4.3. It is important to note that the transmissivity of glass is essentially zero for long wavelength radiation, whereas glass is transparent for the visible range in which solar radiation intensity is the highest.

This is the reason why a greenhouse covered by only one sheet of glass can give

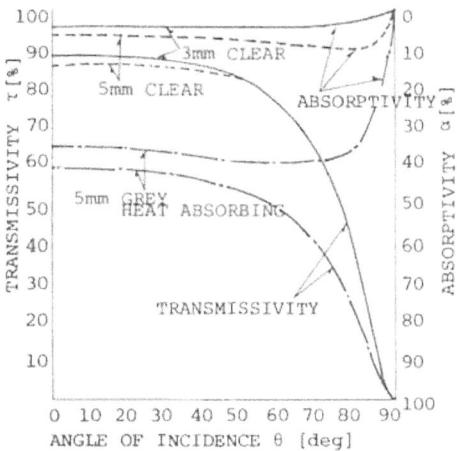

Fig. 4.2. Transmissivity and absorptivity of glass for solar radiation with angle of incidence.

a considerable warmth inside. The glass covering admits a large amount of solar radiation for the plants inside and absorbs the long wavelength radiation emitted by the plants, thus reducing the heat loss. Glass windows of buildings also exert the same effect as a greenhouse, because they not only introduce sunlight into the occupied space but also reduce the heat loss by absorbing radiation from objects in the room. In general, for this reason, this effect is called the greenhouse effect.

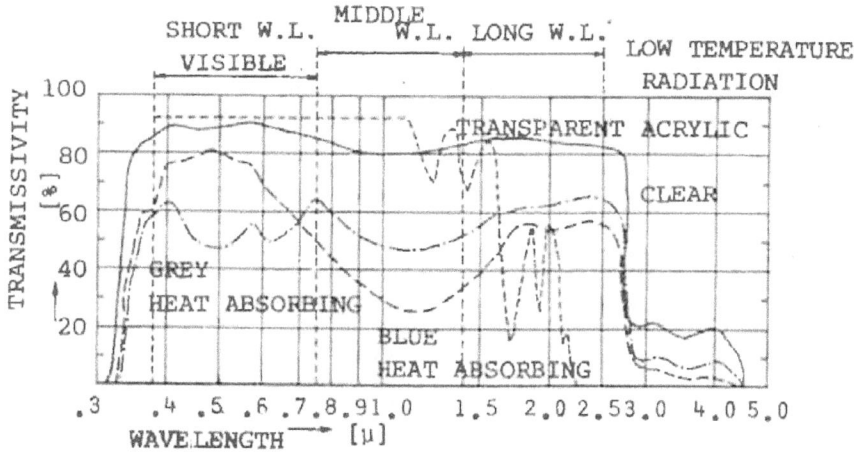

Fig. 4.3. Spectral transmissivity of various kinds of glass.

In air conditioning practices, however, it is seldom made to consider what the transmissivity of glass against wavelength is. As this is sometimes rather important, some simplification is attempted by the author to give approximate figures for four wavelength bands of solar spectrum as shown in Table 4.1.

Again referring to Fig. 4.1, an unit energy incident at A, $(1-r)a$ is absorbed and $(1-r)(1-a)$ reaches point B, where $(1-r)(1-a)r$ is reflected back towards C and $(1-r)^2(1-a)$ refracted towards the inside space to become a part of the transmitted component. Looking at the process of reflection and refraction further from point B to point C at the outer surface, $(1-r)(1-a)ra$ is absorbed and $(1-r)^2(1-a)^2r$ refracted toward the outside becoming a part of the reflected component in relation to the original unit input energy. Subsequent repetition of reflection and refraction takes place, while energy is absorbed in the sheet glass. As a result, absorptivity α, reflectivity ρ and transmissivity τ of the sheet glass can be given as the summation of the infinite series of respective components during the process to be expressed as follows:

Table 4.1
Transmissivity of various kinds of glass for different range of wavelength

Range of wavelength	Energy ratio	Clear 3 (mm)	Clear 5 (mm)	Grey heat absorbing 5 (mm)	Blue heat absorbing 5 (mm)	Clear acrylic 3 (mm)
Short wavelength radiation	0·5	0·88	0·85	0·52	0·70	0·92
Middle wavelength radiation	0·4	0·82	0·76	0·50	0·35	0·89
Long wavelength radiation	0·1	0·83	0·80	0·61	0·50	0·40
Solar radiation, average	1·0	0·85	0·81	0·52	0·59	0·90
Low temperature radiation	0·0	0·0	0·0	0·0	0·0	0·0

$$\alpha = a(1-r)[1 + r(1-a) + r^2(1-a)^2 + \cdots]$$
$$= \frac{a(1-r)}{1-r(1-a)} \qquad (4.3)$$

$$\rho = r\{1 + (1-a)^2(1-r)^2[1 + (1-a)^2 r^2 + \cdots]\}$$
$$= r\left(1 + \frac{(1-a)^2(1-r)^2}{1-r^2(1-a)^2}\right) \qquad (4.4)$$

$$\tau = (1-r)^2(1-a)[1 + r^2(1-a)^2 + \cdots]$$
$$= \frac{(1-r)^2(1-a)}{1-r^2(1-a)^2} \qquad (4.5)$$

The absorptivity, reflectivity and transmissivity depend on the angle of incidence i and angle of refraction i' as can be understood from the relationships given by eqns.

(4.1)–(4.5). As Snell's law states that:

$$n = \frac{\sin i}{\sin i'} \tag{4.6}$$

where n is refractivity and α, ρ and τ may be expressed in the functions of angle of incidence, using the relationship:

$$\alpha + \rho + \tau = 1 \tag{4.7}$$

The transmissivity and the absorptivity of sheet glass for diffuse radiation could be obtained by integrating the transmissivity for different angle of incidence over hemispherical solid angle.

$$\tau_d = 2 \int_0^{\pi/2} \tau_i \sin i \cos i \, di \tag{4.8}$$

$$\alpha_d = 2 \int_0^{\pi/2} \alpha_i \sin i \cos i \, di \tag{4.9}$$

where τ_i = transmissivity for angle of incidence i, α_i = absorptivity for angle of incidence i, τ_d = transmissivity for diffuse radiation, α_d = absorptivity for diffuse radiation.

When the window consists of two panes of glass, overall transmissivity, overall reflectivity and overall absorptivity must be considered taking multiple repetitions of transmission, reflection and absorption by each pane as shown in Fig. 4.4. These items can be expressed by the summation of infinite series as follows:

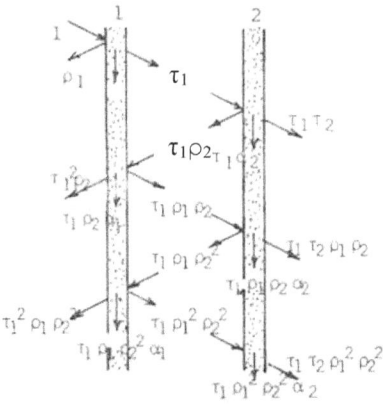

Fig. 4.4. Oveall transmissivity, reflectivity and absorptivity of double glazing.

$$\tau_{12} = \tau_1 \tau_2 + \tau_1 \tau_2 \rho_1 \rho_2 + \tau_1 \tau_2 \rho_1^2 \rho_2^2 + \cdots \tag{4.10}$$

$$= \frac{\tau_1 \tau_2}{1 - \rho_1 \rho_2} \tag{4.11}$$

$$\rho_{12} = \rho_1 + \frac{\tau_1^2 \rho_2}{1 - \rho_1 \rho_2} \tag{4.12}$$

$$\alpha_{i2} = \alpha_1 \left(1 + \frac{\tau_1 \rho_2}{1 - \rho_1 \rho_2}\right) \tag{4.13}$$

$$\alpha_{1\dot{2}} = \frac{\tau_1 \alpha_2}{1 - \rho_1 \rho_2}$$

where τ_{12} = overall transmissivity for double glazing, ρ_{12} = overall reflectivity for double glazing, α_{i2} = overall absorptivity by pane 1 for double glazing, $\alpha_{1\dot{2}}$ = overall absorptivity by pane 2 for double glazing, τ_1, τ_2 = transmissivity of pane 1 and pane 2 respectively, ρ_1, ρ_2 = reflectivity of pane 1 and pane 2 respectively and α_1, α_2 = absorptivity of pane 1 and pane 2 respectively.

4.2. Solar Heat Gain from Glass Windows of Different Orientation

Windows are oriented to different directions depending upon the placing of a building in relation to the building site. Solar radiation for different orientations can be estimated by the formulas given in Chapter 1 both for direct and diffuse components. Combining the transmissivity of sheet glass as described in the preceding section with the amount of solar radiation for the orientation of the window, the solar radiation transmitted through glass can be obtained. In addition, the solar radiation absorbed by the window glass is partly transferred to the room by convection and radiation. Thus, the so-called solar heat gain from a glass window q_G is defined as the summation of the transmitted component q_τ, and the surface heat transfer component of the solar radiation absorbed by the glass q_α as shown in Fig. 4.5, namely,

$$q_G = q_\tau + q_\alpha \tag{4.14}$$

where q_G = solar heat gain from glass windows (Wm^{-2}),

$$q_\tau = \tau_D I_D + \tau_d I_d \tag{4.15}$$

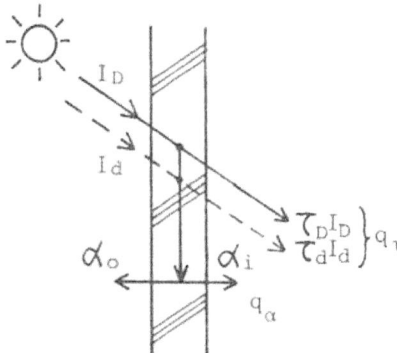

Fig. 4.5. Absorption and transmission of solar radiation upon glass.

where τ_D = transmissivity of glass for direct solar radiation, I_D = direct solar radiation upon the glass (Wm^{-2}), τ_d = transmissivity of glass for diffuse solar radiation and I_d = diffuse solar radiation upon the glass (Wm^{-2}),

$$q_\alpha = \frac{\alpha_i}{\alpha_o + \alpha_i}(\alpha_D I_D + \alpha_d I_d) \qquad (4.16)$$

where α_o = outside film coefficient (Wm^{-2} deg C^{-1}), α_i = inside film coefficient (Wm^{-2} deg C^{-1}), α_D = absorptivity of glass for direct solar radiation and α_d = absorptivity of glass for diffuse solar radiation.

The values of τ_D in eqn. (4.15) and α_D in eqn. (4.16) should be consistent with the angle of incidence of the direct solar radiation upon the glass surface in reference to the relationship as shown in Fig. 4.2.

The value of q_G for a single pane of regular clear glass of 3 mm thick is being used as a standard solar heat gain from a glass window. The idea is that the solar heat gain from a particular type of window or windows with shading is obtained by multiplying the standard solar heat gain by a shading coefficient, viz.,

$$q_G = k_s q_{GS} \qquad (4.17)$$

where q_G = solar heat gain from a given window (Wm^{-2}). q_{GS} = standard solar heat gain from glass window (Wm^{-2}), and k_S = shading coefficient.

The actual values of standard solar heat gain from a glass window for principal window orientations and for standard locality and shading coefficient data for different shading arrangements are usually prepared, so that one can easily estimate solar heat gain from the window concerned.

Table 4.2 shows a list of the standard solar heat gain values from a glass window prepared by SHASE (Society of Heating, Air-conditioning and Sanitary Engineers of Japan) for Tokyo as a representative urban area in the latitude of 35° N because most of the large cities of Japan lie in the vicinity of that latitude.

One might inquire as to how to incorporate the effect of nocturnal radiation with eqn. (4.16) where the combined film coefficient is involved. This is a good point, but the answer to this inquiry is rather simple; that is if the effect of nocturnal radiation is expressed in the form of equivalent temperature drop, this effect is to be taken into account in the heat gain across glass window due to the temperature difference between inside and outside as can be understood from eqn. (3.37). This procedure may be considered in a first approximation method, but for more accurate calculations the iteration procedure must be used as explained in Section 3.5 instead

Table 4.2
Standard solar heat gain from a glass window (Wm^{-2}) (SHASE for latitude 35° N [4.1])

Season	Orientation	Solar time															Daily total
		5	6	7	8	9	10	11	12	13	14	15	16	17	18	19	
Summer (23 July)	Horizontal	1	50	180	326	445	541	604	624	604	541	445	326	180	43	1	4917
	N shade	0	63	40	24	29	34	36	37	36	34	29	24	40	63	0	488
	NE	0	252	330	300	205	87	36	37	36	34	29	24	18	10	0	1398
	E	0	277	409	424	374	268	118	37	36	34	29	24	18	10	0	2059
	SE	0	129	239	295	304	268	188	89	36	34	29	24	18	10	0	1664
	S	0	10	18	24	46	87	121	134	121	87	46	24	18	10	0	746
	SW	0	10	18	24	29	34	36	89	188	268	304	295	239	129	0	1664
	W	0	10	18	24	29	34	36	37	119	268	374	424	409	277	0	2059
	NW	0	10	18	24	29	34	36	37	36	87	205	300	330	251	0	1398
Autumn (24 October)	Horizontal			12	100	233	340	403	425	403	340	233	101	12			2602
	N shade			4	10	15	17	20	21	20	18	15	10	4			154
	NE			61	91	25	17	20	21	20	17	15	10	4			301
	E			139	369	364	268	110	21	20	17	15	10	4			1337
	SE			131	402	475	464	404	303	159	40	15	10	4			2406
	S			36	181	294	374	422	438	422	374	294	181	36			3052
	SW			4	10	15	39	159	303	404	464	475	402	131			2405
	W			4	10	15	17	20	21	110	268	364	369	139			1337
	NW			4	10	15	17	20	21	20	17	25	91	61			301
Winter (21 January)	Horizontal				45	154	259	325	347	325	259	154	45				1913
	N shade				5	9	11	13	14	13	11	9	5				89
	NE				40	9	11	13	14	13	11	9	5				121
	E				324	347	254	99	14	13	11	9	5				1076
	SE				391	504	502	444	348	212	70	9	5				2486
	S				213	348	433	484	501	484	433	348	213				3460
	SW				5	9	70	212	348	444	502	504	391				2485
	W				5	9	11	13	14	99	254	347	324				1076
	NW				5	9	11	13	14	13	11	9	40				125
Spring (20 April)	Horizontal			18	128	285	417	516	582	605	582	516	417	286	128	18	4500
	N shade			19	12	17	22	26	28	28	28	26	22	17	12	19	276
	NE			167	304	267	153	45	28	28	26	22	17	12	5		1103
	E			206	434	460	404	290	121	28	28	26	22	17	12	5	2054
	SE			118	297	371	386	353	272	149	43	26	22	17	12	5	2071
	S			5	12	40	105	175	223	240	223	175	105	40	12	5	1358
	SW			5	12	17	22	26	43	149	271	353	386	371	297	118	2071
	W			5	12	17	22	26	28	28	121	290	404	460	434	206	2054
	NW			5	12	17	22	26	28	28	45	153	267	304	167		1103

of relying on the standard solar heat gain from glass windows.

The data for shading coefficients of different shading arrangements have been published. The ASHRAE Handbook of Fundamentals offers a good range of shading coefficients data. Most of these data are derived from the experimental studies carried out by Pennington, Parmelee and others over a long period of time. Table 4.3 shows a list of shading coefficients useful for estimating solar heat gain from glass windows.

Table 4.3

Shading coefficients [4.1]

Glass	Blind	Shading coefficient		
		Convection SC_C	Radiation SC_R	Total SC
Regular single pane	Without	0.05	0.95	1.0
	Light	0.4	0.25	0.65
	Medium	0.5	0.25	0.75
Heat absorbing single pane	Without	0.1	0.7	0.8
	Light	0.35	0.25	0.6
	Medium	0.45	0.25	0.7
Regular double pane, blind between	Light	0.2	0.2	0.4
Regular double pane	Without	0.05	0.85	0.9
	Light	0.38	0.22	0.6
	Medium	0.48	0.22	0.7
Outside heat absorbing and inside regular double pane	Without	0.1	0.6	0.7
	Light	0.35	0.18	0.5
	Medium	0.43	0.18	0.6

4.3. EXPERIMENTAL DETERMINATION OF COOLING LOAD ASSOCIATED WITH SOLAR HEAT GAIN

Solar heat gain is the instantaneous rate of heat flow into the occupied space in the form of radiation and convection and is different from the cooling load. The cooling load is the rate of flow of heat to be extracted from the space to maintain the room air temperature at the required level. Thus, the convection component of the solar heat gain can be regarded as becoming a cooling load instantaneously, whereas the radiation component would appear as a cooling load with a time delay after being stored in the building structure instead of being directly transferred to the room air. Then, the diurnal variation of cooling load caused by solar radiation from windows shows a different pattern from the variation of solar heat gain.

In air conditioning design practice the storage load factor proposed by the Carrier Company [4.2] has been quite extensively used for determination of peak cooling load caused by solar heat gain. The storage load factor is defined as the variable ratio of solar cooling load to the maximum fixed value of solar heat gain for a given orientation and is denoted as SLF$_n$ for time $t = n\Delta t$ to be expressed as follows:

$$\text{SLF}_n = \frac{\text{cooling load due to solar radiation at time } n}{\text{maximum instantaneous solar heat gain}} \tag{4.18}$$

It is not clear, however, whether the storage load factor is based on any special experiments or only on theoretical studies.

A comparison was made between the published SLF$_n$, and the calculated SLF$_n$ form the data obtained by an experiment with the prototype calorimeter room with 2m^2 of glass window facing west, with a 12cm thick concrete slab, and with a fan-coil unit to extract heat from the space. Figure 4.6 illustrates the section of the prototype calorimeter room of Waseda University [4.3] and Fig. 4.7 shows the results of comparison.

It can be seen that the variation of SLF for August 13 is almost equal to that of August 14. These results seem to be somewhat larger than Carrier's data around peak conditions, but in general both data are close enough to give a realistic reference for air conditioning design when the storage effects of the building structure are to be considered.

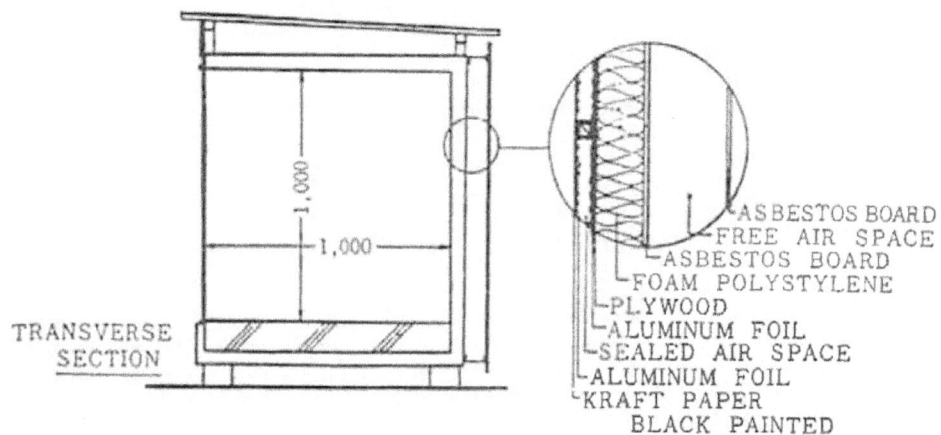

Fig. 4.6. Prototype calorimeter room to measure solar heat from window at Waseda University [4.3]. Dimensions in millimeters.

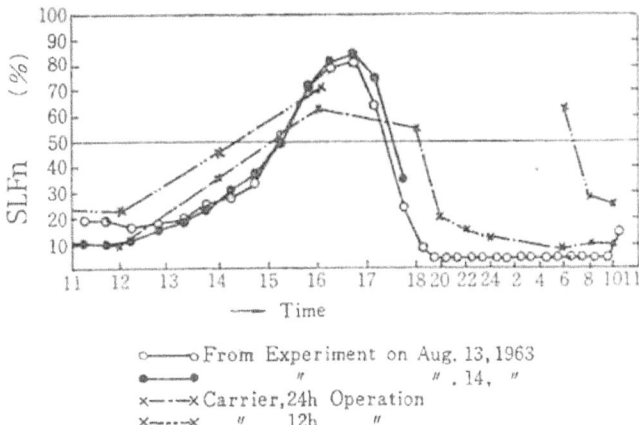

Fig. 4.7. Comparison of SLF [4.3]. (○—○) From experiment on Aug.13, 1963; (●—●) from experiment on Aug. 14, 1963; (×———×) Carrier, 24h operation; (×------×) Carrier 12h operation.

There is a second version of a calorimeter room to measure the cooling load caused by solar radiation upon the windows surface located in the Ohbayashi-gumi Engineering Research Laboratory [4.4]. This is a revolving type so that the glass window surface can be oriented to any direction to do experiments with different window orientations and with window orientations of any actual building. Figure 4.8(a) shows the view from outside and Fig. 4.8(b and c) show two sections of the calorimeter room. The inside dimensions of the room are 4m×4m×2m and the room is constructed of 12cm thick precast concrete panels. Two fan-coil units are placed inside to supply air regulated by an electropneumatic type of PID activated controller, maintaining the space temperature constant. Two-way valves are used to pick up warm water and cold water in the storage tanks beneath the floor of machine room to the proportion indicated by the variation of space cooling load. The guard space is provided presupposing the room to be part of a multi-storied building and the air temperature there is controlled to be equal to that of the room air. The schematic diagram of the piping system is shown in Fig. 4.9.

A great number of thermocouples were embedded in the precast concrete panels to measure the temperature so that the rate of heat transfer between inside surface and room air could be estimated. Eppley pyrheliometers were installed inside and outside of the glass to measure solar radiation upon the vertical surface of the glass.

Figure 4.10 shows the experimental results obtained with the revolving air conditioning test room on August 20, 1966 when the window was oriented to the east. The room air temperature was maintained at 26°C for a week prior to this experiment. Curve (1) represents the solar radiation transmitted through glass, measured by an Eppley pyrheliometer placed inside with the sensor surface set vertically, multiplied by $8m^2$ of glass area. Curve (2) represents the heat extraction by the fan-coil units measured by a calorimeter knowing the water flow rate and the

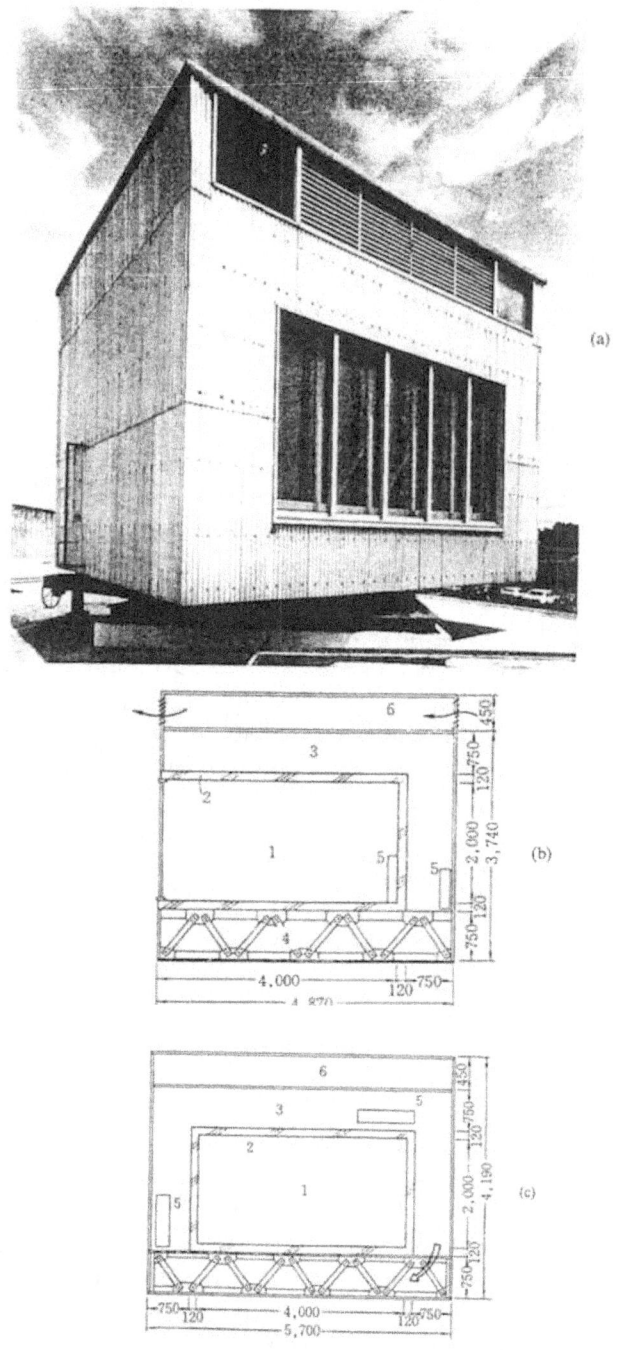

Fig. 4.8. Revolving air conditioning test room in Ohbayashi-gumi research laboratory [4.4], (a) Outside view, (b and c) sections. 1. Test room space; 2.12 cm thick precast reinforced concrete panel; 3. upper guard space; 4. lower guard space; 5. fan-coil unit; 6. ventilated plenum. All dimensions are in millimeters.

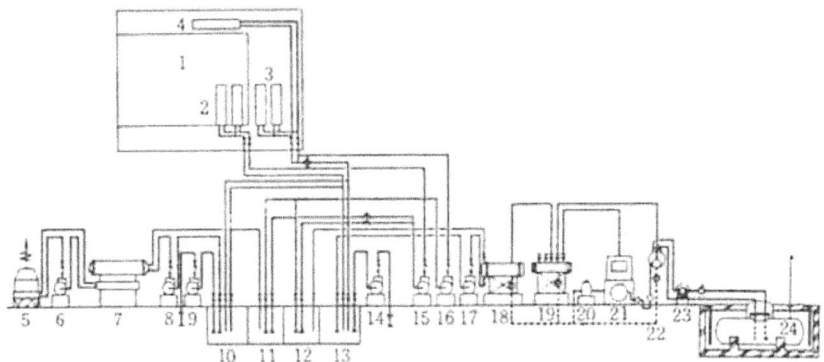

Fig. 4.9. Diagram of air conditioning system of revolving air conditioning test room [4.4]. 1. Test room; 2. fan-coil unit; 3. guard space; 4. fan-coil unit in guard space 5. cooling tower; 6. condenser water pump; 7. refrigerating machine; 8. chilled water pump; 9. drainage pump; 10. cold water storage tank (higher temperature); 11. cold water storage tank (lower temperature); 12. warm water storage tank (higher temperature); 13. warm water storage tank (lower temperature); 14. drainage pump; 15. pump to supply warm or cold water to test room; 16. pump to supply warm or cold water to guard space; 17. warm water circulation pump; 18. heat exchanger; 19. steam header; 20.vaacuum pump; 21. boiler; 22. oil service pump; 23. oil gear-pump; 24. oil tank.

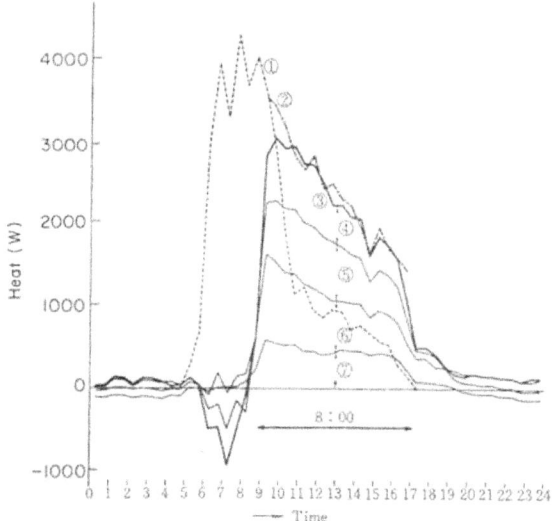

Fig. 4.10. Total cooling load vs. heat extraction (Aug. 20, 1966) [4.4]. (1) Transmitted solar radiation through glass; (2) heat extraction by fan-coil unit; (3) total convective heat transfer to the room air (= (4) + (5) + (6) +(7)); (4) convective heat transfer from wall surfaces to room air; (5) convective heat transfer from ceiling surface to room air; (6) convective heat transfer from floor surface to room air; (7) convective heat transfer from glass surface to room air. Time in day hours.

temperature rise across the coil. Curve (3) represents the total space cooling load estimated from the temperature data measured inside which is supposed to coincide with curve (2). Curves (4), (5), (6) and (7) are a breakdown of curve (3). The inside surface temperature was measured at about 50 points and averaged surface by surface. Then the convective heat transfer to the room air from the wall surfaces was calculated from the temperature difference between the surface and the room air multiplied by the convective heat transfer coefficient of $9 \cdot 3$ Wm^{-2} deg C^{-1} and the surface area, which is shown as curve (4). Similarly, curves (5), (6) and (7) represent the convective heat transfer to the room air from the ceiling surface, floor surface and glass surface respectively. The fact that the total convective heat transfer coincided with the heat extraction by the fan-coil units when the value of convective heat transfer coefficient was assumed to be $9 \cdot 3$ Wm^{-2} deg C^{-1} indicates that the air movement in this room was quite large compared with what would have been the situation in a normal room.

Figure 4.11 shows the results obtained from the experiments made on January 14 to January 19, 1967, when the glass surface was facing south [4.5]. All six days were clear as would be seen from the measured data in the curve. The room air temperature was maintained at a constant 20°C from 9 a.m. to 5 p.m. on the 14th through to the 16th by intermittent operation and from 9 a.m. on the 17th to 6 p.m. on the 18th the system was operated continuously. As shown in the curves of temperature for the inside air, average temperature of wall surface and the average temperature of concrete panel sections, heating was required to maintain 20°C inside in spite of the increase of solar incidence. This was considered reasonable because the structure itself was not yet warm enough for continuous operation. Here the values of convective heat transfer coefficients were assumed to be $4 \cdot 7$ Wm^{-2} deg C^{-1} when the measured heat extraction coincided with the total cooling load theoretically derived using the surface temperature measurements.

4.4. Cooling Load Weighting Factors for Solar Heat Gain

If the solar heat gain from windows and the space cooling load associated with it are both expressed as a time series, the most straightforward way of relating one to the other may be to use a convolution technique where weighting factors are to be introduced. The cooling load weighting factors for solar heat gain can be defined in the following convolution form:

$$q_{CL}(n) = \sum_{j=0}^{\infty} W_G(j) q_G(n-j) \qquad (4.19)$$

where $q_{CL}(n)$ = space cooling load at time $t = n\Delta t$ associated with solar heat gain

(Wm^{-2}), $q_G(n)$ = solar heat gain from glass window at time $t = n\Delta t$ (Wm^{-2}), $q_G(n-j)$ = solar heat gain at time $j\Delta t$ hours prior to time $t = n\Delta t$, $W_G(j)$ = cooling load weighting factors for solar heat gain (dimensionless).

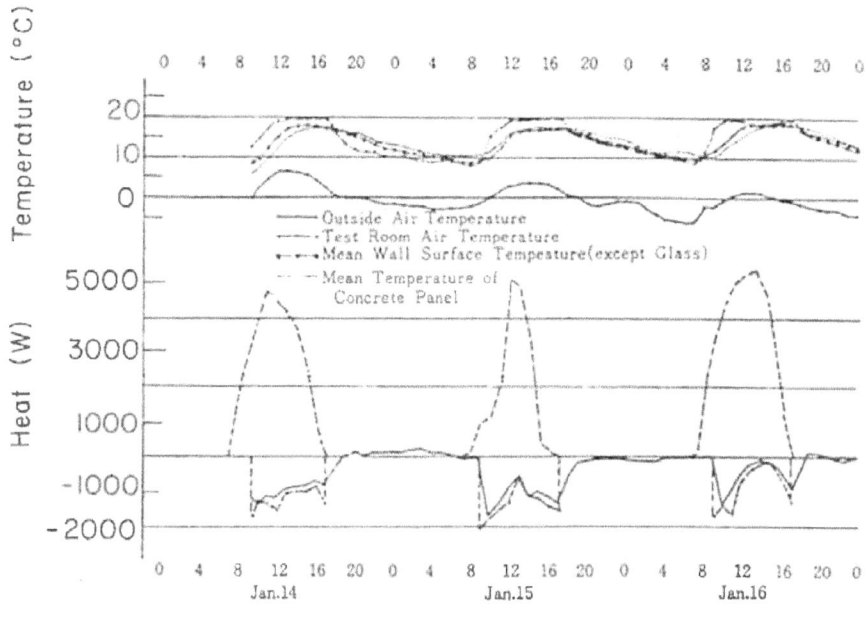

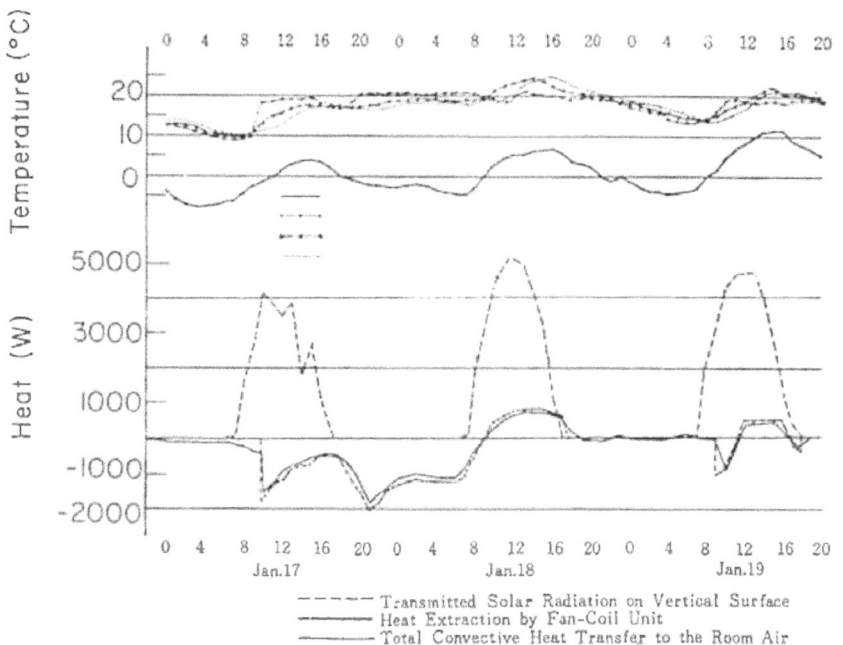

Fig. 4.11. Variation of cooling load and temperature in winter experiment [4.5].

The relationship between Carrier's storage load factor SLF_n and weighting factors $W_G(j)$ can be interpreted by the following expression:

$$SLF(n) = \sum_{j=1}^{\infty} W_G(j) \cdot \sigma_G(n-j) \qquad (4.20)$$

where

$$\sigma_G(n) = \frac{q_{GS}(n)}{q_{GS,\max}} \qquad (4.21)$$

where $q_{GS}(n)$ is the standard solar heat gain from glass window for a given orientation and $q_{GS,\max}$ is the maximum value of $q_{GS}(n)$. It must be remembered that $SLF(n)$ varies with window orientation and that $W_G(j)$ is independent of window orientation. The major differences between the two is that $SLF(n)$ is used only for design purposes to obtain maximum probable solar heat gain, whereas the weighting factors method can be used for any random or irregular excitations as far as they are given in the form of a time series.

Theoretical determination of the weighting factors is discussed by Ishino and the author [4.6] and will be introduced in Chapter 6.

Experimental determination has been attempted by Miyagawa and the author with the revolving air conditioning test room as explained in the preceding section. The principle to derive the weighting factors is simple, as eqn. (4.19) can be rewritten as follows:

$$q_{CL}(n) = W_G(0)q_G(n) + W_G(1)q_G(n-1) + W_G(2)q_G(n-2) + \cdots$$
$$q_{CL}(n-1) = W_G(0)q_G(n-1) + W_G(1)q_G(n-2) + W_G(2)q_G(n-3) + \cdots$$
$$\vdots \qquad \vdots \qquad \vdots \qquad \vdots$$
$$(4.22)$$

If $q_{CL}(n)$ and $q_G(n)$ are measured at as many times as possible, the unknowns $W_G(1)$, $W_G(2)$, ... can be obtained by solving the simultaneous equations. The results by this method often give rise to unrealistic values of $W_G(j)$. It has been found more appropriate to restrict the number of terms of $W_G(j)$ and to use common ratios for $W_G(j)$ for large j values.

Since it may be approximated as:

$$W_G(j) = C \cdot W_G(j-1) \qquad (4.23)$$

for $j > k$ where k is an integer chosen to suit the particular case. Usually $k = 3$ or 4 is adequate. Then the number of simultaneous equations to be prepared would be $k + 2$, because:

$$\begin{bmatrix} q_{CL}(n) \\ q_{CL}(n-1) \\ \vdots \\ q_{CL}(n-k) \\ q_{CL}(n-k-1) \end{bmatrix} = \begin{bmatrix} q_G(n) & q_G(n-1) & q_G(n-k) & q_G(n-k-1) \\ q_G(n-1) & q_G(n-2) & q_G(n-k-1) & q_G(n-k-2) \\ \vdots & \vdots & \vdots & \vdots \\ q_G(n-k) & q_G(n-k-1) & q_G(n-2k) & q_G(n-2k-1) \\ q_G(n-k-1) & q_G(n-k-2) & q_G(n-2k-1) & q_G(n-2k-2) \end{bmatrix} \begin{bmatrix} W_G(0) \\ W_G(1) \\ \vdots \\ W_G(k) \\ C W_G(k) \end{bmatrix}$$

(4.24)

Solving these simultaneous equations for $W_G(0)$, $W_G(1)$, ..., $W_G(k)$ and $C.W_G(k)$, the weighting factors together with the common ratio can be obtained.

Table 4.4 shows various values of weighting factors determined by this procedure using the experimental data obtained from the revolving air conditioning test room. This includes the weighting factors not only for a clear glass window, but also for windows with internal shading devices.

Table 4.4
Cooling load weighting factors for transmitted solar radiation through a glass window obtained from experimental results

(a) Clear glass only

Date tested	Orientation	W_0	W_1	W_2	W_3	W_4	W_5
25.5.1967	E	0·505	0·175	0·098	0·051	0·021	
26.5.1967	E	0·502	0·156	0·096	0·032		
4.7.1967	E	0·520	0·203	0·192	0·028		
19.7.1967	E	0·540	0·180	0·107	0·020	0·020	0·009
20.7.1967	E	0·422	0·209	0·084	0·052	0·046	0·021
22.8.1968	E	0·462	0·255	0·139	0·079	0·031	
23.12.1967	S	0·305	0·196	0·080	0·067	0·059	0·022
30.12.1967	S	0·310	0·126	0·106	0·083	0·043	
3.2.1968	S	0·488	0·272	0·078	0·052	0·029	

(b) Clear glass and slat type blind

Date tested	Orientation	Type of blind	Slat angle	W_0	W_1	W_2	W_3	W_4
17.5.1967	E	H	45°	0·727	0·051	0·007		
18.5.1967	E	H	closed	0·727	0·020	0·010		
23.5.1967	E	H	open	0·705	0·069	0·052	0·022	
31.5.1967	E	V	45°	0·753	0·020	0·009		
1.6.1967	E	V	45°	0·720	0·061	0·020		
3.6.1967	E	V	open	0·740	0·045	0·017		
15.6.1967	E	V	closed	0·654	0·073	0·059	0·027	
10.10.1967	E	V	open	0·650	0·072	0·049	0·037	
17.12.1967	S	V	45°	0·744	0·007			
25.1.1968	S	H	closed	0·780	0·046	0·025		
26.1.1968	S	H	closed	0·763	0·082	0·010		
7.2.1968	S	H	45°	0·915	0·036			
14.2.1968	S	H	open	0·860	0·061			

H = Horizontal venetian blind.
V = Vertical cloth blind.

4.5. SOLAR HEAT GAIN FROM WINDOWS WITH INSIDE VENETIAN BLINDS

The slat type of sun-shade, the so-called venetian blind, is widely used in modern buildings to intercept mainly direct solar radiation. They are usually installed on the inside of glass window and they are generally considered less effective in reducing the solar heat gain through windows than the external shade. The reason why these blinds are so commonly used is that they are moderate in price, convenient to use and easy to maintain. It is rather difficult, however, to estimate the solar heat gain from windows with inside venetian blinds when designing the air conditioning system for spaces. In practice the shading coefficient is commonly used to obtain it by multiplying the solar heat gain from a standard glass window by the shading coefficient which is different for different types of internal shading devices as well as depending on the type of glass. It is rather doubtful, however, whether it can be used for calculation of cooling load under natural weather conditions, Parmelee et al. presented convenient graphs on shading performance of slat-type sunshades obtained through geometrical analysis [4.7, 4.8]. They give the values of transmittance and absorptance of slat-type sun-shades regarded as an assembly of a semi-opaque layer, with perfectly specular and perfectly diffuse slats, for slats with different absorptance, different geometry of slat assembly against direct solar radiation and diffuse solar radiation.

Figure 4.12 shows one of Parmelee's charts for estimating the transmittance and the absorptance of a slat assembly with variation of the absorptivity of slat material for different profile angles. The profile angle ϕ is defined as:

$$\tan\phi = \frac{\tan\beta}{\cos\gamma} \tag{4.25}$$

where β = solar altitude (degrees), γ = wall solar azimuth (degrees). These relationships are illustrated in Fig.4.13.

Figure 4.14 shows the geometry of the slat assembly, where w is slat width, s is slat spacing and m is sunlit width of slat depending on profile angle ϕ and slat angle ψ to be given by the following formula:

$$\frac{m}{w} = \frac{s\cos\phi}{w\sin(\phi+\psi)} \tag{4.26}$$

In determining a part of direct solar radiation transmits through the slat assembly, a factor L is defined here as:

$$L = 1 - \frac{w\sin(\phi+\psi)}{s\cos\phi} \tag{4.27}$$

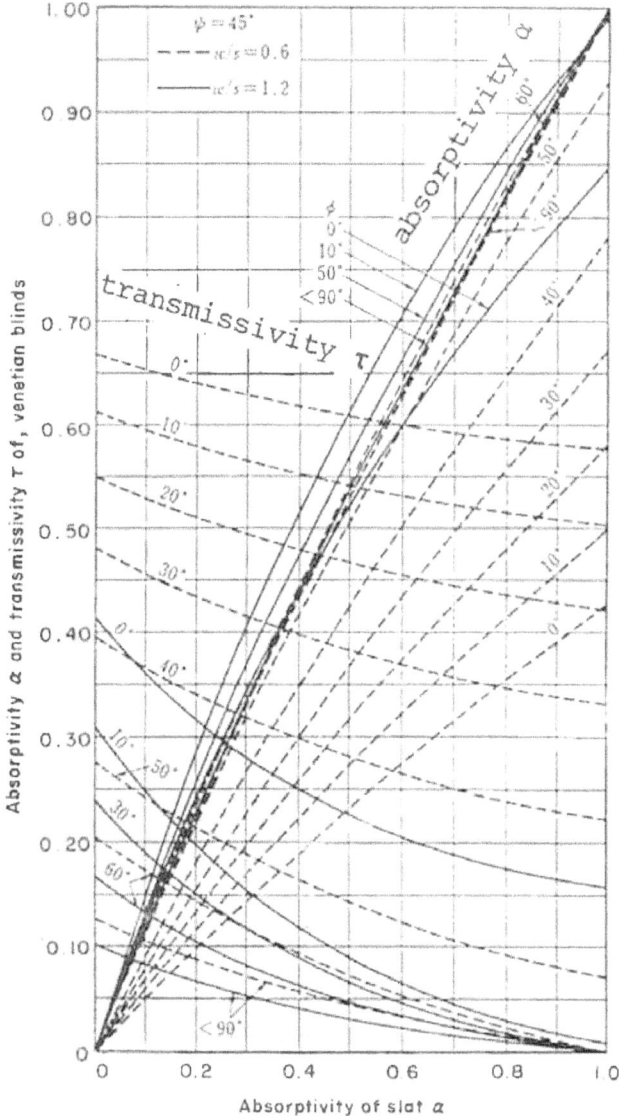

Fig. 4.12.   Absorptivity and transmissivity of venetian blinds [4.7]. (Reprinted by permission of the American Society of Heating Refrigeration and Air Conditioning Engineers, Inc., from *ASHRAE Transactions*.)

Then the transmittance τ, and the absorptance α of the slat assembly can be given by the following formulas depending on whether L is positive or negative, viz.,

For $L \geq 0$

$$\tau = 1 - \frac{w\sin(\phi+\psi)}{s\cos\phi}$$
$$\times \left(1 - F_1(1-a) - \frac{F_2(1-a)}{1-F_2^2(1-a)^2}[F_3 + F_1F_2(1-a)]\right) \quad (4.28)$$

$$\alpha = 1 - \frac{aw\sin(\phi+\psi)}{s\cos\phi}\left(1 + \frac{F_2(1-a)}{1-F_2(1-a)}\right) \quad (4.29)$$

For $L < 0$

$$\tau = (1-a)F_4 + 1 + \frac{F_5(1-a)^2}{1-F_2^2(1-a)^2}[F_3 + F_1F_2(1-a)^2] \quad (4.30)$$

$$\alpha = a\left(1 + \frac{F_5(1-a)}{1-F_2(1-a)}\right) \quad (4.31)$$

where a = absorptivity of slat surface and F_1, F_2, F_3, F_4 and F_5 are form factors [4.7, 4.8].

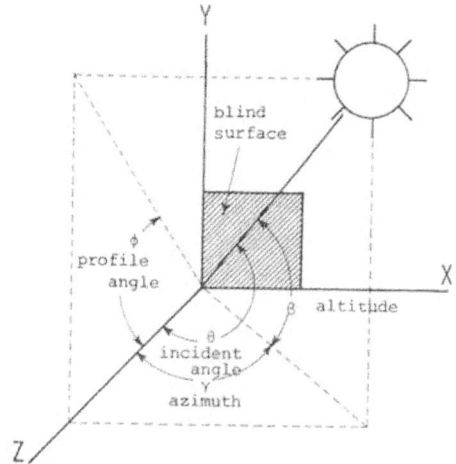

Fig. 4.13.   Profile angle

It is necessary to consider the mechanism of heat transfer across the fenestration as a combination of glass and venetian blind. The absorbed solar heat in the venetian blind can be calculated from the solar radiation upon the vertical plane for window orientation multiplied by the value of overall absorptance of the slat assembly. It is necessary to establish the method to estimate how much of the absorbed solar heat would be transferred to the room air to bring about the actual heat gain. Then, a thermal system model is assumed where the temperature distribution from outside to inside across the glass and venetian blind are given as shown in Fig. 4.15.

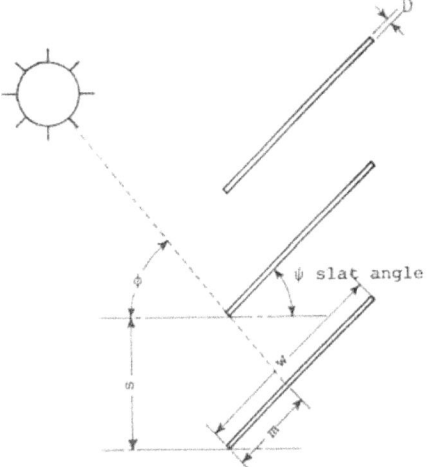

Fig. 4.14. Slat detail.

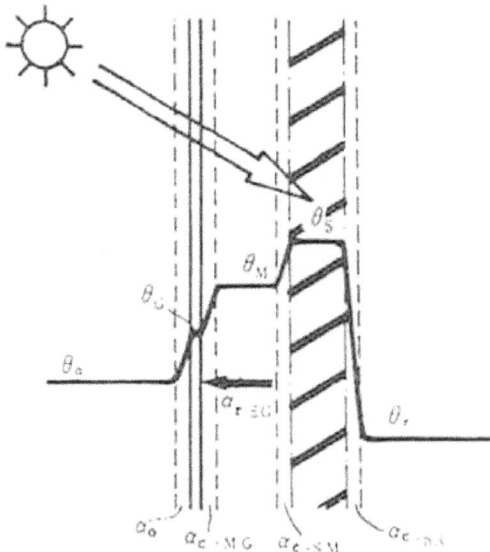

Fig. 4.15. Assumed temperature distribution within the thermal system consisting of glass, venetian blind and air space [4.16].

Using the superposition principle that convective and radiative heat transfer coefficients would not change with temperature in the thermal system by assumption, the heat gain q (Wm^{-2}) can be expressed by the following:

$$q = K_{GV}(\theta_a - \theta_r) + k_V q_{Va} + k_G q_{Ga} \qquad (4.32)$$

where q_{Va} = solar radiation absorbed by the slat assembly (W m^{-2}), q_{Ga} = solar radiation absorbed by the glass (W m^{-2}), θ_a = ambient air temperature (°C) and θ_r = room air temperature (°C), K_{GV} is the overall heat transfer coefficient including the thermal resistance of air space between glass and venetian blind expressed as:

$$K_{GV} = \frac{1}{R_o + R_a + R_i} \tag{4.33}$$

$$R_o = \frac{1}{\alpha_o}$$

$$R_a = \frac{1}{\alpha_{rsG} + \dfrac{1}{1/\alpha_{csM} + 1/\alpha_{cMG}}} \tag{4.34}$$

$$R_a = \frac{1}{\alpha_{csr} + \alpha_{rsr}}$$

In these equations, it is rather difficult to assume the value of α_{csM} and α_{csr}. Tests have shown that the value of α_{csr} is roughly 23 Wm^{-2} degC^{-1} in the case of 45° of slat angle. The value k_V is the fraction of heat gain of the solar radiation absorbed by the slat assembly of venetian blind and can be expressed as:

$$k_V = \frac{R_o}{R_o + R_a + R_i} \tag{4.35}$$

The value k_G is the fraction of heat gain of the solar radiation absorbed by the glass and can be expressed as:

$$k_G = \frac{R_o}{R_o + R_a + R_i} \tag{4.36}$$

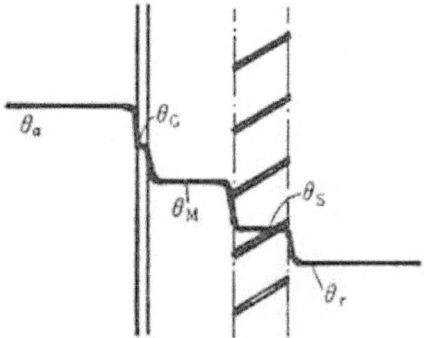

Fig. 4.16. Presumed temperature distribution when the blind receives less radiation [4.16].

When the solar radiation is relatively small, a temperature distribution like that of Fig. 4.15 would not be realized but that in Fig. 4.16 may be realistic. Such a temperature distribution as in Fig. 4.16 can be realized in the case where absorbed total solar radiation is smaller than the transferred heat to the room out of the absorbed solar radiation. Heat-absorbing glass would result in the temperature distribution shown in Fig. 4.17. In either case eqn. (4.32) would be valid. It is considered almost impossible to estimate the heat transfer to the room with a strict theoretical analysis. With such rough assumptions, the result of calculations would seem to suggest validity in assumed values to some extent.

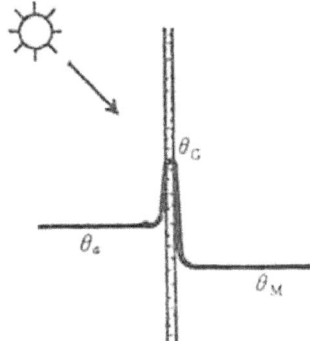

Fig. 4.17. Presumed temperature distribution when heat-absorbing glass is used [4.16].

In applying the theoretical equation as expressed in eqn. (4.32), the real problem is to estimate the convective heat transfer coefficient along the hypothetical surface of the slat assembly especially α_{csr}, which could be called the equivalent convective heat transfer coefficient.

4.6. EXPERIMENTAL DETERMINATION OF THERMAL CHARACTERISTICS OF VENETIAN BLINDS

It is generally considered that an aluminium venetian blind has better heat-intercepting characteristics with the high reflectivity of its slats than a painted one, especially when installed on the inside of the glass. Since the reflectivity depends very much on how well the blind is maintained and there is no standard test for heat interception, there is no criterion by which test results can be evaluated. What is tested here is the performance of an aluminium venetian blind, which had been used for about two weeks, as an arbitrary test. Utilising the prototype calorimeter room at Waseda University, the test was made with the venetian blind installed 5 cm from the inside surface of the glass window of a test room facing west.

Figure 4.18 shows the results of temperature measurement in the case of a blind with 45° slat angle recorded by multi-point electronic recorders using thermocouples [4.9]. Though the performance of the automatic control in keeping the room temperature constant was not so satisfactory, the following tendency can be recognised from the results obtained.

Temperature of the glass is found to be somewhat higher than presumed for the case in which there is no venetian blind, and to approach closer to the ambient air temperature as time passes. This is considered due to the absorption of re-radiation from the blind. The glass temperature becomes almost equal to the ambient air temperature when the solar altitude becomes lower after 3 p.m. and the solar radiation absorbed by the blind increases. Air space temperature between glass and venetian blind gets noticeably high, which would indicate the existence of a kind of insulating effect of the blind. The curve G-M-R shows the effect of the slat assembly in blocking the air movement through the openings between slats.

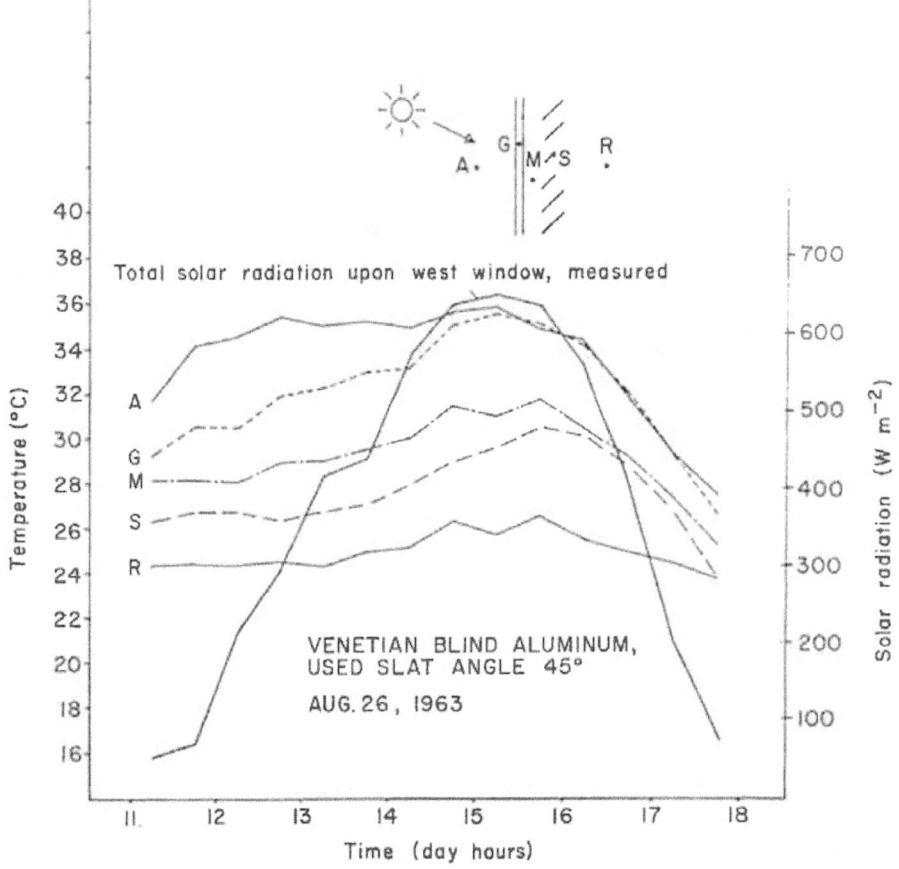

Fig. 4.18. Temperature variation with venetian blind of 45° slat angle [4.16].

Another experiment with a venetian blind painted in a light colour was made to obtain the values of the equivalent convective heat transfer coefficient between the slat assembly and the room air and the values of the overall transmittance of a combination of glass and venetian blind. Figure 4.19 shows the results of the experiment with the prototype calorimeter room with the glass windows facing west, when the slat angle was set at 45° and 90° (closed position). The equivalent convective heat transfer coefficient α_{csr} as used in eqn. (4.34) is shown in Fig. 4.19(a) and the overall transmittance is shown in Fig. 4.19(b). Total measured solar radiation upon the west vertical surface is shown in Fig. 4.19(c) and temperatures of ambient air (θ_a), room air (θ_r) and slat (θ_s) are shown in Fig. 4.19(d). All these data are average values during 30 min. The value of α_{csr} and τ_{sG} are obtained from the following formulae:

$$\alpha_{csr} = \frac{a_s I - \alpha_{rsG}(\theta_s - \theta_G) - \alpha_{rsw}(\theta_s - \theta_w)}{\theta_s - \theta_r} \tag{4.37}$$

$$\tau_{sG} = \frac{q_b}{I_o} \tag{4.38}$$

where I_o = total solar radiation on glass surface measured (Wm^{-2}), I = total solar radiation through glass estimated from I_o (Wm^{-2}), a_s = overall absorptance of slat assembly obtained from Parmelee's chart in Fig. 4.12 for 50% of slat reflectivity at corresponding profile angle, α_{rsG} = radiative heat transfer coefficient between slat and glass (Wm^{-2} degC^{-1}), α_{rsw} = radiative heat transfer coefficient between slat and inside room surfaces (Wm^{-2} degC^{-1}), q_b = short and long wave length radiation measured by Beckman and Whitney radiometer (Wm^{-2}).

It can be seen that, when solar radiation intensity tends to be high, the value of the equivalent convective heat transfer coefficient remains quite stable at 20–23 Wm^{-2} degC^{-1} for 45° of slat angle and at 9–12 Wm^{-2} degC^{-1} for 90° of slat angle. The state of closed position somewhat resembles to that of a flat plate and the value obtained here seems realistic. In the case of 45° of slat angle, it can be considered that heat flow occurs due to the air flow between the slats and this effect is included in the value of α_{csr}.

The overall transmittance of a combination of glass and venetian blind is the ratio of the transmitted short wave length solar radiation after multiple reflections among slats plus the long wave length radiation from the slat surfaces that absorbed solar radiation to the total solar radiation upon the glass surface. This transmitted component of solar heat gain tends to be stored in the building structure, whereas the convective heat transfer component becomes a space cooling load instantaneously.

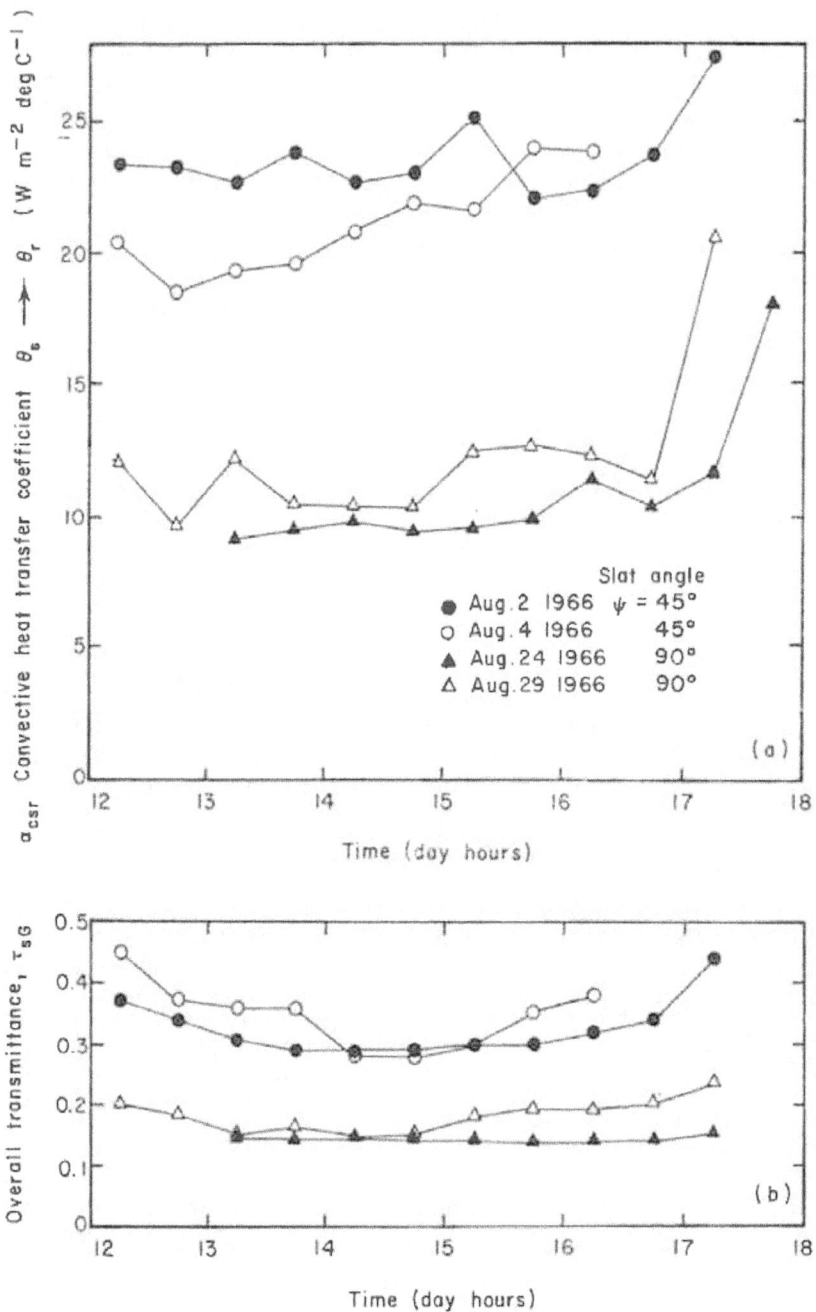

Fig. 4.19. Test results of (a) convective heat transfer coefficient from venetian blind to room air; (b) overall transmittance of combination of venetian blind and glass; (c) total solar radiation upon the west vertical surface and (d) temperatures of ambient air, room air and slat [4.16].

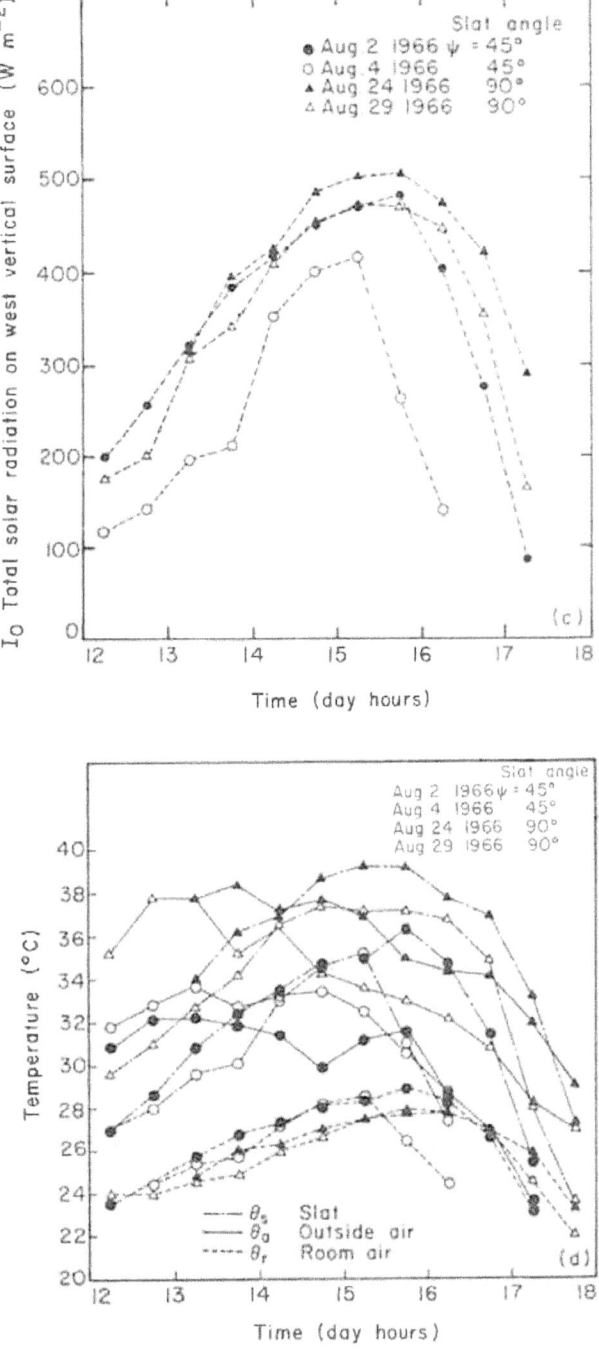

Fig. 4.19 – *continued*:

4.7. EXPERIMENTAL DETERMINATION OF THE EFFECT OF RE-RADIATION FROM EXTERNAL SHADING

Sun-shade devices architecturally integrated with building facades known as brise-soleil, are being used a great deal all over the world. As with the estimation of incident solar radiation transmitted through the sun-shades and glass window, it is mathematically possible to calculate the direct solar radiation directly transmitted through the openings of sun-shades at a certain instant from the position of the sun and the geometrical shape of the sun-shades as well as to calculate the radiation reflected at the surface of the sun-shades and transmitted through glass into the room. It is complex and difficult, however, to estimate the cooling load due to the re-radiation from the surfaces of sun-shades warmed by the absorbed solar radiation.

If one tries to determine the effect of re-radiation from sunlit shades by experiment, it is also difficult to extract the solar heat gain affected only by the re-radiation from the result of the experiments. In comparison with the case in which there is no sun-shade, this effect might be estimated using the following expression:

q_{RR} = solar heat gain effected only by re-radiation
from sun-shade surfaces

$$q_{RR} = \alpha_i(\theta_G - \theta_r) - \alpha_i(\theta'_G - \theta_r) = \alpha_i(\theta_G - \theta'_G) \quad (4.39)$$

where α_i = inside film coefficient, θ_r = room air temperature, θ_G = glass temperature measured when the glass is warmed by absorbing re-radiation from sunlit louvre surfaces, θ'_G = glass temperature estimated if no sun-shades were installed.

$$\theta'_G = \frac{\alpha_o \theta_a + \alpha_i \theta_r}{\alpha_i + \alpha_o} \quad (4.40)$$

where θ_a = ambient air temperature.

In the value q_{RR}, however, the direct and reflected radiation absorbed in the glass are included. It is considered necessary, therefore, for a reasonable estimation to measure the surface temperature of glass and surface temperature at several positions of the louvre and to calculate the radiative heat transfer from louvre to glass.

Figure 4.20 shows the variation of solar heat gain and total solar radiation obtained from experiments made with wooden louvres installed on a west facing glass window of 1m×2m in size of the prototype calorimeter room as illustrated in Fig. 4.21. The wooden louvres used as test pieces are of lauan board 12 mm thick and 15 cm wide and painted grey (N7). There can be seen solar heat gain during the period when the louvre would seem to be perfectly intercepting direct solar radiation judging from the geometrical proportion, which shows the effects of reflection and re-radiation from the louvres. The more direct radiation that is transmitted through the louvre, the more the heat gain increases in absolute value. When both the amount of solar radiation upon louvre and the temperature rise of the louvre surfaces are less, the effect of re-radiation is consequently reduced.

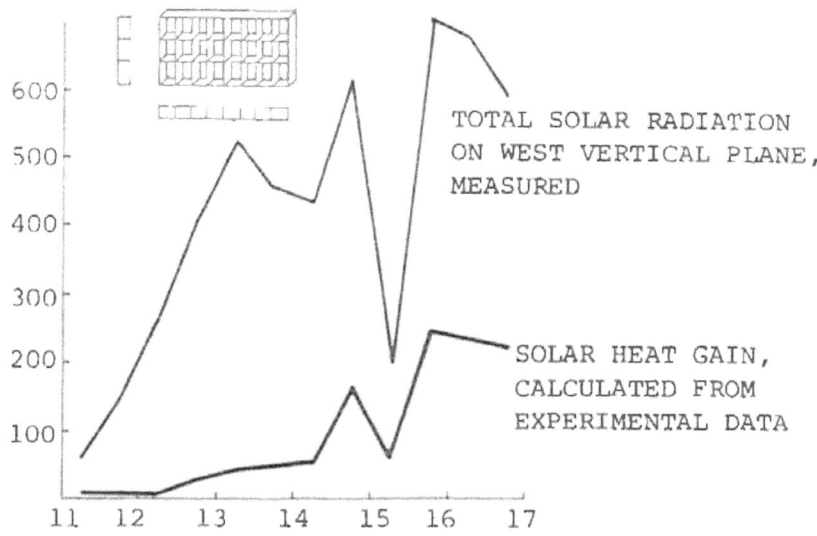

Fig. 4.20. Tested shading performance of egg-crate louvre [4.16]. Ordinate: rate of heat gain (Wm^{-2}). Abscissa: time (day hours).

Fig. 4.21. Egg-crate louvre on the window of prototype calorimeter room.

Under the conditions of intense solar radiation, the temperature of the louvre gets higher and the effect of re-radiation increases, although it intercepts much of solar radiation. Figure 4.22 shows the diurnal temperature variation of various surfaces of an egg-crate louvre, which illustrates the situation very well. In relation to the graphs in this figure, it should be mentioned that the heat gain from the solar radiation directly transmitted through louvres increases after 3 p.m. when surface temperature does not get high and that the heat gain is less before 2 p.m. when surface temperature is very high due to a great deal of absorption of solar radiation.

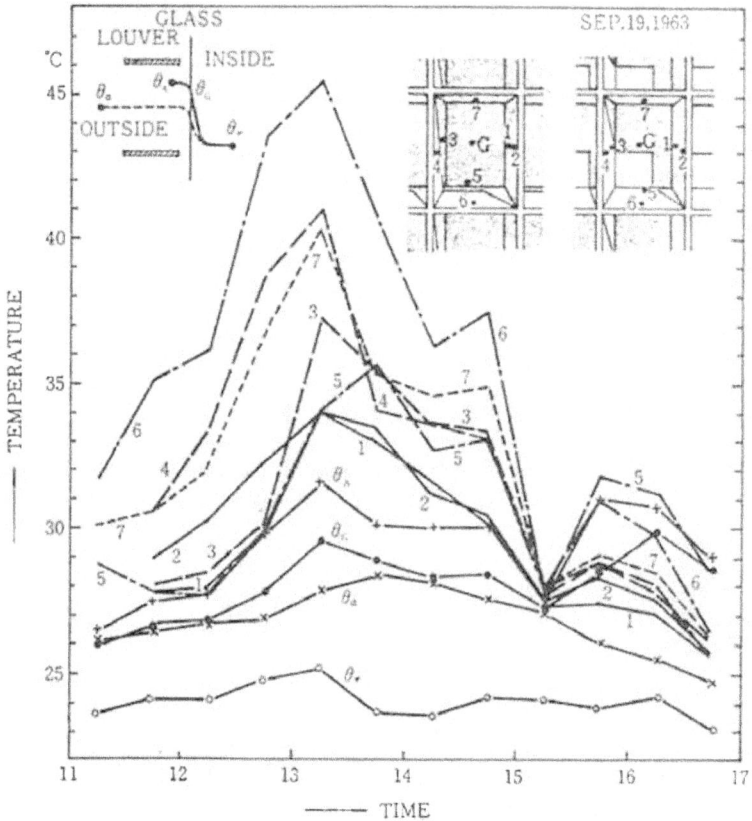

Fig. 4.22. Temperature variation of egg-crate louvre [4.16]. θ_a = Outside air temperature; θ_A = air temperature between louvre; θ_G = glass temperature; θ_r = room air temperature; 1, 2, 3, 4, 5, 6, 7 = surface temperature of louvre as illustrated in the drawing. Time in day hours.

Thus, a maximum of total solar heat gain occurs when the radiation transmitted through the louvres is the greatest and the re-radiation is small enough to be neglected. The result of such an unbalanced heat gain should depend upon the design of louvres. The louvre tested can be regarded as an example of poor design from the viewpoint of heat intercepting performance. The louvre should be designed so that no radiation, or at least as little as possible, would be transmitted at anytime, and then the heat gain due to re-radiation would be large enough to be taken into consideration.

The rate of solar heat gain with sun-shades on the outside of the glass window could be analysed into three components: solar radiation directly transmitted through the louvres into the room (q_{DT}), solar radiation reflected from the surface of the louvre and transmitted through glass into the room (q_{RT}) and the overall heat transfer from outside to inside across the glass including the effect of radiative heat transfer from the surfaces of the louvre warmed by the absorption of solar radiation to the glass surface (q_{Gr}). Of these three components, q_{Gr} can be expressed by the heat transfer from glass to room air. Attempting to analyse the components of q_{Gr} from the heat balance equation at the glass surface:

$$q_{Gr} = q_{AG} + q_{LG} + q_{RG} + q_{SG} - q_{Ga} \tag{4.41}$$

can be obtained where q_{AG} = the convective heat transfer to glass surface from the outside air close to the glass surface which is warmed by convection from the surface of the louvre irradiated by the sun, q_{LG} = the radiative heat transfer from every part of the louvre surface to glass surface, q_{RG} = component of heat absorbed by the glass of the reflected radiation at the louvre surface, q_{SG} = the component of heat absorbed by the glass of the direct solar radiation without being intercepted by the louvres, q_{Ga} = the radiative heat transfer from glass surface to the atmosphere.

Figure 4.23 shows the variations of the components of heat transfer calculated from the results of temperature measurements as shown in Fig. 4.22. Every value in Fig. 4.23 is obtained from the following:

④ q_{RT} = solar radiation reflected from the surface of the louvre and transmitted through the glass into the room;

⑤ q_{DT} = solar radiation directly transmitted through glass into the room without being intercepted by louvre;

⑥   solar heat gain calculated from the measured temperatures of inside room surfaces which includes the effect of thermal storage in the floor slab;

⑦   transmitted solar radiation estimated from the measured solar radiation upon the glass surface;

② q_{ar} = the rate of overall heat transfer derived from the temperature difference between inside and outside, calculated from $q_{ar} = K_G(\theta_a - \theta_r)$, where $K_G = 6.25$ Wm^{-2}degC^{-1} in which $\alpha_o = 23.3$ and $\alpha_i = 10.5$ are assumed;

③ $q_{Gr} = \alpha_i(\theta_G - \theta_r)$;

① = ③ − ②: the increased overall heat transfer effected by the louvre irradiated by the sun. The breakdown of ① can be converted into the equivalent temperature differential, which is shown in Fig. 4.24;

⑧   the total equivalent temperature differential corresponding to ① in Fig. 4.23, calculated from $\Delta\theta_{er} = q_{Gr}/K_G \times (\theta_a - \theta_r)$;

⑨, ⑩, ⑪, ⑫ = components of ⑧ corresponding to q_{SG}, q_{RG}, q_{AG}, q_{LG}

respectively. For example ⑫ is calculated from

$$\Delta\theta_{er} \cdot \frac{q_{LG}}{q_{SG} + q_{RG} + q_{AG} + q_{LG}}$$

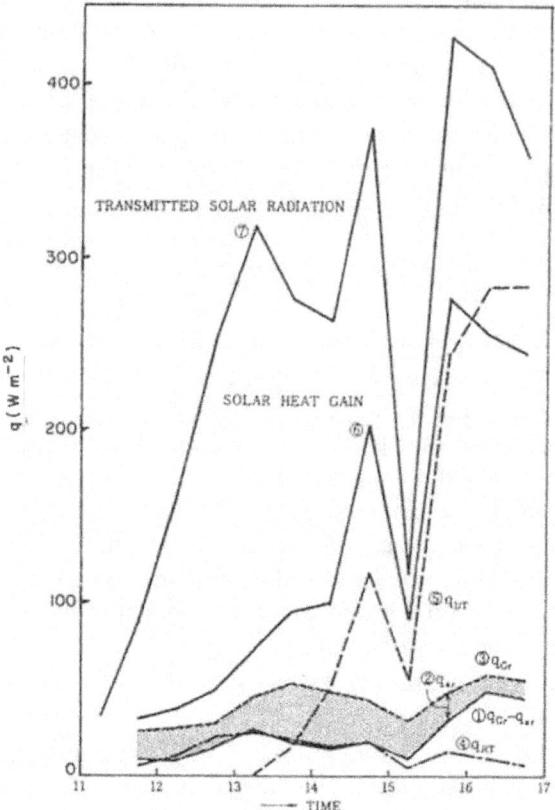

Fig. 4.23. Analysis of solar heat gain variation from experimental data for west faced glass window with egg-crate louvre [4.16]. Time in day hours.

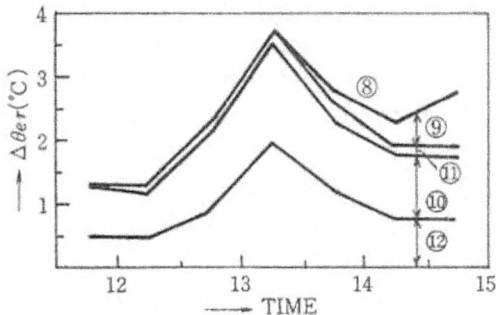

Fig. 4.24. Equivalent temperature differential ($\Delta\theta_{er}$) of re-radiation effect from louvres [4.16]. Time in day hours.

The comparison of Figs. 4.22, 4.23 and 4.24 suggests that the effect of re-radiation is considerable when much solar radiation falls on the louvre and makes the surface temperature higher, while the effect of re-radiation is too small to be counted when solar radiation without being intercepted by the louvre is significant enough to have q_{DT} increased to a considerable extent and the surface temperature of the louvre does not get so high.

4.8. SIMPLIFIED CALCULATION PROCEDURE OF SOLAR HEAT GAIN FROM GLASS WINDOWS WITH EXTERNAL SHADING USING WEIGHTING FACTOR TECHNIQUE

This section describes the method of calculation of heat gain from the glass window combined with the sun-shade when the geometry of the window and the shade is given [4.10]. There are three basic components of heat gain that appear on the inside; direct solar radiation transmitted through the shade and glass, diffuse solar radiation transmitted through the shade and glass including the reflected component from the sunlit surface of the shade and the heat transfer from outside across the glass, including the long wavelength re-radiation from surfaces of the shade, the temperature of which may get considerably higher than the air temperature because of the absorption of solar radiation. Figure 4.25 shows the overall phase of direct and diffuse solar radiation that produces heat gain through the combination of the shade assembly and glass.

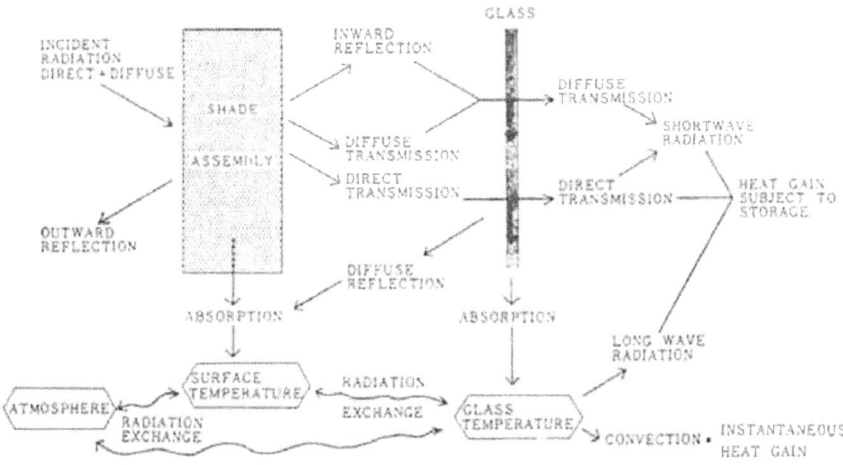

Fig. 4.25. Route of the incident solar radiation converted into heat gain through the shade assembly and the glass [4.10].

The direct transmission component can be calculated using the profile angle and wall solar azimuth in relation to the geometry of the sun-shades. The diffuse component including the reflected radiation at the surfaces of the shade can be calculated with the view factor formulas. As the rigorous calculation of the re-radiation component is very complicated, attempts were made to simplify the situation and estimate it in the form of equivalent temperature rise based on sol-air temperature concept against the glass surface using the weighting factor technique as used for the space cooling load calculation. Part of incident solar-radiation is transmitted through the shade as shown in Fig. 4.25 and the remainder naturally falls upon the surfaces of the shade.

Part of the radiation absorbed in the shade material is stored but eventually discharged to the air by convection and to the glass surface by radiation, the remainder being emitted to the sky. The radiation component from sunlit shade surface to the glass is defined as re-radiation and the effect of it can be estimated approximately by a weighting factor technique.

Referring to Fig. 4.26 the weighting factor $W_s(j)$ relating the heat discharged from all the surfaces of the shade to the incident solar radiation into the shade assembly can be expressed by the following equations using the response factors of shade material X_j and Y_j. Namely:

$$W_s(0) = 1 - (X_0 - Y_0) \cdot \frac{a_s}{\alpha_{s0}} \tag{4.42}$$

for $j \geq 1$

$$W_s(j) = -(X_j - Y_j) \cdot \frac{a_s}{\alpha_{s0}} \tag{4.43}$$

where a_s is the absorptivity of shade assembly and α_{s0} is the film coefficient along the shade surface.

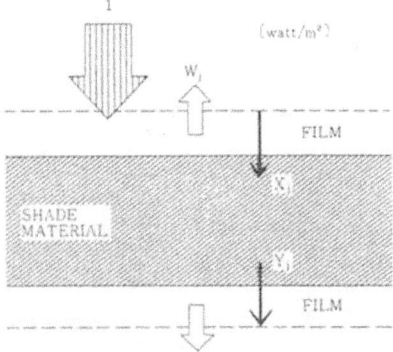

*Fig.*4.26 Weighting factors relating incident solar-radiation into shade assembly to the heat discharged from shade surface [4.10].

Then $q_s(n)$ the heat discharged from the shade surfaces per unit window area at time $t = n\Delta t$ (Wm^{-2}), where Δt = time interval, can be obtained by:

$$q_s(n) = \sum_{j=0}^{\infty} W_s(j) \cdot I_s(n-j) \qquad (4.44)$$

where $I_s(n)$ is the incident solar radiation into the shade assembly including the reflection from glass as shown in Fig. 4.25 per unit of window area at time $t = n\Delta t$.

A sample calculation is made with the brise-soleil whose shape is shown in Fig. 4.27. Table 4.5 shows the results of the calculation for a clear day in summer. In this case, the re-radiation effect becomes quite large and the equivalent temperature rise amounts to over 4°C especially when the shade intercepts a considerable amount of incident solar radiation. This is quite similar to the experimental result with a wooden louvre that showed the equivalent temperature rise was 3–4°C at maximum in summer.

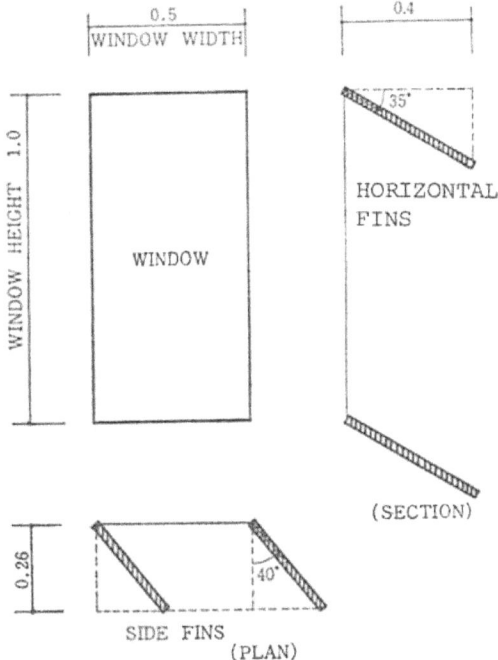

Fig. 4.27. Geometry of glass window and external shade [4.10].

It may be concluded, therefore, that this simplified calculation method using the equivalent temperature differential concept to express the radiation absorbed by the glass from the irradiated surface of the external shade could be applied to the heat gain calculations for glass windows with external shading.

Table 4.5
Calculation example

Time	Weather data			Output information			Equivalent temperature rise		
	Direct solar radiation	Diffuse solar radiation	Outside air temperature °C	Direct radiation transmitted	Diffuse radiation transmitted	Heat transferred across	Radiation absorbed by glass °C	Re-radiation from shade °C	Atmospheric radiation °C
	$W\,m^{-2}$			$W\,m^{-2}$					
9	2·3	39·5	28·6	0	12·8	8·1	0·16	0·19	−1·28
10	3·5	57·0	29·6	0	24·4	18·6	0·28	0·49	−1·30
11	82·6	65·1	30·3	0	33·7	26·7	0·39	1·05	−1·31
12	250·0	66·3	30·7	0	39·5	36·1	0·46	2·02	−1·32
13	395·4	65·1	31·1	0	43·0	45·4	0·51	3·19	−1·33
14	494·2	62·8	31·0	26·7	43·0	54·7	1·27	4·13	−1·32
15	529·1	59·3	30·7	33·7	40·7	58·1	1·42	4·74	−1·32
16	483·7	54·7	30·5	18·6	34·9	54·7	0·91	4·91	−1·31
17	334·9	45·4	29·6	0	25·6	43·0	0·29	4·41	−1·30
18	62·8	25·6	28·4	0	8·1	25·6	0·10	2·94	−1·28

Chapter 5

Effects of Heat from Lights on Air Conditioning

Heat generated by lights is a major component of the cooling load in modern air-conditioned buildings. It happens quite often that the sunlight coming into the occupied space from large glass windows causes too much glare for the comfort of the occupants, necessitating the use of venetian blinds. In consequence, artificial lighting has to be used even in the daytime to maintain a comfortable level of illumination in interior spaces. The illumination level itself tends to increase because people who have been accustomed to working under higher illumination will not accept a lower level of illumination. If the illumination level is doubled, the sense of light felt by the human eyes may be considered to increase only 30% or so according to Weber–Fechner's law in psychology in spite of the doubling of the illumination and the amount of power consumption. The idea of permanent supplementary artificial lighting of interiors (PSALI) [5.1] recommends an even higher illumination level by artificial lighting in interiors to avoid the high contrast in brightness which occurs when darker objects in the interior could be seen against the brighter surface of a large window in the background.

A higher rate of light flux from lighting fixtures also gives rise to a higher rate of thermal radiation effect on the human body in terms of thermal sensation. If the space is to be thermally comfortable, this means that a lower room air temperature is required to compensate for the radiation increase from higher illumination than if the space had less artificial lighting. Recessed luminaire with translucent or louvred coverings reduces glare, but shows poor efficiency in light output against power input.

All of these effects contribute to the increase in power consumption for lighting and, of course, the increase in energy consumption for air conditioning. It is very important, therefore, to understand the real features of the heat from lighting from the viewpoint of air conditioning load.

5.1. ILLUMINATION LEVEL AND HEAT GENERATED BY LIGHTS

Illumination level is an index representing luminous density on the working surface and may be defined as the light energy flux per unit area of the surface receiving the light. The electric power supplied to the lamps which illuminate the working area is almost proportional to the illumination level and is expressed by:

$$W \div k_w E = \frac{bC}{\eta K} E \tag{5.1}$$

where W = electric power consumed by lights (W m^{-2}), E = illumination level (1x), η = luminous efficiency (lm/W), K = utilance, a useful fraction of the luminous flux (dimensionless), C = compensation factor for luminous reduction of lamps and fixtures on account of aging (dimensionless) and b = coefficient of ballast loss, the ratio of total power consumption including ballast to power input to the lamp.

The approximate figures for the coefficient k_w in eqn. (5.1) are listed in Table 5.1 for different types of lighting and for fluorescent and incandescent lamps.

Table 5.1
Approximate figures of k_w and utilance

	Utilance K(−)			(lm / W)	(−)	(−)
	Indirect lighting	Overall diffuse lighting	Direct lighting	η	C	b
Fluorescent	0·2	0·1	0·5	60–70	1·5–1·8	1·15–1·25
Incandescent	0·5	0·3	0·1	10–30	1·1–1·3	1
Utilance (K)	0·1–0·2	0·3–0·4	0·5–0·6			

Figure 5.1 shows a nomograph to obtain the power generation from lights corresponding with eqn. (5.1), except that the chart gives the power in the case of $C = 1$ and $b = 1$.

The utilance is a key factor to show the efficiency in terms of light output to light input: the ratio of the useful light actually falling on the working surface such as on the top surface of desks to the light emitted from the lamp in the fixture. A part of the light emitted from the lamp is absorbed by the surface of the fixture and part of the light coming out of fixture into the room space is absorbed by the various surfaces of the room by multiple reflection among the surfaces until part of the light falls on the desk surface. The utilance, therefore, depends on the following factors:

1. types of lighting fixtures such as direct lighting and indirect lighting fixtures,
2. reflectivity of the surfaces of ceiling, wall, floor and so on,
3. dimensions of the room and relative position of receiving surface to the lighting fixtures.

Convenient tables giving the values of utilance for different cases are included in various reference books on lighting.

Luminous efficiency also contributes to the energy economy of lighting. The value of luminous efficiency of fluorescent lamps is about three times higher than that of incandescent lamps. Among fluorescent lamps the ones that have higher fidelity to

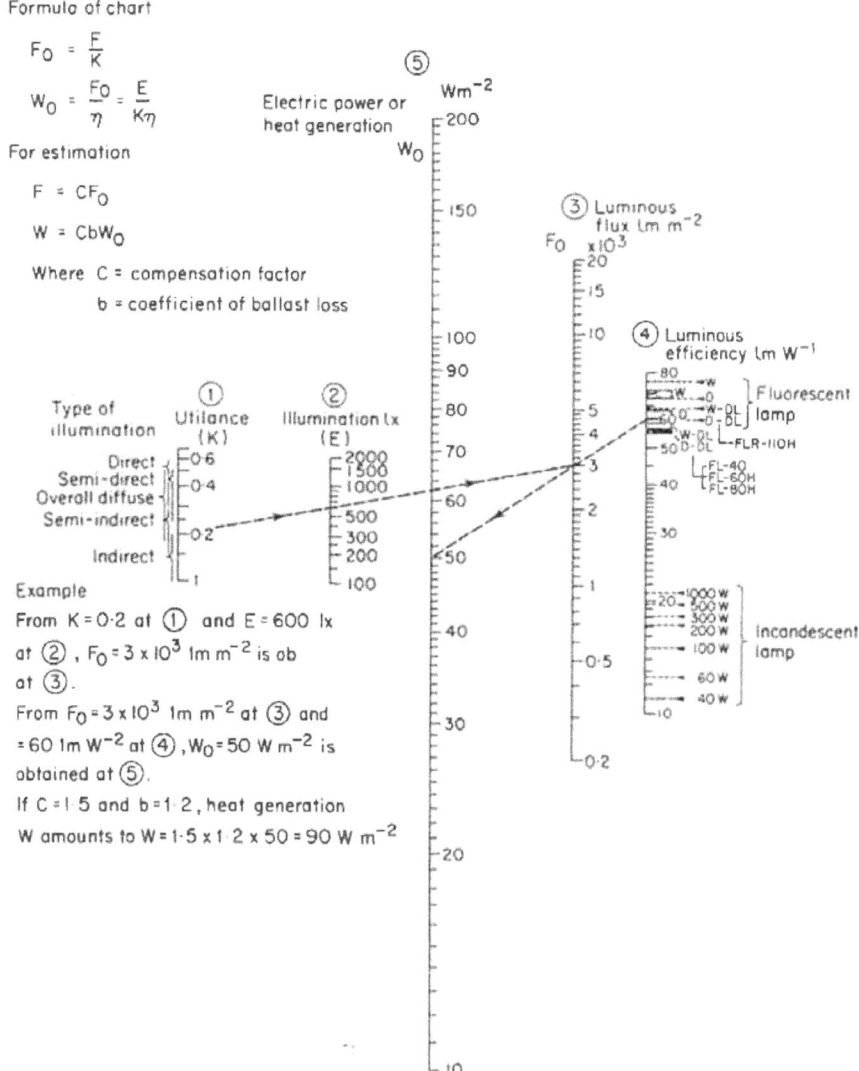

Fig. 5.1. Nomograph of heat generation from lights [5.11].

the natural sunlight show lower luminous efficiency. Among incandescent lamps the ones of smaller wattage have lower luminous efficiency.

It can be estimated, therefore, that a 40 W fluorescent lamp and a 150 W incandescent lamp deliver nearly the same amount of light. The total input of electrical power to both lamps eventually becomes heat, but the energy distribution around the lamp as shown in Fig. 5.2 can be broken down into four components: visible light, invisible ultraviolet and infrared radiation, ballast loss, and heat by convection and conduction. The approximate percentage values of these four components are shown in Table 5.2.

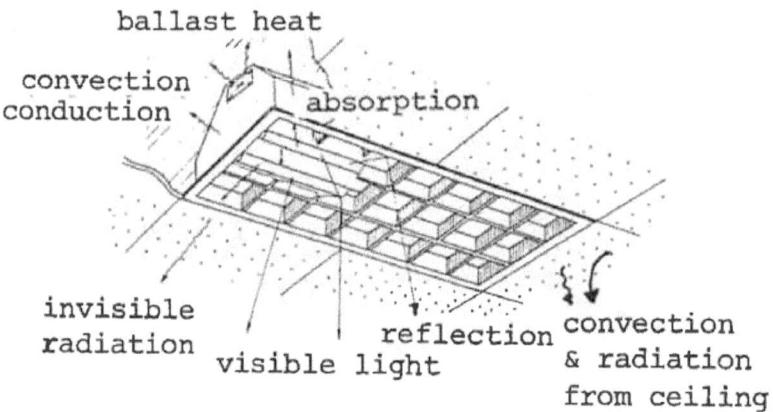

Fig. 5.2.   Components of lighting energy.

In the actual lighting systems, lamps are usually housed in the fixture and a combination of fixture and lamps is called luminaire. Since part of the energy from lamps is absorbed by the surfaces in the fixtures before coming into the room, the energy distribution pattern of a luminaire is quite different from that of a lamp. In the case of recessed luminaires as commonly used in modern buildings, a large portion of the energy from the lamp is trapped in the fixture. From the viewpoint of theoretical analysis, it is necessary to estimate as accurately as possible upward and downward percentages of energy of the total electrical power input to the lamps.

Table 5.2
Energy distribution of lamps [5.7]

	150 W incandescent lamp	40 W fluorescent lamp
Visible light	10 %	18 %
Invisible radiation	70 %	31 %
Ballast loss	—	18 %
Heat by convection and radiation	20 %	33 %

Assuming a half of the radiation energy, both visible and invisible, is trapped by the fixture instead of coming down to the occupied space, the following method, which applies the percentage values in Table 5.2, may be used for estimating the energy breakdown of a fluorescent luminaire. Namely:

upward fraction:

$$18 \times 0{\cdot}5 + 31 \times 0{\cdot}5 + 18 + 33 = 75{\cdot}5\%$$

downward fraction:

$$18 \times 0{\cdot}5 + 31 \times 0{\cdot}5 = 24{\cdot}5\%$$

5.2. INTEGRATED LIGHTING–AIR CONDITIONING SYSTEM

The results of the preceding estimations indicate that almost three quarters of electrical power input is trapped above the ceiling in the case of recessed luminaires, whereas all power input to a lamp is dissipated within the occupied space, in the case of exposed types of fixtures such as hanging units. Thus, it is obvious that, if part of the trapped heat from the power input to lights could be removed by the air flowing through fixtures, that part of the energy would not contribute to the space cooling load. This suggests the idea of integrated lighting and air conditioning system as a kind of energy conservation system. A special type of luminaire must be used for this purpose so that the air can pass through it to take up the heat of the lights. Such a luminaire is called an air handling troffer, or simply a troffer. There are many different kinds of troffers and Fig. 5.3 shows the basic types of integrated lighting-air conditioning systems.

Another advantage of this system is its ability to maintain the luminous efficiency of lamps at the desired temperature level by cooling the lamp surfaces with air flow, because fluorescent lamps show highest efficiency when the lamp surface temperature is around 40°C. Typical characteristics are shown in Fig. 5.4.

The heat extracted from the lights by the return air can be used for space heating in winter through recirculation of warmer return air. Figure 5.5 shows the characteristics of heating and cooling loads against outside air temperature on the year-round basis. It can be seen that the pattern of heating and cooling loads during the year will be changed by the removal or utilisation of the heat from the lights.

Let us check the air temperature in the plenum space for the case as shown in Fig. 5.3(a) where the return air picks up the trapped heat from the light in the fixture and goes out of the plenum as a return air chamber. The thermal system model for this case is shown in Fig. 5.6.

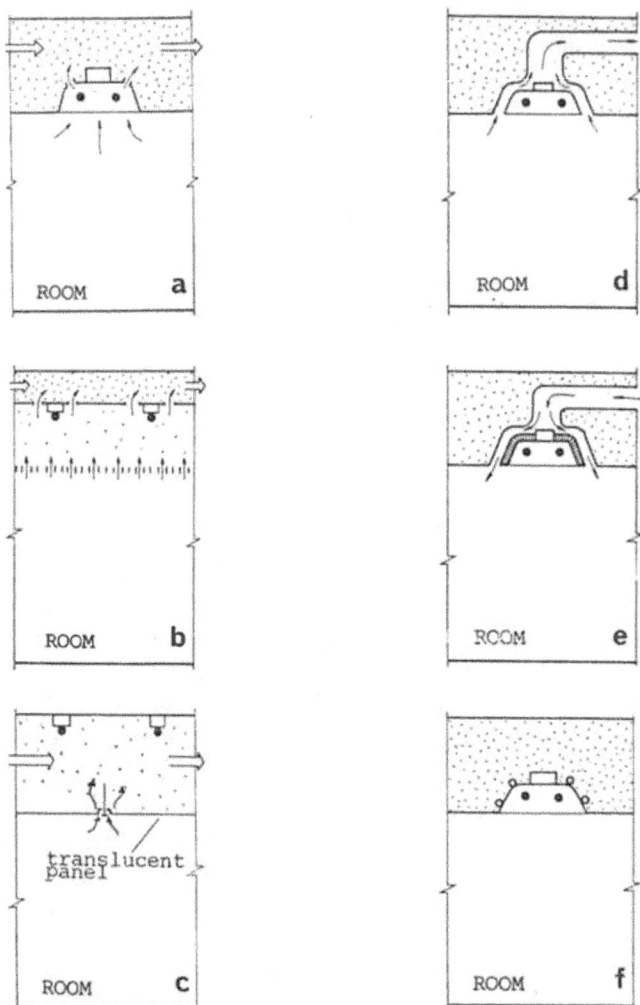

Fig. 5.3. Basic types of lighting-air conditioning systems [5.11]. (a) Recessed luminaire and ceiling plenum as a return chamber; (b) louvre-all lighting and return duct or plenum above; (c) luminous ceiling and return chamber; (d) troffer with inlet and return air duct; (e) troffer with outlet and supply air duct; (f) water-cooled luminaire.

The heat balance equation with this model can be expressed by:

$$\rho H = (K_1 + K_2)(\theta_c - \theta_r) + H_c \tag{5.2}$$

where H = rate of heat generated from lights per unit floor area (W m^{-2}), ρ = heat removal efficiency of luminaire, K_1, K_2 = thermal transmittance from the ceiling plenum to the room through floor slab and through ceiling panel respectively (W m^{-2} deg C^{-1}), θ_c = ceiling plenum air temperature (°C), θ_r = room air temperature (°C) and H_c = rate of heat carried by return air per unit floor area (W m^{-2}).

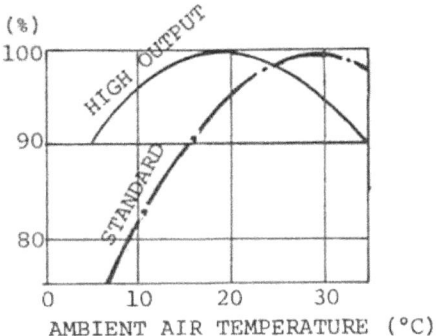

Fig. 5.4. Relative luminous flux (ordinate) of fluorescent lamp vs. ambient air temperature [5.11]

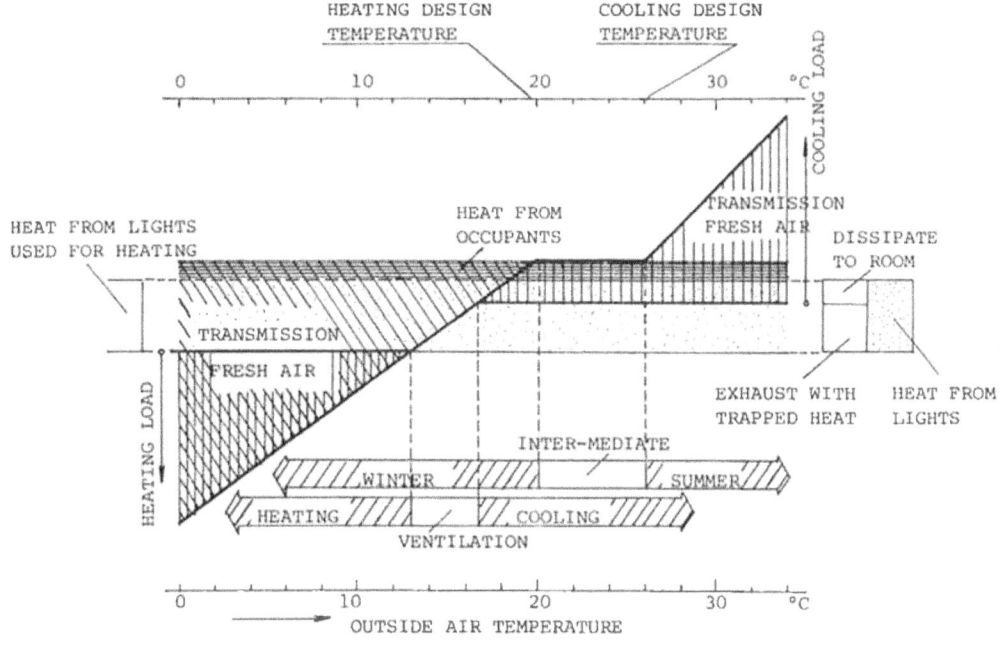

Fig. 5.5. Heat from lights and heating/cooling loads vs. outside air temperature [5.11].

H_c may be given by the following:

$$H_c = C_p \gamma Q(\theta_c - \theta_r) \qquad (5.3)$$

where C_p = specific heat of room air (J kg^{-1} deg C^{-1}), γ = mass density of room air (kg m^{-3}) and Q = rate of return air volume per unit floor area (m^3 h^{-1} m^{-2}).

Substituting eqn. (5.3) into eqn. (5.2), the plenum air temperature can be obtained as follows:

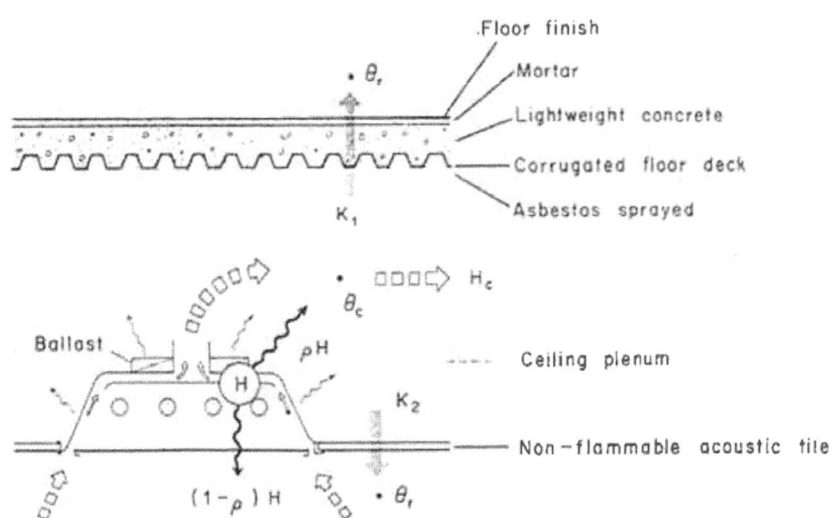

Fig. 5.6. Thermal system model in the ceiling plenum [5.11].

$$\theta_c = \theta_r + \frac{\rho H}{K_1 + K_2 + C_p \gamma Q} \quad (5.4)$$

If we take the following values for example, viz.,
$\theta_r = 27°C$, $H = 40$ W m^{-2}, $\rho = 0\cdot 7$, $K_1 = 2\cdot 5$ W m^{-2} degC^{-1}, $K_2 = 2\cdot 0$ W m^{-2} degC^{-1}, $C_p = 1\cdot 0$kJ kg^{-1} degC^{-1}, $\gamma = 1\cdot 2$ kg m^{-3}, $Q = 20$m^3 h^{-1} m^{-2}, the plenum air temperature θ_c can be calculated as:

$$\theta_c = 27 + \frac{0\cdot 7 \times 40}{2\cdot 5 + 2 + 1000 \times 1\cdot 2 \times 20 \div 3600}$$
$$= 27 + \frac{28}{4\cdot 5 + 6\cdot 67} = 27 + 2\cdot 5 = 29\cdot 5°C$$
$$H_c = 1000 \times 1\cdot 2 \times 20 \div 3600 \times 2\cdot 5 = 16\cdot 7 \text{Wm}^{-2}$$
$$H_c / H = 16\cdot 7 \div 40 = 0\cdot 42$$

This indicates that 70% of power input to lights is initially trapped by the return air, but the percentage of power eventually carried by the return air, which may be called the heat removal efficiency of the system, is only 42%. The effect of thermal resistance of floor slab and ceiling is also important. This formula is based on a steady state basis and radiation and convection heat exchange is not rigorously taken into account. However, it may be considered that this gives an approximate solution for the problem.

5.3. EXPERIMENTAL DETERMINATION OF HEAT REMOVAL EFFICIENCY OF TROFFERS WITH RETURN AIR INTAKE [5.5]

In order to estimate the real effect of the integrated lighting-air conditioning system, information on the heat removal efficiency for different types of troffer and for different types of air system is essential.

There are published data on the performance of commercialised troffers as assessed by manufacturers. Basic studies have been conducted to generalise the performance of troffers with different detail arrangements and some of the findings obtained from the experiments conducted by Maekawa, Kimura and others at the Takenaka Technical Research Laboratory are introduced here. The test apparatus used is shown in Fig. 5.7. It consists of a heavily insulated plenum box equipped with a return air type of troffer on the bottom, which is made of a commonly used ceiling material, and an exhaust duct with a fan to measure the air flow rate. The ambient air temperature is maintained constant. The sections of the troffers tested are shown in Fig. 5.8.

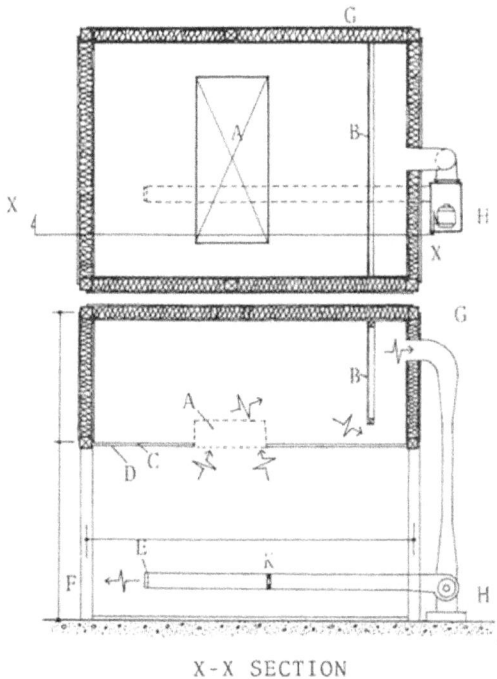

X-X SECTION

Fig. 5.7. Test apparatus [5.5, 5.11]. A: troffer; B: buffer plywood; C: plywood; D: non-flammable acoustic tile; E: velometer; F: wooden post; G: plywood 6 mm + foam polystyrene 50 mm × 2 + plywood 6 mm; H: fan; K: orifice.

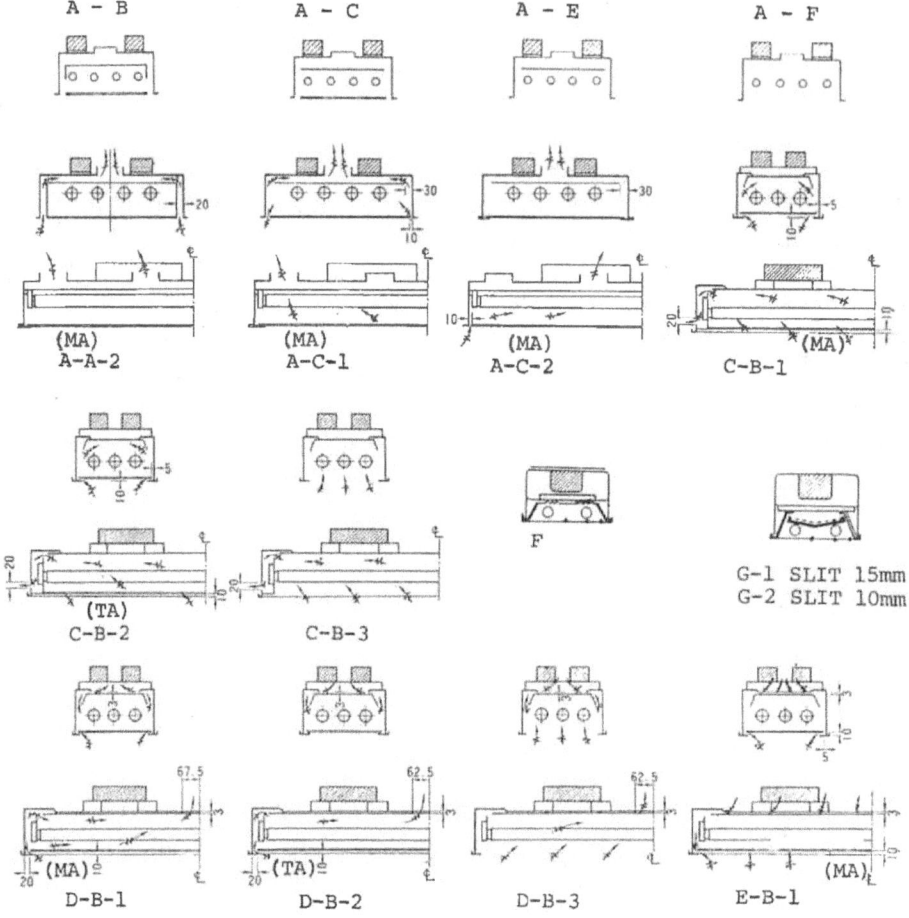

Fig. 5.8   Troffers tested [5.5, 5.11].
(MA), Milk-white acrylic lens; (TA), Transparent acrylic lens.

. Figures 5.9(a)–(d) show extracted results on the heat removal efficiency of systems with different types of troffers and with two types of ceiling in relation to exhaust air flow rate. The heat loss through the insulated box is negligible except for that through the ceiling. The heat removal efficiency of complete systems obtained from the experiment is different from the heat removal efficiency of troffers alone, which could be regarded as nearly equal to the heat removal efficiency of an actual system for a large exhaust air flow rate with heavily insulated ceiling and floor slab.

It must be stressed, therefore, that the ceiling should be made of a high thermal resistance material.

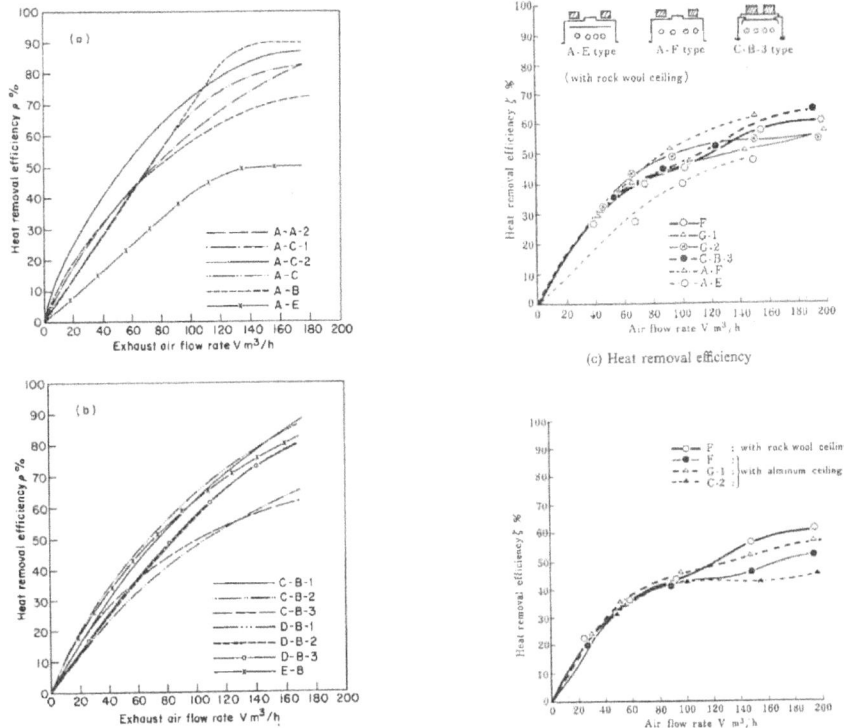

Fig. 5.9. Test results on heat removal efficiency of troffers [5.5, 5.11].

Heat removal efficiency of systems is the value obtained from the following equation using measured data.

$$\zeta = \frac{C_p \gamma V (\theta_c - \theta_r)}{P \times 3600} \times 100 \quad (\%) \tag{5.5}$$

where θ_e = air temperature measured at the exit of the plenum (°C), θ_r = room air temperature (°C), C_p = specific heat of room air (J kg^{-1} °C^{-1}), γ = mass density of room air (kgm^{-3}), V = air flow rate through troffer (m^3 h^{-1}) and P = power input to lights (W).

There are many complicated problems of heat transfer around the troffers and it is quite difficult to generalise proper solutions in terms of radiation and convection components transferred upward and downward from the surfaces of the troffers.

5.4. Theory of Cooling Load Caused by Lights†

In the preceding sections heat removal of the energy from luminaires by means of exhaust air flow through them was discussed on a steady state basis. In reality, however, the lights are switched on and off according to a schedule determined by practical considerations of space usage. It is necessary, therefore, to deal with the problem on an unsteady state basis because some of the heat from the lights is stored by the building structure, particularly in the floor slab, and it appears as a cooling load after the lights are switched off.

A thermal system model for the case with a luminaire recessed into a suspended ceiling may be set up assuming that the rooms above and below are identical to the room in question in reference to Fig. 5.10 as attempted by Stephenson and the author [5.2].

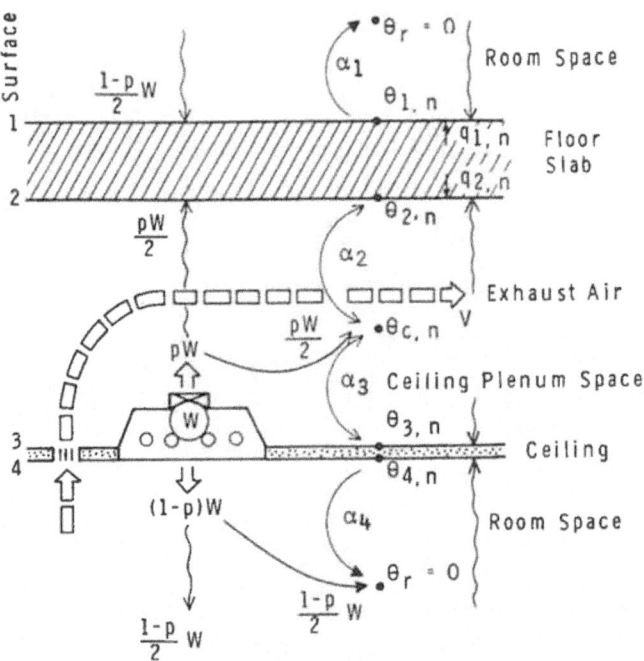

Fig. 5.10. Thermal system of suspended ceiling with recessed lights [5.2]. (Reprinted by permission of the American Society of Heating Refrigeration and Air Conditioning Engineers, Inc., from *ASHRAE Transactions*.)

† Parts of the passages in this Section are taken from the paper by Kimura et al. in ASHRAE Transactions [5.2] by permission of the American Society of Heating, Refrigeration and Air Conditioning Engineers, Inc.

The power to the lights is assumed to be dissipated as shown in Fig. 5.10: a fraction p, of the input going up and $(1-p)$ going down into the room. Each of these components is assumed to be divided equally between convection to the air and radiation absorbed by the floor surface. The fraction $(1-p)/2$ of the input power that goes directly to the room air allows for the heat transfer by convection from the light fixture and part of the radiation from the lights to be absorbed by the furniture. This presupposes that the radiation absorbed by the furniture appears as a cooling load almost immediately, because of the low heat storage capacity of the furnishings. All of the heat storage capacity is assumed to be in the floor slab, the suspended ceiling being treated as a thermal resistance.

The temperature at each surface of the floor and ceiling and in the space above the ceiling can be found by solving five sets of heat balance equations for the four surfaces and the ceiling cavity, using response factors for the slab and the room air temperature as the zero base:

(1) At the upper surface of floor slab:

$$q_{1(n)} + \frac{1-p}{2}W - \alpha_1 \theta_{1(n)} + \alpha_{r41}[\theta_{4(n)} - \theta_{1(n)}] = 0 \qquad (5.6)$$

where

$$q_{1(n)} = \sum_{j=0}^{\infty} \theta_{2(n-j)} Y_j - \sum_{j=0}^{\infty} \theta_{1(n-j)} X_j \qquad (5.7)$$

(2) At the lower surface of floor slab:

$$q_{2(n)} + \frac{p}{2}W + \alpha_2[\theta_{c(n)} - \theta_{2(n)}] + \alpha_{r32}[\theta_{3(n)} - \theta_{2(n)}] = 0 \qquad (5.8)$$

where

$$q_{2(n)} = \sum_{j=0}^{\infty} \theta_{1(n-j)} Y_j - \sum_{j=0}^{\infty} \theta_{2(n-j)} Z_j \qquad (5.9)$$

(3) At the upper surface of ceiling panel:

$$\frac{\lambda_c}{l_c}[\theta_{4(n)} - \theta_{3(n)}] + \alpha_3[\theta_{c(n)} - \theta_{3(n)}] - \alpha_{r32}[\theta_{3(n)} - \theta_{2(n)}] = 0$$

$$(5.10)$$

(4) At the lower surface of ceiling panel:

$$\frac{\lambda_c}{l_c}[\theta_{3(n)} - \theta_{4(n)}] - \alpha_4 \theta_{4(n)} - \alpha_{r41}[\theta_{4(n)} - \theta_{1(n)}] = 0$$

$$(5.11)$$

(5) At the ceiling plenum:

$$\alpha_2[\theta_{2(n)} - \theta_{c(n)}] + \alpha_3[\theta_{3(n)} - \theta_{c(n)}] + \frac{p}{2}W - C_p\gamma V\theta_{c(n)} = 0$$

(5.12)

In the above five equations $\theta_{1(n)}$ = upper surface temperature of floor slab (°C), $\theta_{2(n)}$ = lower surface temperature of floor slab (°C), $\theta_{3(n)}$ = upper surface temperature of ceiling panel (°C), $\theta_{4(n)}$ = lower surface temperature of ceiling panel (°C), $\theta_{c(n)}$ = average air temperature in ceiling plenum (°C), $q_{1(n)}$ = outward conductive heat flux to surface 1 (W m^{-2}), $q_{2(n)}$ = outward conductive heat flux to surface 2 (W m^{-2}). Second subscript n denotes time after lights are switched on. α_1 = convective heat transfer coefficient at surface 1 (W m^{-2} degC^{-1}), α_2 = convective heat transfer coefficient at surface 2 (W m^{-2} degC^{-1}), α_3 = convective heat transfer coefficient at surface 3 (W m^{-2} degC^{-1}), α_4 = convective heat transfer coefficient at surface 4 (W m^{-2} degC^{-1}), α_{r32} = radiative heat transfer coefficient between surfaces 3 and 2 (W m^{-2} degC^{-1}), α_{r41} = radiative heat transfer coefficient between surfaces 4 and 1 (W m^{-2} degC^{-1}), λ_c, λ_s = thermal conductivity of ceiling panel and floor slab respectively (W m^{-1} degC^{-1}), l_c, l_s = thickness of ceiling panel and floor slab respectively (m), $C_p\gamma$ = product of specific heat and mass density of return air (J m^{-3} degC^{-1}), p = fraction of power input to be transferred to plenum, W = power supplied to lights per unit floor area (W m^{-2}), V = rate of ventilated air flow through plenum per unit floor area (m^{3}s^{-1}m^{-2}), X_j, Y_j, Z_j = response factors (W m^{-2} deg C^{-1}) of floor slab.

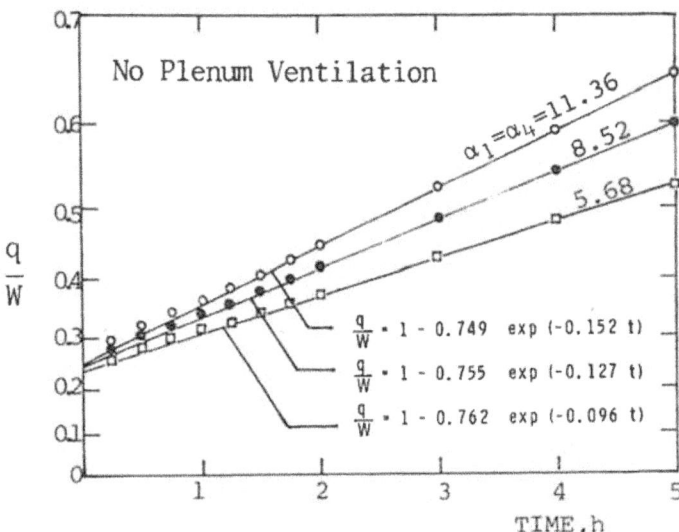

Fig. 5.11. Cooling load for unventilated plenum, calculated using different convection coefficients [5.2]. (Reprinted by permission of the American Society of Heating Refrigeration and Air Conditioning Engineers, Inc., from *ASHRAE Transactions*.)
$p = 0\cdot6$, $l_s = 0\cdot15$m, $\lambda_c/l_c = 5\cdot68$W m^{-2} deg C^{-1}, $\alpha_2 = \alpha_3 = 2\cdot84$W m^{-2} deg C^{-1}.

The above heat balance equations can be converted into the following simultaneous equations expressed in matrix forms to be solved for $\theta_{1(n)}$, $\theta_{2(n)}$, $\theta_{3(n)}$, $\theta_{4(n)}$ and $\theta_{c(n)}$.

$$[M][\theta] = [K] \qquad (5.13)$$

$$[M] = \begin{bmatrix} -\alpha_1 - \alpha_{r41} - X_0 & Y_0 & 0 & \alpha_{r41} & 0 \\ Y_0 & -\alpha_2 - \alpha_{r32} - Z_0 & \alpha_{r32} & 0 & \alpha_2 \\ 0 & \alpha_{r32} & -\lambda_c/l_c - \alpha_{c3} - \alpha_{r32} & \lambda_c/l_c & \alpha_3 \\ \alpha_{r41} & 0 & \lambda_c/l_c & -\lambda_c/l_c - \alpha_4 - \alpha_{r41} & 0 \\ 0 & \alpha_2 & \alpha_3 & 0 & -\alpha_2 - \alpha_3 - 2C_p\gamma V \end{bmatrix} \qquad (5.14)$$

$$[\theta] = \begin{bmatrix} \theta_{1(n)} \\ \theta_{2(n)} \\ \theta_{3(n)} \\ \theta_{4(n)} \\ \theta_c \end{bmatrix} \qquad (5.15)$$

$$[K] = \begin{bmatrix} -\dfrac{1-P}{2}W + \sum_{j=1}^{\infty}\theta_{1(n-j)}X_j - \sum_{j=1}^{\infty}\theta_{2(n-j)}Y_j \\ -\dfrac{P}{2}W + \sum_{j=1}^{\infty}\theta_{2(n-j)}Z_j - \sum_{j=1}^{\infty}\theta_{1(n-j)}Y_j \\ 0 \\ 0 \\ -\dfrac{P}{2}W \end{bmatrix} \qquad (5.16)$$

Then the cooling load due to lights after switched on per unit floor area at time n q_n (W m^{-2}) can be obtained by the following equation:

$$q_n = \alpha_1\theta_{1(n)} + \alpha_4\theta_{4(n)} + \dfrac{1-P}{2}W \qquad (5.17)$$

The first term represents the convective heat transfer from the upper surface of floor slab to the room air; the second term, the transfer from the lower surface of the ceiling to the room air; and the third term, the instantaneous heat gain from fixtures.

Figure 5.11 shows the calculated cooling load vs. time after lights are turned on for a fluorescent fixture recessed into an unventilated ceiling space. The variation of cooling load with time q(Wm^{-2}) can be closely approximated by an expression of the form:

$$\frac{q}{W} = 1 - A\exp(-Bt) \qquad (5.18)$$

where A, B = constants dependent on parameters in the approximate representation of the cooling load and t = time after lights turned on, in hours.

The rate at which heat is being stored is:

$$W - q = WA\exp(-Bt) \qquad (5.19)$$

Thus, the total heat stored when steady state conditions are reached is:

$$\int_0^\infty WA\exp(-Bt)dt = WA/B \qquad (5.20)$$

This stored heat is released to the room air over quite a long period after the lights are switched off. Thus, the cooling load does not stop even though the power input has stopped. If it is assumed that the heat transfer coefficients remain the same whether the lights are on or off, the cooling load after the lights are turned off is given by:

$$\left(\frac{q}{W}\right)_{t>M} = [1 - A\exp(-Bt)] - \{1 - A\exp[-B(t-M)]\}$$
$$= A\{\exp(BM) - 1\}\exp(-Bt) \qquad (5.21)$$

where the lights were on from $t = 0$ to $t = M$.

The usual values of B are small enough that $\exp(-Bt)$ is not negligible when $t = 24$h. Thus, there is a carry-over effect from day to day when the lights are operated on a regular daily schedule.

Assuming that the lights are on for M hours and off for $24 - M$ hours the cumulative cooling load is:

$$\sum_d \left(\frac{q}{W}\right)_{t\leq M} = 1 - A\exp(-Bt)$$
$$+ \{1 - A\exp[-B(t+24)]\} - \{1 - A\exp[-B(t+24-M)]\}$$
$$+ \{1 - A\exp[-B(t+48)]\} - \{1 - A\exp[-B(t+48-M)]\}$$
$$+ \cdots \qquad (5.22)$$

This infinite geometric series can be summed to give:

$$\sum_d \left(\frac{q}{W}\right)_{t\leq M} = 1 - A\exp(-Bt)\frac{1-\exp[-B(24-M)]}{1-\exp(-24B)} \qquad (5.23)$$

and when $M < t < 24$

$$\sum_d \left(\frac{q}{W}\right)_{M<t<24} = \frac{A[\exp(BM)-1]\exp(-Bt)}{1-\exp(-24B)} \tag{5,24}$$

In the case of an integrated lighting-air conditioning system the cooling load of the room approaches a steady state value q_∞ that is less than W, and the heat extracted from the plenum approaches $W - q_\infty$.

Figure 5.12 shows the calculated results with the same arrangement of floor and ceiling as in the case of a ventilated plenum.

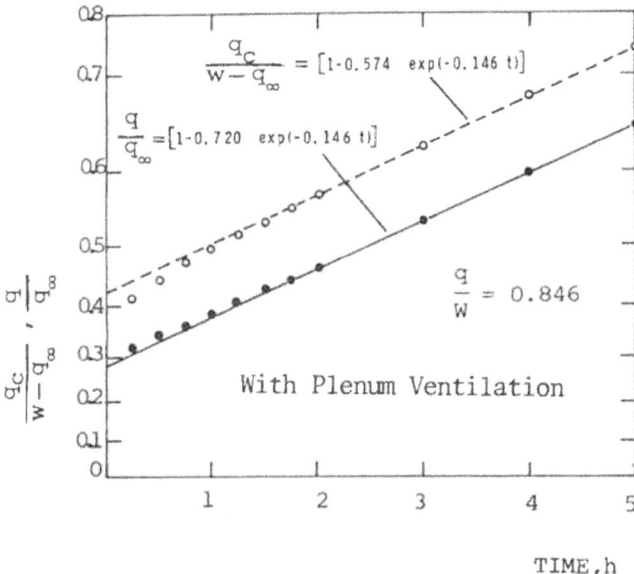

Fig. 5.12. Cooing load and heat removed by exhaust air [5.2]. (Reprinted by permission of the American Society of Heating Refrigeration and Air Conditioning Engineers, Inc., from ASHRAE Transactions.) $V = 3\text{m}^3\text{h}^{-1}\text{m}^{-2}$, $l_s = 0\cdot15\text{m}$, $\lambda_c/l_c = 5\cdot68\text{Wm}^{-2}\text{degC}^{-1}$, $\alpha_2 = \alpha_3 = 5\cdot68\text{Wm}^{-2}\text{degC}^{-1}$, $\alpha_1 = \alpha_4 = 8\cdot52\text{Wm}^{-2}\text{degC}^{-1}$.

These plots indicate that the space cooing load can be represented by:

$$\frac{q}{W} = [1 - A\exp(-Bt)]\frac{q_\infty}{W} \tag{5.25}$$

And the heat extraction from the ceiling space, q_c,

$$\frac{q_c}{W} = [1 - C\exp(-Bt)]\left(1 - \frac{q_\infty}{W}\right) \tag{5.26}$$

Taking the carry-over effect from day to day into consideration when lights are on for M hours, the cumulative cooling load and the cumulative heat removed by ventilating air can be derived from the summation of the infinite geometric series as expressed by the following:

$$\sum_d \left(\frac{q}{W}\right)_{t\leq M} = \left(1 - A\exp(-Bt)\frac{1-\exp[-B(24-M)]}{1-\exp(-24B)}\right)\frac{q_\infty}{W} \tag{5.27}$$

$$\sum_d \left(\frac{q}{W}\right)_{M<t<24} = \frac{A[\exp(BM)-1]\exp(-Bt)}{1-\exp(-24B)} \cdot \frac{q_\infty}{W} \tag{5.28}$$

$$\sum_d \left(\frac{q_c}{W}\right)_{t\leq M} = \left(1 - C\exp(-Bt)\frac{1-\exp[-B(24-M)]}{1-\exp(-24B)}\right)\left(1 - \frac{q_\infty}{W}\right) \tag{5.29}$$

$$\sum_d \left(\frac{q_c}{W}\right)_{M<t<24} = \frac{C[\exp(BM)-1]\exp(-Bt)}{1-\exp(-24B)}\left(1 - \frac{q_\infty}{W}\right) \tag{5.30}$$

Storage load factor (SLF) is proposed by Carrier Company [5.10] for air conditioning design purposes to estimate cooling load variation caused by lights. Storage load factor values are given in percentages at every hour after the lights are switched on against a unit power input to the lights. Data of SLF are presented for a room with three weight classes of building structure and for 10, 18 and 24h of lighting during a day under 24h operation of air conditioning.

It is interesting to compare the calculated results based on theoretical formulas and the SLF values published by Carrier Company for both cases of unventilated plenum and ventilated plenum.

Example comparison is made for the case when lights are on for 10h a day. Figure 5.13 shows the results of the comparison for an unventilated plenum, where the values of SLF for the room with 488kg m^{-2} of floor area of structure are plotted and fitted to the curve so that eqns. (5.23) and (5.24) can be applied. These equations could be used to modify the published values of SLF for any other value of M.

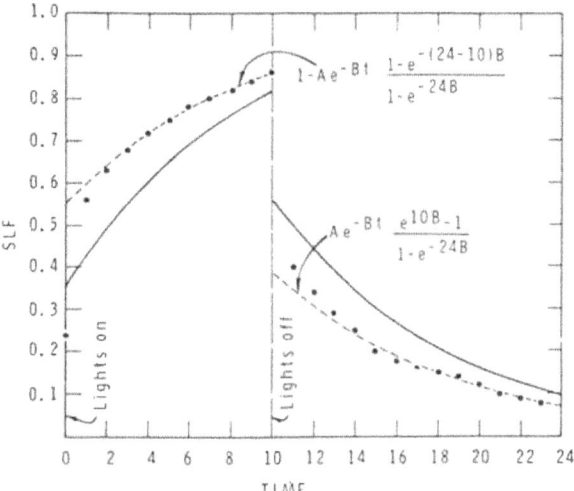

Fig. 5.13. Storage load factor for unventilated plenum [5.2]. (Reprinted by permission of the American Society of Heating Refrigeration and Air conditioning Engineers, Inc., from ASHRAE Transactions.) $p = 0\cdot6$, $l_s = 0\cdot15$m, $\lambda_e/l_c = 5\cdot68\text{Wm}^{-2}\text{degC}^{-1}$, $\alpha_2 = \alpha_3 = 2\cdot84\text{Wm}^{-2}\text{degC}^{-1}$, $\alpha_1 = \alpha_4 = 8\cdot52\text{Wm}^{-2}\text{degC}^{-1}$. Time in day hours.

Figure 5.14 shows the results of the comparison for a ventilated plenum on the same basis as in the above.

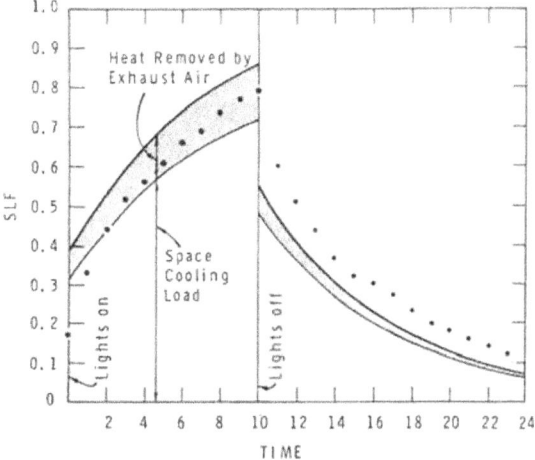

Fig. 5.14. Storage load factor for ventilated plenum [5.2]. (Reprinted by permission of the American Society of Heating Refrigeration and Air conditioning Engineers, Inc., from ASHRAE Transactions.) $p = 0\cdot6$, $V = 3\text{m}^3\text{h}^{-1}\text{m}^{-2}$, $l_s = 0\cdot15$ m, $\lambda_e/l_c = 5\cdot68$ W m^{-2} deg C^{-1}, $\alpha_2 = \alpha_3 = 5\cdot68$ W m^{-2} deg C^{-1}, $\alpha_1 = \alpha_4 = 8\cdot52$ W m^{-2} deg C^{-1}. Time in day hours.

It can be seen from these comparisons that theoretical values and SLF values differ in both cases and particularly that SLF does not take into account the heat removed by exhaust air in the case of the ventilated plenum.

In any case, it is found that the characteristics of this thermal system are very much dependent on the factors A, B and C. From the results of further calculations with different cases, it is pointed out by Stephenson and Kimura that the value A is sensitive to p, the upward fraction of the power input to lights and not sensitive to α_1, and α_4, the convective heat transfer coefficient on ceiling and floor surfaces, whereas the value B is sensitive to α_1 and α_4 and not sensitive to p. In addition, neither A nor B is very sensitive to changes in the convective heat transfer coefficients in the space above the ceiling.

The values of both A and B depend on the thermal resistance of the ceiling and the thickness of the floor. Changing the thickness of the floor (i.e. the heat storage capacity of the room) has the greatest effect on B.

For the ventilated plenum, however, the values C and q_∞ are dependent on all factors to some extent, although the sensitivity of the values A and B is similar to the case for the ventilated plenum.

5.5. Cooling Load Weighting Factors for Power Input to Lights

The cooling load due to lights can be calculated easily by the weighting factor method even though the lights are operated on an irregular schedule as in the case of solar heat gain. The cooling load $q_{CL}(t)$ at any time, t, is:

$$q_{CL}(t) = \sum_{j=0}^{\infty} W(j) \cdot q_p(t - j\Delta) \tag{5.31}$$

where $q_p(t - j\Delta)$ is the average power input to the lights during the interval between $t - j\Delta$ and $t - (j + 1)\Delta$.

The weighting factors, $W(j)$ are simply the values of cooling load at $t = (j + 1)\Delta$ for the case where the lights of a unit power were on from $t = 0$ to $t = \Delta$ and are off thereafter:

$$\text{for } j = 0 \quad W(0) = 1 - A\exp(-B\Delta) \tag{5.32}$$

$$\text{for } j \geq 0 \quad W(j) = A[1 - \exp(-B\Delta)] - \exp(-jB\Delta) \tag{5.33}$$

The values of $W(j)$ get progressively smaller as j increases so that they become negligible for large values of j. Thus, the summation for $q_{CL}(t)$ can be stopped after a finite number of terms; the actual number of terms depending on the magnitude of $B\Delta$ and the precision required.

The initial value of weighting factors $W(0)$ is usually much larger than the other values of $W(j)$. Suppose that a plot of $W(j)$ is made on a semi-log sheet. The plot converges to a straight line for $j \geq 1$. From these two characteristics, it suggests the use of only $W(0)$, $W(1)$ and common ratio c for easier calculation of the cooling load with fairly good accuracy. Thus, the relationship between heat gain and cooling load expressed by:

$$q_{CL}(n) = \sum_{j=0}^{\infty} W(j) \cdot q_{HG}(n-j) \qquad (5.34)$$

can be rewritten as:

$$q_{CL}(n) = W(0) \cdot q_{HG}(n) + [W(1) - cW(0)] q_{HG}(n-1) + c \cdot q_{CL}(n-1) \qquad (5.35)$$

where $q_{CL}(n)$ = cooling load at time $t = n$, $q_{HG}(n)$ = heat gain at time $t = n$, $W(j)$ = cooling load weighting factors for heat gain and c = common ratio.

Based on the above principle, Ishino [5.3] attempted to use basic cooling load weighting factors for unit heat gain that occurs at five different locations of the room. Combining these basic cooling load weighting factors according to the character of heat gain at a reasonable proportion for respective excitations, the cooling load response factors can be obtained. The five basic components of a unit power input are P_1, P_2, P_3, P_4 and P_5 and have a relationship:

$$P_1 + P_2 + P_3 + P_4 + P_5 = 1 \qquad (5.36)$$

where P_1 = radiation absorbed by the lower surface of floor slab, P_2 = energy absorbed by the air in the plenum, P_3 = radiation absorbed by the lower surface of ceiling, P_4 = heat absorbed by room air and P_5 = radiation absorbed by the upper surface of floor slab. Figure 5.15 shows these components.

For every input heat gain, $1 Wm^{-2}$ in the form of a unit triangle pulse, the output cooling load of the room is calculated by solving the simultaneous equations expressed in time series response factors for unknown temperatures at the lower surface of slab(1), ceiling plenum space(2), the lower surface of ceiling panel(3), room space(4) and the upper surface of slab(5). This output cooling load is a combination of basic cooling load weighting factors for every heat gain component at the five locations.

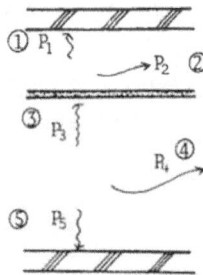

①②③④⑤ : Locations of Excitation
P_i (i=1,...,5) : Basic Components of Unit Power Input

Fig. 5.15. Basic components or unit power input [7.4].

Table 5.3 shows $W_i(j)$, the basic cooling load weighting factors for basic components of unit power input to the locations of excitation as indicated in Fig. 5.15 for three grades of building structure.

Determination of heavy, medium and light construction is not so simple in general. It may be defined in such a way that it depends on the maximum value of Y response factors of a representative component of room enclosure $Y(k)$, viz.,

if $k \geq 4$ heavy structure, H,
if $4 > k \geq 3$ medium structure, M,
if $k < 3$ light structure, L.

Table 5.3
Basic cooling load weighting factors [5.4]

Location of excitation (i)	Structure	$W_i(0)$	$W_i(1)$	c_i
(1)	H	0·059 6	0·047 2	0·949 8
	M	0·065 3	0·069 3	0·925 9
	L	0·101 9	0·120 0	0·866 4
(2)	H	0·157 4	0·054 1	0·935 8
	M	0·161 8	0·071 5	0·914 8
	L	0·184 3	0·114 0	0·860 2
(3)	H	0·396 2	0·943 7	0·927 7
	M	0·398 9	0·054 5	0·909 3
	L	0·397 5	0·085 1	0·858 7
(4)	H			
	M	1·000 0	0·0	0·0
	L			
(5)	H	0·225 4	0·072 5	0·906 4
	M	0·227 6	0·082 1	0·893 7
	L	0·190 0	0·119 4	0·852 5

Knowing the value of P_i ($i = 1, \ldots, 5$) for any type of heat gain, the cooling load weighting factors $W(j)$ can be obtained from the following formula:

$$W(j) = \sum_{i=1}^{5} P_i W_i(j) \qquad \text{for } j = 0, 1 \qquad (5.37)$$

By definition of weighting factors:

$$\begin{aligned} 1 &= W(0) + W(1) + cW(1) + c^2 W(1) + \cdots \\ &= W(0) + \frac{W(1)}{1-c} \end{aligned} \qquad (5.38)$$

The common ratio c can be calculated from

$$c = 1 - \frac{W(1)}{1 - W(0)} \qquad (5.39)$$

It is quite difficult to determine the value of P_i for different types of heat gain. Table 5.4 gives tentative information of P_i for making a first approximation not only of heat gain from lights, but also for heat gain from solar radiation through windows, from occupants and from heat generating appliances on the basis of a common approach to the problem.

Table 5.4
Tentative values of Pi

Type of heat	Gain elements	P_1	P_2	P_3	P_4	P_5
Fluorescent lamp	recessed	0.25	0.25	0.0	0.3	0.2
	semi-recessed	0.15	0.15	0.0	0.4	0.3
	exposed	0.0	0.0	0.0	0.6	0.4
Incandescent lamp	indirect lighting	0.0	0.0	0.4	0.3	0.3
	direct lighting	0.0	0.0	0.2	0.4	0.4
Solar radiation	without blinds	0.0	0.0	0.1	0.2	0.7
through windows	with blinds	0.0	0.0	0.6	0.2	0.2
Occupants		0.0	0.0	0.25	0.5	0.25
Appliances	high temperature	0.0	0.0	0.3	0.4	0.3
	medium temperature	0.0	0.0	0.2	0.6	0.2
	low temperature	0.0	0.0	0.1	0.8	0.1

Table 5.5 shows the values of cooling load weighting factors for heat gain from lights for five different types of lamps and fixtures obtained from the procedure as given by eqns. (5.37) and (5.39).

Table 5.5
Cooling load weighting factors for heat gain from lighting [5.4]

Lamp	Type of fixture	Structure	$W_L(0)$	$W_L(1)$	c_L
Fluorescent lamp	recessed	H	0·399 3	0·039 8	0·933 7
		M	0·402 3	0·051 6	0·913 7
		L	0·409 5	0·982 4	0·860 5
	semi-recessed	H	0·500 2	0·036 9	0·926 1
		M	0·502 4	0·045 7	0·908 1
		L	0·499 9	0·070 9	0·858 1
	exposed	H	0·690 1	0·029 0	0·906 4
		M	0·691 1	0·032 0	0·893 7
		L	0·676 0	0·047 8	0·852 5
Incandescent lamp	indirect lighting	H	0·526 1	0·039 2	0·917 3
		M	0·527 9	0·046 4	0·901 6
		L	0·516 0	0·069 9	0·855 6
	direct lighting	H	0·569 4	0·037 7	0·912 4
		M	0·570 8	0·043 7	0·898 1
		L	0·555 5	0·064 8	0·854 2

Table 5.6
Cooling load weighting factors for solar radiation through windows [5.4]

Type of window	Structure	$W_s(0)$	$W_s(1)$	c_s
Window without blinds	H	0·377 4	0·055 1	0·908 6
	M	0·399 0	0·062 9	0·895 3
	L	0·372 8	0·099 1	0·842 0
Window with blinds	H	0·482 8	0·047 3	0·908 6
	M	0·484 9	0·053 9	0·895 3
	L	0·476 5	0·082 7	0·842 0

Table 5.7
Cooling load weighting factors for heat gain from occupants [5.4]

Structure	$W_m(0)$	$W_m(1)$	c_m
H	0·655 4	0·029 0	0·915 8
M	0·656 6	0·034 2	0·900 5
L	0·646 9	0·051 1	0·855 2

Table 5.8
Cooling load weighting factors for heat gain from appliances [5.4]

Temperature level	Structure	$W_E(0)$	$W_E(1)$	c_E
High	H	0·586 5	0·034 8	0·915 8
	M	0·588 0	0·041 0	0·900 5
	L	0·576 2	0·961 4	0·855 2
Medium	H	0·724 3	0·023 2	0·915 8
	M	0·725 3	0·027 3	0·900 5
	L	0·717 5	0·040 9	0·855 2
Low	H	0·862 2	0·011 6	0·915 8
	M	0·862 7	0·013 7	0·900 5
	L	0·858 7	0·020 5	0·855 2

Tables 5.6, 5.7 and 5.8 show the values of cooling load weighting factors for heat gain from solar radiation through windows, heat gain from occupants and heat gain from appliances respectively obtained from the same procedures as above.

For practical calculations to save computer running time, it could be considered advantageous to have the value of common ratio fixed for all of the different heat gain elements that would occur in a given room and to have the values of the term of weighting factors derived from eqn. (5.39). The calculation operation can be simplified as follows:

$$H_{CLT}(n) = \sum_k W_k(0) H_{HGk}(n) + \sum_k [W_k(1) - cW_k(0)] H_{HGk}(n-1) + cH_{CLT}(n-1) \quad (5.40)$$

where $H_{CLT}(n)$ = total cooling load of the space at time n (W), $H_{HGk}(n)$ = kth kind of heat gain of the space at time n(W), $W_k(0)$, $W_k(1)$ = the first two terms of cooling load weighting factors for kth kind of heat gain(−).

Gintautas P. Mitalas
(? - 1995)

Photo by the author in 1970

Born in Lithuania, Mr. Mitalas immigrated to Canada towards the end of World War II and worked hard as an automobile mechanic for a while. He was a diligent student at Department of Mechanical Engineering, University of Toronto to obtain M.Sc. Joined Division of Building Research, National Research Council in Ottawa, he worked on heat transfer and experiments under Dr. Stephenson He wrote a number of excellent papers on dynamic heat transfer in buildings. ASHRAE fellow

Calorimeter Room designed by the author under construction at the laboratory of Division of Building Research to measure dynamic heat load response to power input of lights as described in Chapter 5. The photo shows the concrete slabs are being installed for the ceiling plenum chamber of the room space (1968 – 1969). Control system and measuring devices were made by G. P Mitalas, who wrote the final paper on this experiment with measured results. [Ref. 5.12]

Chapter 6

Infiltration and Exfiltration Caused by Wind and Stack Effects

Infiltration is unwanted outside air coming into the space through cracks of window sashes or other miscellaneous small holes that exist on the exterior skin of a building. The causes of infiltration are both wind and stack effect. When the air pressure outside of the exterior skin is higher than the interior, infiltration takes place. Exfiltration is air leakage from inside to outside resulting from the mass balance of air with infiltration. At any instance infiltration and exfiltration occur simultaneously within the building concerned.

6.1 AIR LEAKAGE CHARACTERSITICS OF OPENINGS AND CRACKS

When the air flow passes through openings or cracks, some amount of dynamic energy is to be lost and converted into heat or sound by friction or vibration. The amount of reduction in dynamic energy is called pressure loss (see Fig. 6.1) and is given by the following formula:

$$\Delta p = \xi \gamma \upsilon^2 / 2 \tag{6.1}$$

where Δp = pressure loss (Nm^{-2}), υ = air velocity (ms^{-1}), γ = specific weight of air (kgm^{-3}), ξ = pressure loss coefficient (–).

Since the theorem of continuity states that:

$$Q = \upsilon A \tag{6.2}$$

where Q = rate of air flow (m^{3}s^{-1}), A = opening area (m^2), the relationship between the pressure loss and the air flow rate can be expressed as:

$$Q = A\sqrt{\frac{2\Delta p}{\xi \gamma}} = A\sqrt{\frac{2}{\xi \gamma}} \Delta p^{1/2} \tag{6.3}$$

Equation (6.3) applies to openings and implies that the rate of air flow through the opening is proportional to the square root of pressure loss.

In the case of narrow cracks such as in complicated parts of a window sash, a simple relationship as expressed by eqn. (6.3) would not hold true, but might be approximated by the formula:

$$Q = al\Delta p^{1/n} \qquad (6.4)$$

where Q = rate of infiltration (m^{3}s^{-1}), l = crack length (m), a and n = sash constants, depending upon the air tightness of the window sash. The tighter the sash, the smaller the values of a and n.

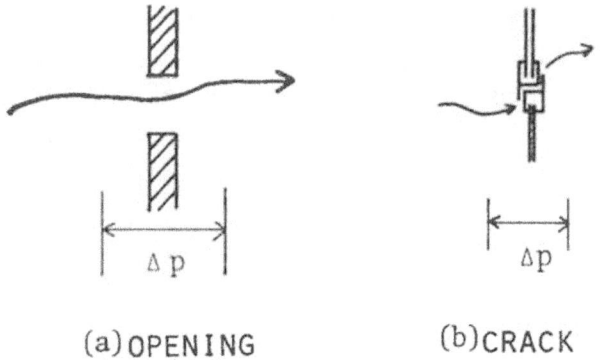

(a) OPENING   (b) CRACK

Fig. 6.1. Air leakage through openings and cracks.

It is interesting to find that $1 < n < 2$. Generally speaking, the case $n = 1$ implies that the flow is proportional to the difference in potential, e.g. conduction of heat in solids with temperature difference or electric current proportional to voltage difference. On the other hand, the case $n = 2$ corresponds to the case of air flow through openings. In the case of window sashes, therefore, $n = 1.5$ is generally accepted unless specific leakage tests were made.

The value of a greatly differs with the type of window sash and following values are generally accepted.

degree of air tightness		
good	1, 2(nominal), 3	
normal	3, 5(nominal), 8	
bad	8, 15(nominal), 40	

Crack length differs with type of window sash, such as hanging type, sliding type, hinged type and so on. The total length indicated by bold lines in Fig. 6.2 is the crack length.

Tamura and Wilson [6.1, 6.2] proposed another way of defining the coefficient of air leakage instead of using al; that is, equivalent orifice area is to be taken over the exterior wall concerned, including the cracks at joints of curtain walls.

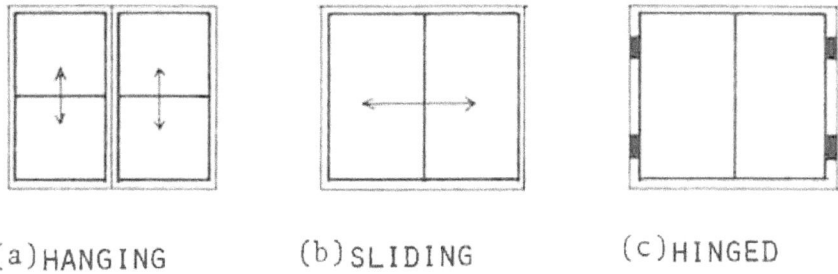

Fig. 6.2. Crack length of different types of window sash.

Putting that

$$\beta S_W = al \qquad (6.5)$$

where S_w = gross wall area (m^2) and β = equivalent orifice area coefficient. Then the rate of air leakage through cracks over the gross exterior wall is to be given by:

$$Q = \beta S_W \Delta p^{1/n} \qquad (6.6)$$

6.2 INFILTRATION BY WIND

Suppose that outside air infiltrates through cracks of a window sash on the windward wall and exfiltrates through those on the leeward wall in such a partitionless space as shown in Fig. 6.3.

The wind pressure on the windward and leeward wall surfaces are $C_1 \gamma v^2/2$ and $C_2 \gamma v^2/2$ respectively, where C_1 and C_2 are wind pressure coefficients. Note that $C_1 > 0$ and $C_2 < 0$. The pressure difference between inside and outside can be given by the following equations:

$$\begin{aligned} \text{windward} \quad & \Delta_1 = C_1 \gamma v^2/2 - p_r \\ \text{leeward} \quad & \Delta_2 = p_r - C_2 \gamma v^2/2 \end{aligned} \qquad (6.7)$$

where p_r = air pressure in the room. Letting the sash constants and crack lengths of windward and leeward window sashes be a_1, n_1, l_1, a_2, n_2, and l_2 respectively.

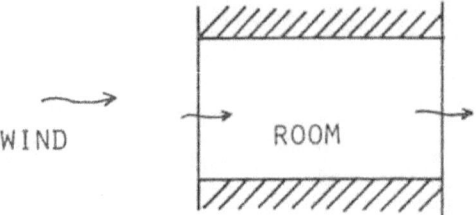

Fig. 6.3. Room with windward and leeward openings.

The pressure balance equations at windward and leeward windows can be obtained as follows, using eqn. (6.3), namely:

$$\left(\frac{Q}{a_1 l_1}\right)^{n_1} = C_1 \gamma v^2 / 2 - p_r$$
$$\left(\frac{Q}{a_2 l_2}\right)^{n_2} = p_r - C_1 \gamma v^2 / 2 \tag{6.8}$$

Eliminating p_r from the above two equations,

$$\left(\frac{Q}{a_1 l_1}\right)^{n_1} + \left(\frac{Q}{a_2 l_2}\right)^{n_2} = (C_1 - C_2) \gamma v^2 / 2 \tag{6.9}$$

Q may be obtained by solving eqn. (6.9). If $n_1 = n_2 = n$, the following equation gives Q quite easily, viz.,

$$Q = \left[\frac{(C_1 - C_2)\gamma v^2 / 2}{\left(\frac{1}{a_1 l_1}\right)^n + \left(\frac{1}{a_2 l_2}\right)^n}\right]^{1/n} \tag{6.10}$$

6.3. PRINCIPLE OF STACK EFFECT

High buildings hold large volumes of air at higher temperatures than outside in the heating season. As in a chimney, the column of hot air rises. The driving force of the air rising, which is due to the difference in specific weight of air between inside and outside and the height of the column, is called the stack effect or chimney action. In fact, the cold outside air comes in when entrance doors are open and the warm room air goes out of cracks of windows in the higher floors. The stack effect is emphasized with higher buildings in cold countries. Revolving doors with ante-rooms are often provided in the vestibule of large buildings for this reason.

The fact that the specific volume of air is greater for a higher temperature is evidenced by the Gay-Lussac's law that states:

$$v(\theta) = v(0)\left(1 + \frac{\theta}{273\cdot16}\right) \quad (6.11)$$

where $v(\theta)$, $v(0)$ = specific volume of gas at temperature θ (°C) and 0 (°C) respectively, θ = temperature of ideal gas (°C).

Assuming the air is similar to the ideal gas, it can be understood that the specific weight of the air is inversely proportional to the absolute temperature of the air. This is derived from eqn. (6.11) to be expressed as:

$$\gamma(T) = \frac{1\cdot293 \times 273\cdot16}{T} \quad (6.12)$$

where T = temperature of the air (K), $\gamma(T)$ = specific weight of the air at T (kg m^{-3}).

It follows, therefore, that the specific weight of the inside air and the outside air, γ_i, and γ_o respectively, are:

$$\gamma_i = \frac{353\cdot20}{T_i} \qquad \gamma_0 = \frac{353\cdot20}{T_0} \quad (6.13)$$

Under standard atmospheric pressure, the values of absolute pressure inside and outside, p_i and p_o (N m^{-2}) respectively, at the height z (m) above the reference point 0, are given by:

$$p_i(z) = (103\,32\cdot3 - \gamma_i z)g, \qquad p_o(z) = (103\,32\cdot3 - \gamma_o z)g \quad (6.14)$$

Thus, the pressure difference between inside and outside is:

$$\Delta p(z) = p_o(z) - p_i(z) = z(\gamma_i - \gamma_o)g = 353.20gz\left(\frac{1}{T_i} - \frac{1}{T_o}\right) \quad (6.15)$$

Figure 6.4 illustrates this relationship common to both chimneys and buildings. Taking the middle point of the total height of a homogeneous column as zero reference, the values of the pressure difference between inside and outside are zero at that height. The zone in the building at this height is called the neutral zone

This pressure difference in the unit of force per unit area is a important potential to cause infiltration through cracks or openings of building walls.

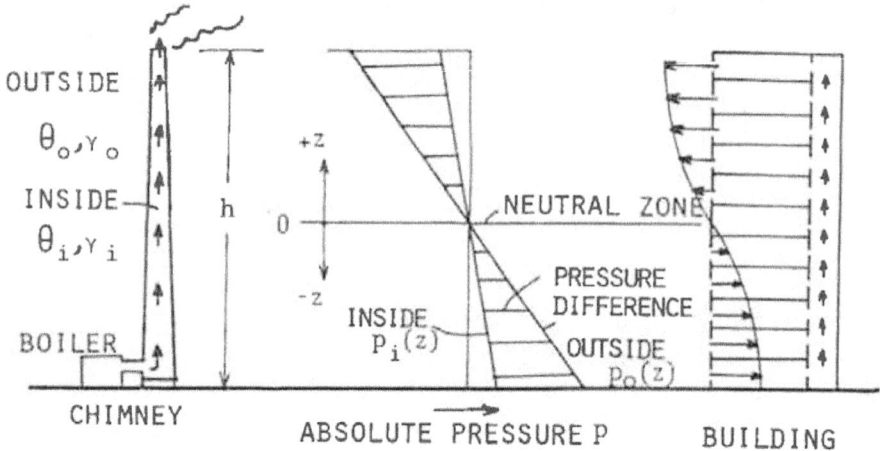

Fig. 6.4. Pressure distribution of building and chimney [6.3].

6.4 INFILTRATION BY STACK EFFECT

When infiltration through cracks at the rate of Q (m³s⁻¹) takes place by the pressure difference across the window Δp (N m⁻²), the rate of infiltration is to be expressed by eqn. (6.4) as previously described.

In the case of a multi-storied building with a vertical shaft created by stairwells or liftshafts as shown in Fig. 6.5, the pressure difference at the kth floor level $\Delta p_o(k)$ (N m⁻²) is expressed by:

$$\Delta p_o(k) = p_o(k) - p(k) = \left(\frac{Q_o(k)}{A_o(k)}\right)^{n_o(k)} \quad (6.16)$$

where $p_o(k)$, $p(k)$ = pressure outside and inside respectively at the kth floor level (N m⁻²), $Q_o(k)$ = infiltration at the kth floor level (m³s⁻¹), $A_o(k)$ ($= a_k l_k$) = equivalent orifice area of the window at the kth floor level (m$^{3-2n_o(k)}$ N$^{n_o(k)}$ s⁻¹). $n_o(k)$ = sash constant of the window at the kth floor level (–).

The same equation applies to the air leakage through cracks of the indoor partitions from room space to shaft space as follows:

$$\Delta p_i(k) = p(k) - p_i(k) = \left(\frac{Q_i(k)}{A_i(k)}\right)^{n_i(k)} \quad (6.17)$$

where $p_i(k)$ = pressure in the vertical shaft at the kth floor level (N m^{-2}), $\Delta p_i(k)$ = pressure difference at the kth floor level between room space and shaft space (N m^{-2}), $Q_i(k)$ = air leakage at the kth level from room space to shaft space (m^{3}s^{-1}), $A_i(k)$ = equivalent orifice area of the partition at the kth floor level (m$^{3-2n_s(k)}$ N$^{n_s(k)}$ s^{-1}), $n_i(k)$ = sash constant of the interior partition at the kth floor level(–).

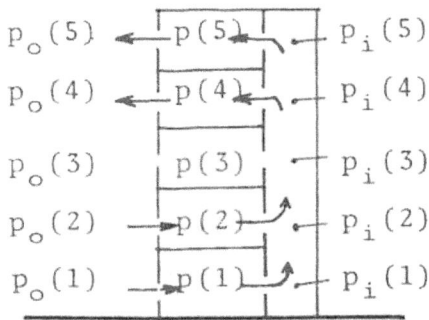

Fig. 6.5. Inside and outside pressures of a five storied building.

If there is no air leakage through the floor slab, it follows:

$$Q_o(k) = Q_i(k) = Q(k) \tag{6.18}$$

A combination of eqns. (6.16) and (6.17) eliminates $p(k)$ and gives the following equation:

$$\left(\frac{Q(k)}{A_o(k)}\right)^{n_o(k)} + \left(\frac{Q(k)}{A_i(k)}\right)^{n_i(k)} = p_o(k) - p_i(k) \tag{6.19}$$

For simplicity, the following assumptions can be made:

$$\begin{aligned} n_o(k) = n_i(k) = n \\ A_o(k) = A \quad A_i(k) = 2A \end{aligned} \tag{6.20}$$

Then the rate of infiltration at the kth floor level can be given as:

$$Q(k) = \left[\frac{p_o(k) - p_i(k)}{\dfrac{1}{A^n} + \left(1 + \dfrac{1}{2^n}\right)}\right]^{1/n} \tag{6.21}$$

In the case of five storied buildings the neutral zone lies in the third level. If the floor to floor height is d (m) for all floors, the numerator of eqn. (6.21) is given by:

$$p_o(k) - p_i(k) = (3-k)d(\gamma_o - \gamma_i) = (3-k)d\left(\frac{1}{T_o} - \frac{1}{T_i}\right) \times 353 \cdot 2 \quad (6.22)$$

Thus, the infiltration at each floor level can be expressed as a function of the inside and outside air temperatures and the height of the space concerned by the following equation:

$$Q(k) = \left[\frac{A^n(3-k)d}{1+\frac{1}{2^n}}\left(\frac{1}{T_o} - \frac{1}{T_i}\right) \times 353 \cdot 2\right]^{1/n} \quad (6.23)$$

As a result $Q(1)$ and $Q(2)$ are positive, $Q(3) = 0$. $Q(4)$ and $Q(5)$ are negative.

In general, when there is a variety of cracks with different air leakage characteristics, i.e. A's and n's are all different, iteration is necessary to find the level of neutral zone first and then to obtain the values of infiltration and exfiltration at each floor level.

Example 1: In the case of a five storied building as shown in Fig. 6.5, calculate the rate of infiltration due to stack effect at every floor level under the conditions:

outside air temperature $=\theta_a = -10°C$
inside air temperature $=\theta_r = 20°C$
equivalent orifice area of the window at kth floor level
$=A_0(k) = A = 50$
equivalent orifice area of the partition at kth floor level
$=A_i(k) = 2A = 100$
sash constant $= n = 1.5$
floor to floor height $= d = 3 \cdot 6$m

Solution: Infiltration at the kth floor level can be calculated by eqn. (6.21) or (6.23), viz.,

$$Q(k) = \left[\frac{p_o(k) - p_i(k)}{\frac{1}{A^n}+\left(1+\frac{1}{2^n}\right)}\right]^{1/n} = \left[\frac{(3-k) \times 3 \cdot 6}{\frac{1}{50^{1.5}}\left(1+\frac{1}{2^n}\right)}\left(\frac{353 \cdot 2}{263 \cdot 16} - \frac{353 \cdot 2}{293 \cdot 16}\right)\right]^{1/1.5}$$

$$= \frac{[(3-k) \times 3 \cdot 6(1 \cdot 342 - 1 \cdot 205)]^{1/1.5}}{0 \cdot 0245} = \frac{[0 \cdot 493(3-k)]^{1/1.5}}{0 \cdot 0245}$$

$Q(1) = 40 \cdot 4 \text{m}^3\text{h}^{-1}$ $\quad Q(2) = 25 \cdot 5 \text{m}^3\text{h}^{-1}$ $\quad Q(3) = 0$
$\quad Q(4) = -25 \cdot 5 \text{m}^3\text{h}^{-1}$ $\quad Q(5) = -40 \cdot 4 \text{m}^3\text{h}^{-1}$

The positive value of Q means infiltration and the negative value of Q exfiltration.

Example 2: Calculate the rate of infiltration for Example 1 except that the orifice area of the ground floor level is 1000 assuming the entrance door.

Solution: If the neutral zone for this case was shifted downwards by x(m) from the middle point of the third floor level, the pressure difference between inside and outside at the kth floor level can be expressed as:

$$p_o(k) - p_i(k) = (1 \cdot 342 - 1 \cdot 205)[(3-k) \times 3 \cdot 6 - x]$$

At the ground floor level the conditions of $A_o(1) = 1000 = 20A$ and $A_i(1) = 2A$ yield the following equations:

$$Q(1)^n = 20^n A^n [p_o(1) - p(1)]$$
$$Q(1)^n = 2^n A^n [p_o(1) - p_i(1)]$$

Therefore

$$Q(1) = \left[\frac{p_o(1) - p_i(1)}{\frac{1}{A^n} + \left(\frac{1}{20^n} + \frac{1}{2^n}\right)} \right]^{1/n} = \frac{[p_o(1) - p_i(1)]^{1/1.5}}{0 \cdot 0102}$$

At the other floor levels $Q(k)$ is given by the same equation as in Example 1.
Now as it follows that:

$$\sum_{k=1}^{5} Q(k) = 0$$

$$\frac{[p_o(1) - p_i(1)]^{1/1.5}}{0 \cdot 0102} + \frac{\sum_{k=2}^{5}[p_o(k) - p_i(k)]^{1/1.5}}{0 \cdot 0245} = 0$$

Therefore

$$\frac{(7 \cdot 2 - x)^{1/1.5}}{0 \cdot 0102}$$
$$+ \frac{(3 \cdot 6 - x)^{1/1.5} - x^{1/1.5} - (3 \cdot 6 + x)^{1/1.5} - (7 \cdot 2 - x)^{1/1.5}}{0 \cdot 0245} = 0$$

By iteration we obtain $x \doteq 1.8$ m, which means that the neutral zone is shifted downwards by 1.8 m. Then the rate of infiltration at every floor level can be derived as follows:

$$Q(1) = 80 \cdot 2 \, \text{m}^3 \text{h}^{-1} \quad Q(2) = 16 \cdot 2 \, \text{m}^3 \text{h}^{-1} \quad (3) = -16 \cdot 2 \, \text{m}^3 \text{h}^{-1}$$
$$Q(4) = -33 \cdot 4 \, \text{m}^3 \text{h}^{-1} \quad Q(5) = -46 \cdot 8 \, \text{m}^3 \text{h}^{-1}$$

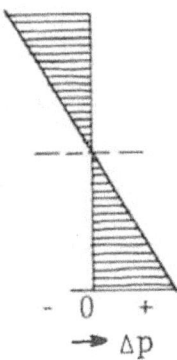

Fig. 6.6. Pressure difference distribution by stack effect only.

6.5. COMBINATION OF WIND AND STACK EFFECTS

Buildings in general are subject to both wind and stack effects simultaneously. In effect, it is the infiltration and exfiltration due to wind and stack effects which are known as natural ventilation. The relationship between the rate of infiltration or exfiltration and the pressure difference across the window as previously described holds true in the case when both effects exist simultaneously. Namely the algebraic sum of the pressure difference due to wind and the pressure difference due to stack effect is related to the total rate of infiltration.

Figure 6.6 shows the vertical distribution of pressure difference between outside and inside caused by stack effect only, where the inside pressure is taken as the zero reference.

When there are both wind and stack effects, the distribution of pressure difference between inside and outside shows different patterns depending n whether the window is windward or leeward as shown in Fig. 6.7. If the room faces the windward side, the positive outside pressure is increased by $C_1 \gamma v^2 / 2$ on top of the pressure distribution due to stack effect, thus bringing the neutral zone upward and adding to the number of floors where infiltration takes place. On the contrary exfiltration increases in the leeward room, because the neutral zone is pulled down by negative pressure difference by $C_2\gamma\upsilon^2/2$.

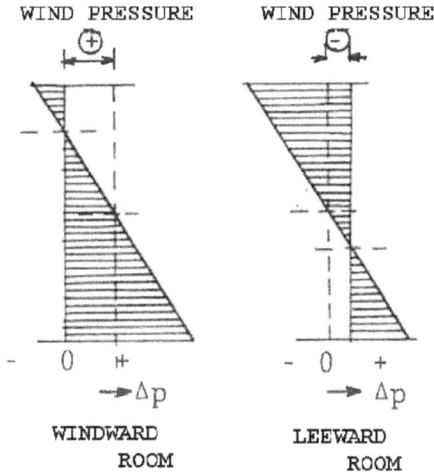

Fig. 6.7. Pressure difference distribution by stack effect and wind.

It must be noted, however, that the wind velocity increases with the height of the building and the vertical distribution of pressure difference caused by wind would not be linear.

George T. Tamura
(1927 -1996)

Photo by the author in 1982

Born in Vancouver as a second generation of Japanese Canadian, Mr. Tamura joined Fire Section, Division of Building Research, National Research Council in Ottawa after receiving M. Sc. From University of Toronto. He is well known authority in smoke movement in high rise buildings from basic theory to a full height multi storied building. ASHRAE Fellow.

Chapter 7

Heat Load of Air Conditioning

In order to maintain comfort in an occupied space, positive or negative heat must be supplied to the space by various means. The amount of heat required for this purpose is known as heat load. There are two kinds of heat load in air conditioning depending on the season: cooling load and heating load [7.1, 7.2]. There are also two kinds of heat load in air conditioning depending on the interest that one takes: heating and cooling demands and energy requirements for heating and cooling. The amounts of maximum probable heating and cooling demands are the basis for selecting boilers, fans, refrigeration machines and other necessary components of an air conditioning system so that the space can be maintained at comfort level even on very cold or hot days. Estimation of heating and cooling demands is made primarily for the air conditioning design purpose. On the other hand, energy requirements for heating and cooling are associated with the total annual operating cost of air conditioning. The owner of the building is evidently interested in knowing how much the operation of air conditioning would cost in a year at the stage of architectural design and air conditioning system design.

Estimation of heating and cooling demands has traditionally been made by manual calculation with the aid of convenient tables and charts, but computers are also being used for this purpose when answers are required to be as accurate as possible. On the other hand, annual energy requirements for heating and cooling could not be estimated without the aid of a computer [7.3, 7.4], because the heat load must be calculated not only for very cold days but also for milder days.

It would be desirable, however, to be able to apply a common physical basis to the estimation of both demands and energy requirements. This chapter describes basic methods of calculating heat load components and diurnal variations of space heating and cooling loads for estimation of energy requirements to be consistent with the method used for estimating the demands.

7.1. HEAT GAIN AND COOLING LOAD

Cooling load is different from heat gain and heating load is different from heat loss. Discussion hereafter deals with heat gain and cooling load, because heat loss and heating load can be considered as negative heat gain and negative cooling load respectively.

Heat gain may be defined as the rate of unwanted heat entering into the space under the condition that the room air temperature would be kept always constant. Cooling load may be defined as the rate of heat required to be removed from the space to maintain the room air temperature at a constant specified level.

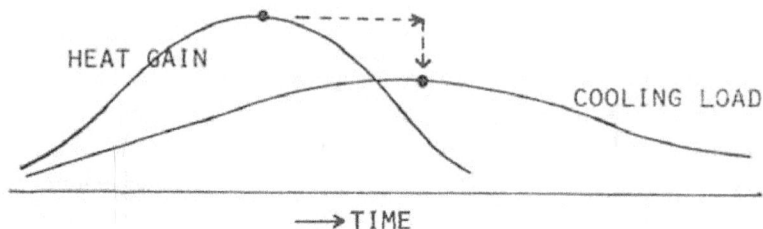

*Fig.*7.1. Heat gain and cooling load.

The reason for having these two treated as different terms is that the thermal storage in the building structure is so significant that all of the heat entering into the space as heat gain might not appear as cooling load instantaneously, part of the heat gain being stored in the building structure, In consequence, the diurnal variation of cooling load shows a certain reduction from the peak and a certain delay from heat gain variation as shown in Fig.7.1.

The component of heat gain to be stored in the building structure is the radiation component, because any flux of radiant energy falling on a surface is at once partially absorbed by the structure and appears as cooling load by convection from the surface to the room air after a while. The radiation components of heat gain are classified as transmitted solar radiation through windows, long wavelength radiation from the inside surface of exterior skin and radiation from interior heat generating objects such as lights, people and electrical appliances. On the other hand, the convective component of heat gain may be considered to become cooling load instantaneously. Convection from the inside surface of exterior, walls and roofs and convection from the interior heat generating objects to the room air are classified in this category.

The thermal storage effect by building structures due to heat gains from solar radiation and lights is discussed in Chapters 4 and 5 respectively. As described in these preceding chapters, it is convenient to use time series expressions for the variables involved in the thermal system for the room enclosure. The relationship between heat gain and cooling load can be expressed by using cooling load weighting factors for heat gain as follows:

$$H_{CL}(n) = \sum_{j=0}^{n} W(j) \cdot H_{HG}(n-j) \tag{7.1}$$

where $H_{CL}(n)$ = cooling load at time $t = n\Delta t$ due to heat gain(W), $H_{HG}(n)$ = heat gain at time $t = n\Delta t$(W), $W(j)$ = cooling load weighting factors for heat gain (–).

When there are different kinds of heat gain for the space concerned, the space cooling load at time n can be considered as the sum of the cooling loads at time n for the respective heat gains. This is based on the superposition principle, and namely the space cooling load can be given by:

$$H_{SCL}(n) = \sum_{k=1}^{M} H_{CL,k}(n)$$
$$= \sum_{k=1}^{M} W_k(j) \cdot H_{HG,k}(n-j) \quad (7.2)$$

where $H_{SCL}(n)$ = space cooling load at time n (W), $H_{CL,k}(n)$ = kth cooling load at time n(W), $H_{HG,k}(n)$ = kth heat gain at time n(W), $W_k(j)$ = cooling load weighting factors for kth heat gain(–). For simple practical calculation cooling load weighting factors may be approximated by the first two terms and common ratio so that the following relationship may be valid in reference to Fig.7.2:

$$W_k(0) + \frac{W_k(1)}{1-c_k} = \sum_{j=0}^{\infty} W_k(j) = 1 \quad (7.3)$$

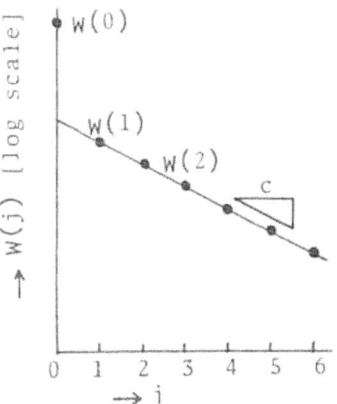

Fig 7.2 Semi-log plot of approximated values of cooling load weighting Factors for heat gain.

Since the heat storage effect in the building structure could be more or less of the same nature for different heat gain components, the common ratio c_k might be taken as a constant value, i.e.

$$c_1 = c_2 = \cdots = c_n = c \quad (7.4)$$

Applying eqns. (7.3) and (7.4) to eqn. (7.2), the space cooling load may be calculated by a very simple equation as in the following:

$$H_{SCL}(n) = cH_{SCL}(n-1) + \sum_{k=1}^{M} W_k(0)H_{HG,k}(n)$$
$$+ \sum_{k=1}^{M}[W_k(1) - cW_k(0)]H_{HG,k}(n-1) \tag{7.5}$$

The cooling load weighting factors for various heat gain components in eqn. (7.5) are given in Tables 5.5–5.8. The simplicity of eqn. (7.5) enables manual calculation to be effected quite easily.

7.2. Components of Space Cooling Load

Cooling load of a given space can be classified in different ways. The interior zone of a space imposes cooling load on the air conditioning systems caused by heat from lights, occupants and heat generating appliances. The perimeter zone of a space, which faces outside, holds a cooling load caused by outside environmental excitations in addition to the interior heat generation, i.e. solar radiation transmitted through glass windows, heat transmission across glass windows, heat transmission across exterior walls and roofs, and infiltration. The summation of several cooling load components pertaining to the space is called space cooling load.

When the air temperature in the space varies with time, a considerable amount of heat transfer occurs between the room air and the building structure because the room air temperature deviates from the set reference point on which the calculation of the space cooling load is based. The sum of the heat transfer caused by the room air temperature deviation and the space cooling load is termed heat extraction, which implies the rate of heat actually extracted from the space by the air conditioning system.

There are two kinds of cooling load, depending on whether moisture transfer accompanies heat transfer or not. Heat transmission across walls, roofs and windows, solar radiation and heat from lights bring about only sensible cooling load, whereas heat generation by occupants and some kinds of appliances, and heat transfer by infiltration bring about both sensible and latent loads because moisture transfer takes place in the respective thermal processes.

Another important feature in cooling load calculation is that some cooling load components arc affected by heat storage in the building structure and others remain the same as instantaneous heat gain. Infiltration belongs to the latter. It is important to note that the convection portion of other cooling load components also can be classified as the latter, while the ones that involve radiation heat transfer are associated with heat storage, belonging to the former for which a convolution process is required in calculation as described in the preceding section.

Figure 7.3 and Table 7.1 are summarized calculations from different views as discussed in the above.

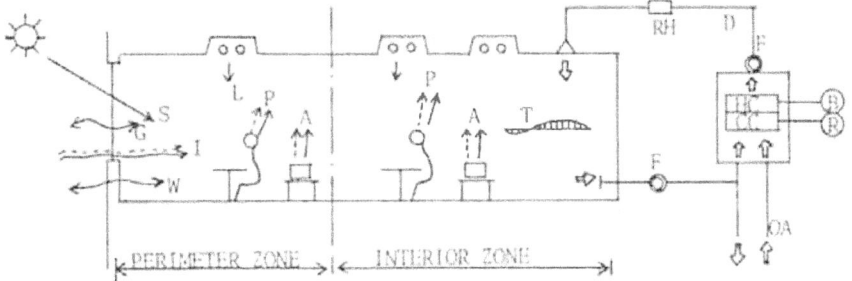

*Fig.*7.3.   Heat load components.

Table *7.1*
Classification of heat load components

		Heat load components	Interior zone	Perimeter zone	Sensible load	Latent load	Instantaneous load	Transient load	Symbols used in Fig. 7.3
Heat load on coils of air conditioner	Heat extraction	Space cooling load	Heat from lights	√	√	√			√	L
			Heat from occupants	√	√	√	√		√	P
			Heat from appliances	√	√	√	√		√	A
			Solar radiation through glass windows		√	√			√	S
			Heat transmission across glass windows	√	√				√	G
			Heat transmission across exterior walls and roofs		√	√			√	W
			Infiltration		√	√	√	√		I
			Heat load due to room air temperature deviation	√	√	√			√	T
		Outside air load for ventilation		√	√	√	√	√		OA
		Heat from fans		√	√	√			√	F
		Heat transmission across duct insulation		√	√	√			√	D
		Terminal reheat		√	√	√			√	RH

163

7.3. Algorithm of Calculating Space Cooling Load

The algorithms for computing space cooling load components according to the procedures used in SHASE program HASP/ACLD/7101 [7.6] to calculate annual energy requirements for air conditioning are as follows:

An algorithm is a set of equations written in sequence of calculation, where output is on the left-hand side and input data, which should be known, are on the right-hand side; a computer program can easily be made from the algorithm merely by replacing symbols and operations with those used in the computer language according to its grammar.

(1) *Cooling load associated with heat from lights*
  (a) Heat gain at time n, $G_L(n)$ (W):

$$G_L(n) = L \cdot P_L(n) \cdot (1 - \rho_L) \tag{7.6}$$

  (b) Cooling load at time n, $H_L(n)$ (W):

$$H_L(n) = W_L(0)G_L(n) + [W_L(1) - c_L W_L(0)] \times G_L(n-1) + c_L H_L(n-1)] \tag{7.7}$$

  where L = power input to lights including ballast loss(W), $P_L(n)$ = fraction of lights turned on at time at on daily schedule, ρ_L = heat removal efficiency of air handling troffers or luminaires, $W_L(0)$, $W_L(1)$ = cooling load weighting factors for heat from lights(–)(See Table 5.5), c_L = common ratio associated with $W_L(0)$, $W_L(1)$.

(2) *cooling load associated with heat from occupants*
  (a) Sensible heat generated by one occupant at reference room air temperature, Q_{PS}(W) (Fig. 7.4):

$$Q_{PS} = Q_0 + (24 - \theta_r)g \tag{7.8}$$

  (b) Latent heat generated by one occupant at reference room air temperature Q_{PL}(W):

$$Q_{PL} = Q_{PT} - Q_{PS} \tag{7.9}$$

  (c) Sensible heat gain at time n, $G_{PS}(n)$ (W):

$$G_{PS}(n) = Q_{PS} \cdot N_p \cdot P_p(n) \tag{7.10}$$

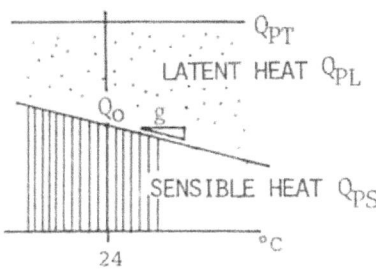

*Fig.*7.4 Sensible and latent heat generated by human body under different room air temperatures [7.4].

(d) Sensible cooling load at time n, $H_{PS}(n)$ (W):

$$H_{PS}(n) = W_P(0)G_{PS}(n) + [W_P(1) - c_P W_P(0)] \times G_{PS}(n-1) + c_P H_{PS}(n-1) \quad (7.11)$$

(e) Latent cooling load at time n, $H_{PL}(n)$ (W):

$$H_{PL}(n) = Q_{PL} \cdot N_p \cdot P_p(n) \quad (7.12)$$

where Q_0 sensible heat generated by a human body at 24°C depending on work strength (W) (Table 7.2), Q_{PT} = total heat generated by a human body under the respective working conditions (W) (Table 7.2), g = gradient of sensible heat generation in reference to room air temperature (W deg C^{-1}) (Table 7.2), θ_r = reference room air temperature (°C), N_p = number of occupants in the room, $P_p(n)$ = fraction of occupants at time n on week days, $W_p(0)$, $W_p(1)$ = sensible cooling load weighting factors for heat gain from occupants (–) (Table 5.7) and c_p = common ratio associated with $W_p(0)$, $W_p(1)$.

Table 7.2
Heat generated by a human body depending on work strength [7.4]

Work strength	Example of building applicable	Q_{PT} (W)	Q_0 (W)	g (W deg C^{-1})
1	Auditorium	79	50	−3·0
2	School	91	53	−3·1
3	Office, hotel, housing	102	54	−3·4
4	Bank	113	55	−3·6
5	Restaurant	125	59	−3·8
6	Factory–light work	170	65	−5·6
7	Dance hall	194	71	−6·0
8	Factory–heavy work	227	85	−6·3
9	Gymnasium	329	118	−5·4

(3) *Cooling load associated with appliances*
   (a) Sensible heat gain at time n, $G_{AS}(n)$ (W):

$$G_{AS}(n) = Q_{AS} \cdot P_A(n) \tag{7.13}$$

   (b) Sensible cooling load at time n, $H_{AS}(n)$:

$$H_{AS}(n) = W_A(0)G_{AS}(n) + [W_A(1) - c_A H_{AS}(0)] \times G_{AS}(n-1) + c_A H_{AS}(n-1) \tag{7.14}$$

   (c) Latent cooling load at time n, $H_{AL}(n)$:

$$H_{AL}(n) = Q_{AL} \cdot P_A(n) \tag{7.15}$$

where Q_{AS} = sensible heat generated by appliances in the room space (W), Q_{AL} = latent heat generated by appliances in the room space (W), $P_A(n)$ = fraction of appliances used at time n, $W_A(0)$, $W_A(1)$ = sensible cooling load weighting factors for sensible heat gain from appliances (–), and c_A = common ratio associated with $W_A(0)$, $W_A(1)$.

(4) *Cooling load associated with solar radiation through glass windows*
   (a) Fraction of direct solar radiation that is transmitted through the standard glass pane and that is absorbed by the standard glass pane and transferred to the room by radiation and convection at tine n, $g_{Di}(n)$:

$$g_{Di}(n) = 2 \cdot 3920 \, c_i(n) - 3 \cdot 8636 [c_i(n)]^2 + 3 \cdot 7658 [c_i(n)]^3 - 1 \cdot 3952 [c_i(n)]^4 \tag{7.16}$$

   (b) Fraction of diffuse solar radiation as heat gain from the standard window glass:

$$g_d(n) = 2\int_0^{\pi/2} g_{Di}(n) \cdot \sin i \cos i \, di \tag{7.17}$$

   (c) Solar heat gain from the standard glass window at time n, $I_G(n)$ (Wm^{-2}):

$$I_G(n) = g_{Di}(n) r_D(n) I_D(n) + g_d(n) r_d(n) I_d(n) \tag{7.18}$$

   (d) Solar heat gain for the given window with shading at time n, $G_S(n)$ (W):

$$G_S(n) = k_s I_G(n) A_G \tag{7.19}$$

   (e) Cooling load associated with solar heat gain at time n, $H_S(n)$ (W):

$$H_S(n) = W_S(0)G_S(n) + [W_S(1) - c_S W_S(0)] \times G_S(n-1) + c_S H_S(n-1) \tag{7.20}$$

where $c_i(n)$ = cosine of incident angle i (degree) of direct solar radiation upon the window glass surface concerned at time $n(-)$, $I_D(n)$, $I_d(n)$ = direct and diffuse solar radiation respectively upon the window glass surface concerned at time n (Wm^{-2}), $r_D(n)$ = fraction of sunlit area of glass window with external shading at time n (–), $r_d(n)$ = form factor of the sky as seen from glass window with external shading (–), A_G = area of grass window (m^2), k_s = shading coefficient of the window (–), $W_S(0)$, $W_S(1)$ = cooling load weighting factors for solar heat gain from windows (–) (Table 5.6) and c_S = common ratio associated with $W_S(0)$, $W_S(1)$.

(5) *Cooling load associated with heat transmission across glass windows*
   (a) Equivalent temperature differential across the glass window concerned at time n, $\Delta\theta_{eG}(n)$ (°C):

$$\Delta\theta_{eG}(n) = \theta_a(n) - \frac{\varepsilon_G \varphi_a R(n)}{\alpha_0} - \theta_r \tag{7.21}$$

   (b) Cooling load at time n, $H_G(n)$ (W):

$$H_G(n) = K_G A_G \Delta\theta_{eG}(n) \tag{7.22}$$

where $\theta_a(n)$ = outside air temperature at time n (°C), ε_G = emissivity of glass, $R(n)$ = effective radiation to the sky from horizontal surface (Wm^{-2}), φ_a = form factor of the sky as seen from glass window (–), α_0 = film heat transfer coefficient on the outside surface of glass window (Wm^{-2} deg C^{-1}), θ_r = reference room air temperature (°C), K_G = thermal transmittance of glass window (Wm^{-2} deg C^{-1}) and A_G = area of glass window (m^2).

(6) *Cooling load associated with heat transmission across exterior walls and roofs*
   (a) Equivalent temperature differential across the exterior walls at time n, $\Delta\theta_{ew}(n)$ (°C):

$$\Delta\theta_{ew}(n) = \theta_a(n) + \frac{a_S I_T(n) - \varepsilon_w \varphi_a R(n)}{\alpha_0} - \theta_r \tag{7.23}$$

   (b) Heat gain from heat transmission through walls at time n, $G_W(n)$ (Wm^{-2}):

$$G_W(n) = \sum_{j=0}^{\infty} Y_W(j) \Delta\theta_{ew}(n-j) \qquad (7.24)$$

(c) Cooling load at time n, $H_W(n)$(W):

$$H_w(n) = A_W G_W(n) \qquad (7.25)$$

where $\theta_a(n)$ = outside air temperature at time n(°C), a_s = absorptivity of outside surface of wall for solar radiation (–), $I_T(n)$ = total solar radiation upon the outside surface of wall at time n (W m^{-2}), ε_w = emissivity of outside surface of wall (–), φ_a = view factor from the wall surface looking at the atmosphere in reference to the horizontal surface to the atmosphere (–), $R(n)$ = long wavelength radiation exchange between the horizontal surface and the atmosphere at time n (W m^{-2}), α_0 = film coefficient along the outside surface of exterior wall (Wm^{-2} deg C^{-1}) and θ_r = reference room air temperature (°C).

(7) *Cooling load associated with infiltration*
   (a) Wind direction relative to the wall orientation, δ_W (degrees):

$$\begin{aligned}\delta_w &= |Or + 180 - I_{WD} \times 22 \cdot 5| \\ \text{If } \delta_w &> 180 \quad \delta_w = 360 - \delta_w\end{aligned} \qquad (7.26)$$

   (b) Wind pressure coefficient, C_W:

   If $\delta_w \leq 30$ $C_w = 0 \cdot 75$
   If $30 < \delta_w \leq 75$ $C_w = 0 \cdot 75 - 0 \cdot 0166(\delta_w - 30)$
   If $75 < \delta_w \leq 90$ $C_w = -0 \cdot 0267(\delta_w - 75)$
   If $\delta_w > 90$ $C_w = -0 \cdot 4$ (7.26a)

   (c) Wind velocity at the height of the space concerned, v_r (ms^{-1}):

$$\begin{aligned}\text{If } H_r &> H_s \quad v_r = v(H_r / H_s)^{1/4} \\ \text{If } H_r &> H_s \quad v_r = v\end{aligned} \qquad (7.26b)$$

   (d) Pressure difference between inside and outside, Δp (Nm^{-2}):

$$\Delta p = 0 \cdot 5 C_W \gamma_a v_r^2 + (\gamma_r - \gamma_a)(H_r - 0 \cdot 5 H_B) g \qquad (7.27)$$

$$\text{If } \Delta p < 0 \quad \Delta p = 0$$

   (e) Rate of infiltration at time n, $Q(n)$(m^{3}h^{-1}):

$$Q(n) = a_G I_G A_G \Delta p^{1/n_G} \tag{7.28}$$

(f) Sensible cooling load at time n, $H_{IS}(n)$(W):

$$H_{IS}(n) = C_{pa} \gamma_a Q(n)[\theta_a(n) - \theta_r]/3 \cdot 6 \tag{7.29}$$

(g) Latent cooling load at time n, $H_{IL}(n)$(W):

$$H_{IL}(n) = r\gamma_a Q(n)[x_a(n) - x_r]/3 \cdot 6 \tag{7.30}$$

where Or = wall orientation, clockwise from south(degrees), I_{WD} = wind direction index(1 − 16), H_r = height of the space concerned (m), H_S = standard height at which wind speed is measured (m), H_B = height of the building(m), υ = wind velocity measured (m s^{-1}), γ_a = specific weight of outside air (kg m^{-3}), γ_r = specific weight of room air (kg m^{-3}), g = gravity acceleration (m s^{-2}), α_G = sash constant (m$^{2(1-1/n_G)}$ h^{-1} N$^{-1/n_G}$), l_G = crack length of window per unit window area(m^{-1}), n_G = sash constant(−), C_{pa} = specific heat of outside air (kJ kg^{-1} deg C^{-1}), $\theta_a(n)$ = outside air temperature at time n (°C), θ_r = reference room air temperature(°C), r = latent heat of water vapour (kJ g^{-1}), $x_a(n)$ = humidity ratio (absolute humidity) at time n (g kg^{-1}) and x_r = reference room air humidity ratio (g kg^{-1}).

7.4. HEAT EXTRACTION AND ROOM AIR TEMPERATURE VARIATION

It is important to remember that the cooling load is calculated under the condition that the room air temperature is kept constant for 24 hours a day. In actual spaces, however, the room air temperatures are not necessarily kept constant even if automatic control systems are provided. The room air temperature deviates from the set point from time to time and varies within the specified range. This phenomenon is often called temperature swing.

When the air conditioning system is operated under intermittent mode, the room air temperature variation is quite dramatic. After the air conditioning system is turned off the room air temperature changes fairly rapidly and gradually gets closer to the outside air temperature until the system is started in the morning on the following day. During the period when the air conditioning system is off, there is no heat supplied to or extracted from the space and the room air temperature naturally varies with time. Since the temperature has deviated from the set point during the unconditioned period, large amounts of energy must be supplied prior to the time when occupancy starts in order to bring the room air temperature to the set point. This period may be called the preconditioning period, when undesirable room air temperature is picked up in the heating mode or pulled down in the cooling node. The amount of heat supplied or extracted during the preconditioning period may be called the preconditioning load. The longer the preconditioning period, the smaller the preconditioning load.

After the room air temperature reachs the set point at the time when occupancy starts, the amount of heat in excess of the cooling load must be extracted to make up for the heat entering into the space from the surfaces of the room enclosure, as heat is stored in the building structure during the unconditioned period when the room air temperature deviates from the set point. This amount is called the heat storage load. The sum of the cooling load and the heat storage load, which is extracted from the space during the conditioned period in order to maintain the room air temperature at the set point, is called heat extraction. Figure 7.5 shows an overview of intermittent air conditioning. Using the time series expression heat extraction may be given by the following equation:

$$H_{HE}(n) = H_{CL}(n) + H_{SL}(n) \tag{7.31}$$

where $H_{HE}(n)$ = heat extraction at time n(W), $H_{CL}(n)$ = cooling load at time n(W) and $H_{SL}(n)$ = heat storage load at time n(W):

$$H_{SL}(n) = \sum_{j=0}^{\infty} W_z(j) \cdot \theta_r(n-j) + K(n) \cdot \theta_r(n) \tag{7.32}$$

where $\theta_r(n)$ = room air temperature deviation from the set point at time n(°C), $K(n)$ = coefficient associated with infiltration for room air temperature deviation at time n (W deg C^{-1}) and $W_Z(j)$ = heat extraction weighting factors for room air temperature deviation (W deg C^{-1}).

The term $K(n)\theta_r(n)$ in eqn.(7.32) implies instantaneous cooling load at time n when the room air temperature is deviated from the set point by $\theta_r(n)$ and is represented by the decrease in cooling load by infiltration due to the room air temperature deviation $\theta_r(n)$, viz.,

$$K(n) = -C_{pa}\gamma_a Q(n) \tag{7.33}$$

where C_{pa} = specific heat of air (J kg^{-1} degC^{-1}), γ_a = specific weight of outside air (kg m^{-3}) and $Q(n)$ = rate of infiltration at time n (m^3 h^{-1}).

$W_z(j)$ implies the heat extraction at time $t = j\Delta t$ if the room air temperature rose 1 deg C above the set point at time $t = 0$. This can be understood rather easily by the following explanation with reference to Fig.7.6. As described in Chapter 2, the response factors $Z(j)$ of the exterior wall are defined as the response in time series of inside surface heat flow when the room air temperature is given as the unit triangle pulse and the outside air temperature remains zero. It is implied that the wall involves the boundary layers on both surfaces. By definition the outward heat flow

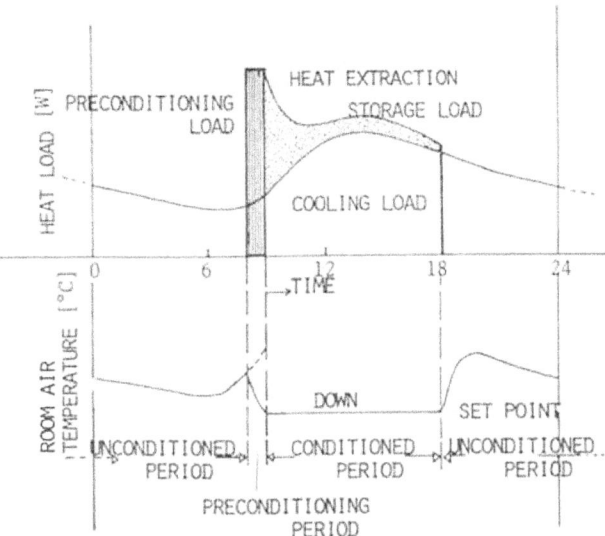

Fig. 7.5 Variation of heat load and room air temperature under intermittent operation of air conditioning.

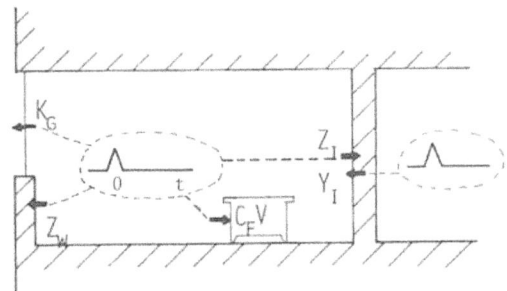

Fig. 7.6 Heat extraction weighting factors for room air temperature as a combination of Z response factors of minus sign.

at the inside surface is positive; the unit positive room air temperature deviation gives rise to outward heat flow at $t = 0$ and inward heat flow at $t = j\Delta t$ ($j \geq 1$). Namely, the heat extraction is required less by $Z(0)$ at $t=0$ and more by $Z(j)$ at $t = j\Delta t$. In consequence $-Z(j)$ identifies the heat extraction weighting factors for room air temperature deviation per unit wall area and the summation of $-Z(j)$ for all exterior walls that enclose the room makes the heat extraction weighting factors for room air temperature deviation for the room, viz.,

$$W_{zw}(j) = -\sum_{i=1}^{kw} Z_w(i,j) A_w(i) \qquad (7.34)$$

where $Z_w(i, j)$ = Z response factors of ith exterior wall (Wm^{-2} deg C^{-1}), $A_w(i)$ = area of ith exterior wall (m^2) and k_w = number of exterior walls. This series $W_{zw}(j)$ is one of the components of $W_z(j)$, heat extraction weighting factors for room air temperature deviation and may be called the exterior wall component of $W_z(j)$.

In general, $W_z(j)$ can be considered to be composed of four major components as given below:

$$W_z(j) = W_{zw}(j) + W_{zi}(j) + W_{zG}(j) + W_{zF}(j) \tag{7.35}$$

Three other components $W_{zi}(j)$, $W_{zG}(j)$ and $W_{zF}(j)$ are to be given by the following description.

When there are adjacent spaces whose air temperature varies simultaneously with that of the space concerned, the Y response factors of the interior walls or floor slabs must be introduced to account for the heat storage effect of the interior walls. Thus, the interior wall component of $W_z(j)$ may be defined by the following expression:

$$W_{zi}(j) = -\sum_{i=1}^{ki}[Z_i(i,j) - Y_i(i,j)]A_i(i) \tag{7.36}$$

where $Z_i(i, j)$, $Y_i(i, j)$, $A_i(i)$ = Z response factors, Y response factors and area of ith interior wall respectively, $W_{zi}(j)$ = interior wall component of $W_z(j)$ (W deg C^{-1}).

In addition the instantaneous cooling load due to the temperature difference between inside and outside as expressed by heat transmission through thin walls, like glass windows, is reduced by the amount corresponding to the room air temperature deviation from the set point at $t = 0$, which makes the reduction of $W_z(0)$ as expressed by the following:

$$W_{zG}(0) = -\sum_{i=1}^{kG} K_G(i)A_G(i)$$

$$W_{zG}(0) = 0 \qquad \text{for } j \geq 1 \tag{7.37}$$

where $K_G(i)$, $A_G(i)$ = thermal transmittance and area of ith glass window respectively, $W_{zG}(j)$ = glass window component of $W_z(j)$.

Assuming that furniture in the room absorbs heat on account of positive room air temperature deviation and discharges heat on account of negative deviation and that the temperature of furniture varies consistently with the room air temperature, the furniture component of $W_z(j)$ may be given by:

$$W_{zF}(0) = -C_F V \times 3600$$
$$W_{zF}(1) = C_F V \times 3600 \tag{7.38}$$
$$W_{zF}(j) = 0 \qquad \text{for } j \geq 2$$

where C_F = heat capacity of furniture (J m^{-3} deg C^{-1}) and V = volume of room space(m^3).

Knowing the heat extraction weighting factors for room air temperature deviation $W_z(j)$, the relationship between heat extraction and room air temperature as expressed by the combination of eqns. (7.31) and (7.32) could be rationalized.

When the air conditioning system is off, room temperature at time $t = n\Delta t$ can be derived by putting $H_{HE}(n) = 0$ in eqn. (7.31). Substitution of eqn. (7.32) into eqn. (7.31) yields the following formula:

$$\theta_r(n) = \frac{-1}{W_z(0) + K(n)} \left(\sum_{j=1}^{\infty} W_z(j) \theta_r(n-j) + H_{CL}(n) \right) \qquad (7.39)$$

7.5. Preconditioning Load and Preconditioning Period

The term preconditioning used here means bringing the room air temperature and humidity to the comfort level prior to the time when occupancy starts early in the morning; pulling down in the case of cooling and picking up in the case of heating are implied by the word preconditioning. The time needed for preconditioning is the preconditioning period and the rate of heat required for preconditioning during this period is the preconditioning load.

During the preconditioning period in the intermittent operation of air conditioning in practice, the constant rate of heat at full capacity is supplied in order to bring the room air temperature to the comfort level within a minimum possible length of time. The shorter the duration of preconditioning period desired, the larger the preconditioning load to be required. In order to investigate the relationship between preconditioning load and preconditioning period, it is necessary to know the characteristics of room air temperature decrease by virtue of the constant unit rate of heat extraction from the room space expressed in time series, which may be defined as the room air temperature weighting factors for unit heat extraction as depicted in Fig. 7.7 [7.7].

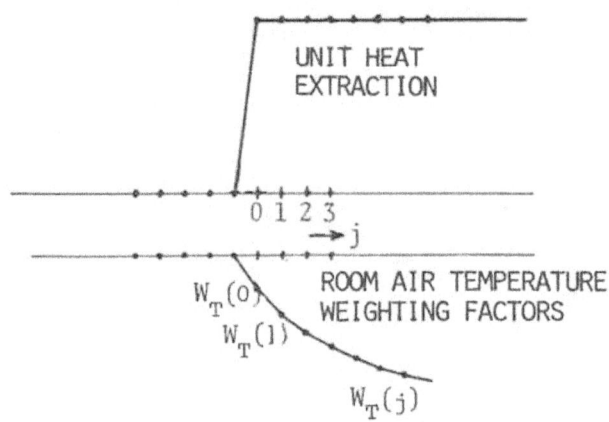

Fig. 7.7. Room air temperature weighting factors for heat extraction.

Table 7.3
Unit heat extraction and room air temperature

n	$H_{HE}(n)$	$\theta_r(n)$
−2	0	0
−1	0	0
0	1	$W_T(0)$
1	1	$W_T(1)$
2	1	$W_T(2)$
3	1	$W_T(3)$
⋮	⋮	⋮

Assuming $K(n)$ in eqn. (7.32) is constant during preconditioning period to be included in $W_z(0)$, eqn. (7.32) is reduced to be:

$$H_{HE}(n) = \sum_{j=0}^{\infty} W_z(j)\theta_r(n-j) \qquad (7.40)$$

When the values of $H_{HE}(n)$ and $\theta_r(n)$ are taken as shown in Table 7.3, referring to Fig. 7.7, the following equations are derived from eqn. (7.40):

$$1 = W_z(0).W_T(0)$$
$$1 = W_z(0).W_T(1) + W_z(1).W_T(0)$$
$$1 = W_z(0).W_T(2) + W_z(1).W_T(1) + W_z(2).W_T(0)$$
$$\vdots$$

(7.41)

Once $W_z(j)$ factors are known, $W_T(j)$ factors can successively be obtained from eqn. (7.41), viz.,

$$W_T(0) = 1/W_z(0)$$
$$W_T(1) = [1 - W_z(1)W_T(0)]/W_z(0)$$
$$W_T(2) = [1 - W_z(1)W_T(1) - W_z(2)W_T(0)]/W_z(0)$$
$$\vdots$$

(7.42)

The superposition principle is applied to the response to multiple excitations. In this case the temperature variation without heat extraction until the start of occupancy must be calculated first. If the temperature deviation at the time when occupancy starts were to be θ_{rb}, the rate of heat extraction required during p hours of preconditioning to pull the temperature down to the reference temperature by θ_{rb} is given by the expression:

$$H_{HE}(p) = \frac{\theta_{rb}}{W_T(p)} \tag{7.43}$$

Hence, if the system capacity of H_{HEX} is given, the duration of preconditioning period p can be obtained from:

$$W_T(p) = \frac{\theta_{rb}}{H_{HEX}} \tag{7.44}$$

where $W_T(p)$ = room air temperature weighting factors for unit heat extraction at $j = p$.

The room air temperature during the preconditioning period $\theta_{rp}(n)$ is to be given by superposing the room air temperature caused only by external excitation without preconditioning $\theta_r(n)$ and the room air temperature caused only by preconditioning $\theta_{rH}(n)$. The former $\theta_r(n)$ is derived from eqn. (7.40) namely:

$$\theta_r(n) = \frac{1}{W_z(0)} \sum_{j=1}^{\infty} W_z(j)\theta_r(n-j) \tag{7.45}$$

The latter $\theta_{rH}(n)$ is given by:

$$\theta_{rH}(n) = H_{HEX} . W_T(n - b + p) \tag{7.46}$$

Superposing $\theta_r(n)$ and $\theta_{rH}(n)$:

$$\theta_{rp}(n) = \theta_r(n) + \theta_{rH}(n) \tag{7.47}$$

Figure 7.8 illustrates this superposition and the total picture of heat extraction and room air temperature variation during a day may result in such a shape as shown in Fig. 7.5.

In the cooling mode, after the air conditioning has stopped, the room air temperature will rise rather rapidly due to solar radiation through windows in the late afternoon and to the release of the heat from lights which has stored in the building structure. During the night room air temperature gradually falls until dawn on the next morning. Pull down starts with maximum heat extraction to bring the room air temperature to the reference level at the time when occupancy starts. The preconditioning period is followed by the conditioned period, when the room air temperature is kept constant at the reference level by heat extraction. This heat is the sum of the space cooling load and the storage load, as illustrated by the hatched area of Fig. 7.5, caused by higher temperature build-up over the long unconditioned period.

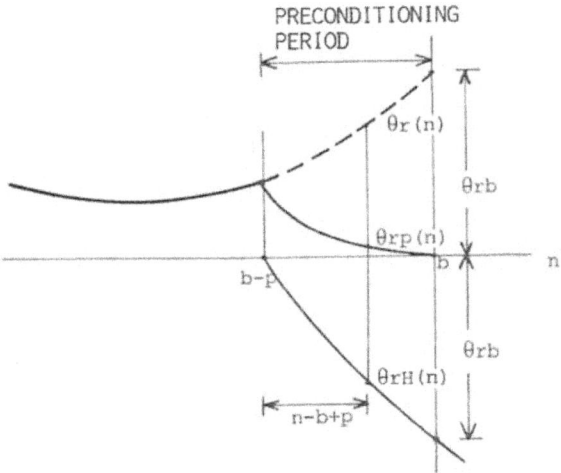

Fig. 7.8. Room air temperature during preconditioning period.

In general, the cumulative heat extracted from the space during a day with intermittent operation is smaller than that with continuous operation for 24 hours. Comparison can be made from the area under the respective curves. It must be noted, however, that a higher rate of heat extraction is needed in intermittent operation than in the case of continuous operation.

In practice, therefore, the large heat storage tank is often used to store the coolness during the night by operating a refrigeration machine with the low utility rate of off-peak electricity. Thus, it is easier to avoid using a heat supply unit of excessive capacity and to maintain a smaller energy consumption on a daily basis than it would be using continuous operation of air conditioning without a storage tank. The advantage of employing a heat storage tank is more significant in the case of heating than cooling. This is because maximum heating load occurs in the early morning which coincides with the preconditioning period, whereas maximum cooling load in summer occurs in the afternoon except in buildings with many large windows facing east.

When the system capacity of heat extraction and the preconditioning period are both given irrespective of severity of weather, it is rather easy to calculate in a straightforward way the room air temperature and heat extraction during the preconditioning period.

The following are the algorithms used in the SHASE program as cited earlier called HASP/ACLD/7101 [7.4, 7.6] for the calculation using heat extraction weighting factors for room air temperature deviation in a right-angled triangular pulse designated as $W_R(j)$. The time series $W_R(j)$ factors can be obtained from the Z response factors for surface temperature excitation given in a right-angled triangular pulse by the procedure similar to the one with an ordinary triangular pulse.

The calculation is divided into three phases:

(1) At the time when preconditioning starts, $n = p$ (Fig. 7.9(a)).
  (a) Room air temperature at $n = p$ if no heat were extracted, $\theta_{rN}(p)(°C)$:

$$\theta_{rN}(p) = -[H_{CL}(p) + G(0)]/W_z(0) \qquad (7.48)$$

  (b) Room air temperature at $n = p$ if rate of heat equal to the system capacity were extracted, θ_{rpx} (°C):

$$\theta_{rpx} = \frac{H_{HEX}}{W_R(0)} \qquad (7.49)$$

  (c) Room air temperature at $n = p$ judged by conditions, $\theta_r(p)$:
    (i) If $\theta_{rN}(p) - \theta_{rpx} \geq \delta$
       $\theta_r(p) = \delta$ and $H_{HE}(p) = H_{HEX}$
    (ii) If $\theta_{rN}(p) - \theta_{rpx} < \delta$ \qquad (7.50)
       $\theta_r(p) = \theta_{rN}(p) - \theta_{rpx}$ and $H_{HE}(p) = \theta_r(p).W_R(0)$

  Similar judgement must be made for heating mode.
  (d) Parameter $G(j)$ for later calculation:

$$G(j) = G(j+1) + \theta_r(p).W_z(j) + H_{HE}(p).W_R(j)/W_R(0) \qquad (7.51)$$

(2) Calculation for the period after the start of preconditioning up to 1 hour before the stopping of the air conditioning.

(a) Room air temperature with no heat extraction at time n, $\theta_{rN}(n)$ (°C):

$$\theta_{rN}(n) = -[H_{CL}(n) + G(0)]/W_z(0) \qquad (7.52)$$

(b) Room air temperature drop by the heat extraction at the rate of system full capacity as an isosceles triangular pulse, θ_{px} (°C):

$$\theta_{px} = -H_{HEX}/W_z(0) \qquad (7.53)$$

(c) (i) If $\theta_{rN}(n) - \theta_{px} \geq \delta$

$$\theta_{rN}(n) = \theta_N(n) - \theta_{px} \quad \text{and} \quad H_{HE}(n) = H_{HEX}$$

(ii) If $\theta_{rN}(n) - \theta_{px} < \delta$

$$\theta_r(n) = \delta \quad \text{and} \quad H_{HE}(n) = \theta_r(n).W_z(0) \qquad (7.54)$$

(d) Parameter $G(j)$ for later calculation:

$$G(j) = G(j+1) - \theta_r(n).W_z(j) \qquad (7.55)$$

The curves of heat extraction after the start or preconditioning are shown as curves A, B and C in Fig. 7.9(b) depending upon the different cases.

(3) Calculation when air conditioning stops at time $n = e$ (Fig.7.9(c)).
  (a) Identical calculations to 2(a), 2(b) and 2(c) are to be made.
  (b) Corrected room air temperature at time $n = e$ by the following equation because heat extraction of a half triangle must be eliminated, $\theta_r^*(e)$ (°C):

$$\theta_r^*(e) = \theta_r(e) - H_{HE}(e).W_R(0) \qquad (7.56)$$

  (c) Calculation of $G(j)$ for $j = 0$–24:

$$G(j) = G(j+1) + \theta_r^*(e).W_z(j) - H_{HE}(e).W_R(j)/W_R(0) \qquad (7.57)$$

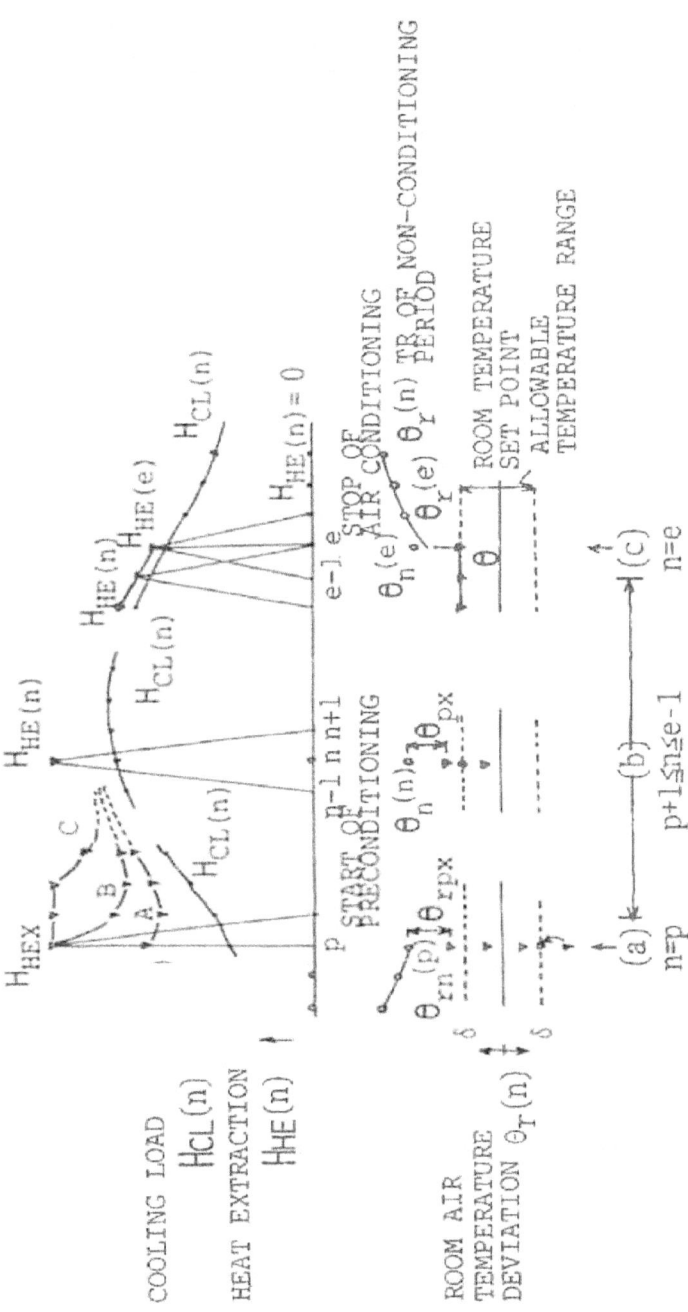

Fig. 7.9. Sequential calculation of heat extraction and room air temperature.
(a) Start of preconditioning $n = p$, (b) conditioned period $p + 1 < n < e - 1$,
(c) stop of air conditioning $n = e$ [7.4, 7.6]

Figure 7.10 shows the basic flow chart to calculate hour by hour heat extraction and room air temperature under intermittent operation of air conditioning for a year. This is used in the computer program to estimate annual energy requirements for air conditioning developed by the Society of Heating, Air Conditioning and Sanitary Engineers of Japan.

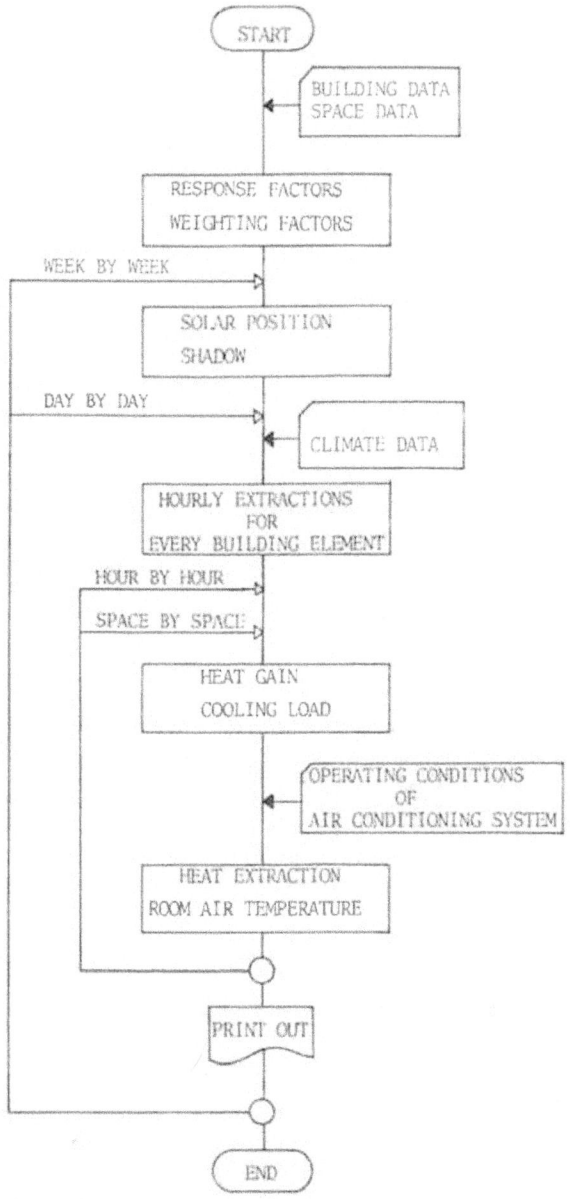

Fig. 7.10. General flow chart to calculate heat gain, cooling load, heat extraction and room air temperature [7.4].

Chapter 8

System Simulation of Air Conditioning

System simulation of air conditioning may be rephrased as the calculation of a simulated air conditioning system. In general, the words 'to simulate a system' mean to obtain the hypothetical operation of a system under given conditions assuming the system in reality would perform under the same conditions. The term 'system' referred to here may be defined as a combination of several elements which all perform together for a particular purpose. The air conditioning system is a combination of refrigeration machines, air conditioners, pumps, fans, duct works, control devices and other miscellaneous components. The air conditioner, for example, is a component of the air conditioning system and at the same time is a system itself, being a combination of heating and cooling coils, filter, fan and other elements. These are called subsystems. A system consists of subsystems and every subsystem consists of sub-subsystems and so on.

A room in the building may also be considered as a thermal system because it responds thermally to environmental excitations. Calculation of room air temperature against heat input into the room space under certain climatic conditions is an example of system simulation. In this sense a room is often called an environmental space system.

It can be summarised, therefore, that system simulation of air conditioning consists of the following three phases:

1. Simulation of environmental space.
2. Simulation of air conditioning networks.
3. Simulation of air conditioning components.

Here, environmental space, air conditioning networks and air conditioning components are the systems of air conditioning to be simulated.

From the results of simulation one can obtain the values of air flow rate, temperature, humidity, water flow rate, heat load and any other items wanted; these are called outputs. On the other hand, the dimensions of the room enclosure, weather data and all other given data needed for simulation are called inputs.

The object of system simulation is to predict the performance of the system at the stage of designing the system, which may then have to be modified in reference to the results of simulation, and to optimise the operation of the system which exists in reality. In the case of air conditioning the results of system simulation are useful for estimating the annual operating cost of air conditioning at the stage of architectural design and air conditioning system design. Optimum design of air conditioning systems and optimum control of existing air conditioning systems may be achieved with the aid of system simulation.

It can be stated, therefore, that system simulation of air conditioning is a tool for evaluating the performance of the air conditioning system so that a desirable comfort level can be attained with a minimum consumption of energy through optimising design and operation of the air conditioning system.

This chapter describes the fundamental concepts and theories of system simulation without going into much detail.

8.1. System Model of Air Conditioning

Use of computers is mandatory for system simulation in most cases. The procedure of system simulation of air conditioning may be broken down into the following four steps:

1. Setting up system models.
2. Preparing input data.
3. Programming.
4. Executing simulation.

Looking at a certain system, the first task for simulation is to set up a system model. As illustrated in Fig. 8.1 a system receives excitations and reacts to yield responses in relation to the characteristics pertinent to the system where constraints prevail. Table 8.1 shows the actual main items of input and output for the three phases of system simulation of air conditioning as previously described.

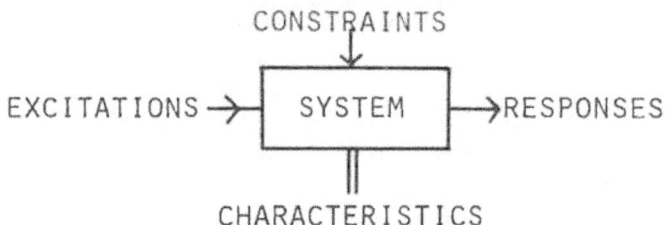

Fig. 8.1. Input and outputs of a system

It can easily be understood from Table 8.1 that the output of one system often appears as the input for another system and all components and networks are interconnected with each other to make an overall system of air conditioning.

Let us take a heat exchanger for an example of a subsystem, as it is one of the most important components of the air conditioning system.

Table 8.1
Input and output items in system simulation of air conditioning

Data \ System	(1) Environmental space	(2) Air conditioning network	(3) A/C components
Input			
Characteristics of system	Building as a whole (location, surroundings) Dimension of space enclosure and building elements (walls, floors, etc.) Thermal properties of building elements (thermal conductivity, etc.)	Dimension of ducts and pipings (length, section, branches, etc.) Composition of duct and piping networks Pressure loss characteristics of ducts and pipings Heat gain from ducts and pipings Characteristics of flow control of dampers and valves Passage of outdoor air intake	Performance of fans and pumps Heat exchange performance of coils Capacity, size, number of components Part load efficiency of boilers and refrigeration machines
Excitations	Natural excitations (temperature, humidity, solar radiation, wind, etc.) Artificial excitations (lights, occupants, appliances)	Space cooling load (output of (1)) Outlet conditions of components (output of (3)) Preconditioning period and/or capacity of heat extraction	Inlet conditions of components (output of (2)) Heat load on components
Constraints	Set point of room air Schedule of usage (light, occupants, appliances)	Control mode Allowable range of room air temperature and humidity	Operation limit
Output			
Major responses	Space cooling load	Heat extraction Reheat load Outdoor air load Coil load Inlet conditions of components (input for (3))	Energy requirement to heat source Outlet conditions of components (input for (2))
Reference conditions	Temperature and humidity of building elements	Room air temperature and humidity Flow rate of air and water Degree of opening of valves and dampers	

Figure 8.2 shows a shell and tube type of water to water heat exchanger, and Fig. 8.3 represents the temperature distribution. In this case the system model for the heat exchanger is a set of mathematically expressed equations concerning the characteristics of the heat exchanger. In every equation for a system model an output stands on the left-hand side of the equal sign while input and known data are all included in the mathematical expressions on the right-hand side.

The problem here is to obtain the rate of heat exchanged and the outlet temperatures of both fluids from the inlet temperatures of both fluids and the configuration of heat exchanger. Defining the symbols to be used as follows:

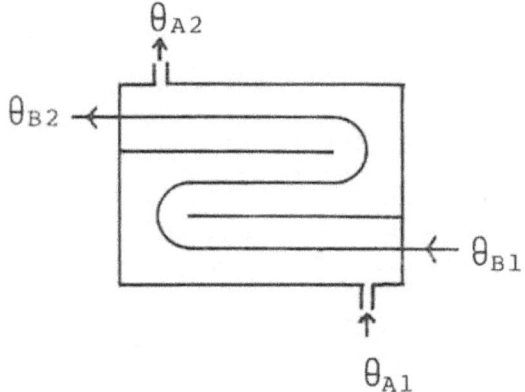

Fig. 8.2. Schematic configuration of shell and tube type of heat exchanger.

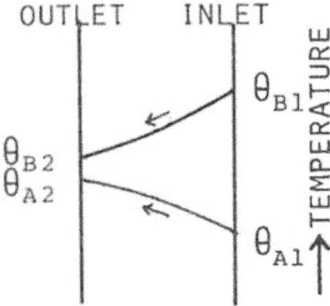

Fig. 8.3. Temperature distribution of both fluids in heat exchanger.

Input

θ_{A1} = inlet temperature of fluid A (°C),
θ_{B1} = inlet temperature of fluid B (°C),
S = surface area where heat is exchanged (m²),
K = thermal transmittance between fluid A and fluid B (W m^{-2} deg C^{-1}),
C_{pA} = specific heat of fluid A (J kg^{-1} degC^{-1}),
C_{pB} = specific heat of fluid B (J kg^{-1} degC^{-1}),
G_A = mass flow rate of fluid A (kg s^{-1}),
G_B = mass flow rate of fluid B (kg s^{-1}).

Output

H = rate of heat exchange (W),
θ_{A2} = outlet temperature of fluid A (°C),
θ_{B2} = outlet temperature of fluid B (°C).

Basic equations

$$H = C_{pA} G_A (\theta_{A2} - \theta_{A1}) \quad (8.1)$$

$$\theta_{A2} = \theta_{A1} + H/(C_{pA} G_A) \quad (8.1a)$$

$$H = C_{pB} G_B (\theta_{B1} - \theta_{B2}) \quad (8.2)$$

$$\theta_{B2} = \theta_{B1} + H/(C_{pB} G_B) \quad (8.2a)$$

$$H = KS \frac{\Delta\theta_1 - \Delta\theta_2}{\log \frac{\Delta\theta_1}{\Delta\theta_2}} \quad (8.3)$$

where $\Delta\theta_1 = \theta_{B1} - \theta_{A1}$, $\Delta\theta_2 = \theta_{B2} - \theta_{A2}$, $(\Delta\theta_1 - \Delta\theta_2) / \log(\Delta\theta_1 / \Delta\theta_2)$ is called logarithmic mean temperature differential.

These five basic equations are well known formulas for a heat exchanger. But these cannot be utilised as a system model by themselves, because the unknown values θ_{A2}, θ_{B2} and H are included in the right-hand side. up a system For setting up model from these relationships, it is necessary to solve the simultaneous equations for the three unknowns θ_{A2}, θ_{B2} and H. Iteration is often used to solve the equations, as in this case, when direct solution is not practical. The following sequence of calculation lends itself easily to the setting up of the system model.

Step 1. Assume the value of θ_{A2} in eqn. (8.1) and calculate H.
Step 2. Using H value from Step 1, calculate θ_{B2} from eqn. (8.2a).
Step 3. Calculate H from eqn. (8.3) into which the values of θ_{A2} and θ_{B2} in the above are to be substituted.
Step 4. Calculate θ_{A2} from eqn. (8.1a) using the new value of H obtained in Step 3 and compare it with the value assumed in Step 1.
Step 5. If the error found in the above comparison is small enough, go on to Step 6. If the error is not small enough, use the new values of θ_{A2} in Step 4 and the new values of H in Step 3, and go back to Step 2.
Step 6. The values of θ_{A2}, θ_{B2} and H currently in use are the output.

The sequence of calculation step by step as described in the above is called "algorithm", which makes it easy to write as a computer program.

8.2. SIMULATION OF THE DUAL DUCT SYSTEM

The dual duct system is considered as an almost ideal system to attain the utmost comfort in a space. Easy and certain control is possible, as there is always a supply of hot air and cold air close to the space concerned. It is often considered, however, that the dual duct system wastes a lot of energy because the process of mixing hot air and cold air always gives rise to some amount of energy loss. Nevertheless, an example of system simulation with the dual duct system is introduced here as it is theoretically clear and easy to be understood.

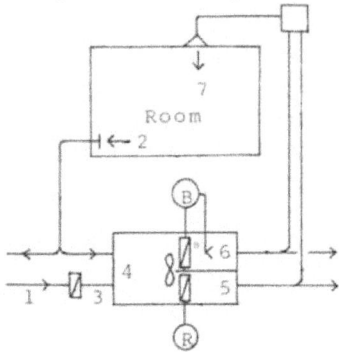

Fig. 8.4.   Basic diagram of dual duct system.

Figure 8.4 shows a typical diagram of a dual duct system. The numbers in the diagram refer to the condition of the air as shown in the psychrometric chart in Fig. 8.5. B stands for boiler and R for refrigerating machine.

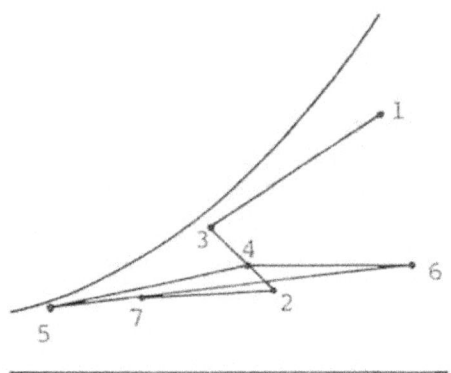

Fig. 8.5.   Change of state in psychrometric chart (umbers correspond to those of Fig. 8.4).

The space cooling load based on constant room air temperature is considered as known for 24 hours a day from the results of simulation of environmental space as listed in Table 8.1:

$$H_{CL}(n) = H_{CLS}(n) + H_{CLL}(n) \tag{8.4}$$

where $H_{CL}(n)$ = total space cooling load at time n(W) and $H_{CLS}(n)$, $H_{CLL}(n)$ = sensible and latent cooling loads respectively at time n(W).

Neglecting heat storage effect for latent heat, it follows:

$$H_{HEL}(n) = H_{CLL}(n) \tag{8.5}$$

where $H_{HEL}(n)$ = latent heat extraction at time n(W).

As described in eqns. (7.31) and (7.32) of the preceding chapter, sensible heat extraction is expressed as:

$$H_{HES}(n) = H_{CLS}(n) + \sum_{j=0}^{\infty} W_z(j) \cdot \theta_r(n-j) + K(n) \cdot \theta_r(n) \tag{8.6}$$

where $H_{HES}(n)$ = sensible heat extraction at time n(W), $\theta_r(n)$ = room air temperature deviation from the reference set point (°C), $W_z(j)$ = heat extraction weighting factors for room air temperature deviation (W degC^{-1}) and $K(n)$ = coefficient associated with infiltration for room air temperature deviation at time n (W degC^{-1}).

Total heat extraction is the sum of sensible and latent heat extractions at all times, namely:

$$H_{HE}(n) = H_{HES}(n) + H_{HEL}(n) \tag{8.7}$$

where $H_{HE}(n)$ = total heat extraction at time n (W).

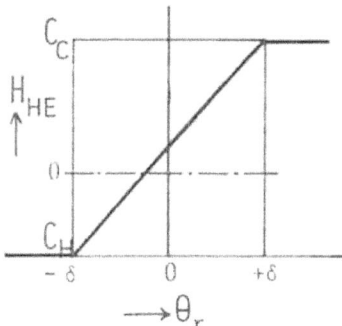

Fig. 8.6. Characteristic of proportional control.

Substituting eqns. (8.4), (8.5) and (8.6) into eqn. (8.7):

$$H_{HE}(n) = H_{CL}(n) + \sum_{j=0}^{\infty} W_z(j) \cdot \theta_r(n-j) + K(n) \cdot \theta_r(n) \tag{8.8}$$

Equation (8.8) is to be applied here to the conditioned period when the room air temperature swings between the upper and lower limits of specified temperature range. The dual duct system under discussion has such characteristics, as the heat extraction is proportionally controlled at the same rate as the room air temperature deviation as shown in Fig. 8.6. This characteristic can be expressed by the following:

$$H_{HE}(n) = A \cdot \theta_r(n) + B \qquad (8.9)$$

$$\text{If } \theta_r(n) \geq \delta \quad H_{HE}(n) = C_C$$
$$\text{If } \theta_r(n) \leq -\delta \quad H_{HE}(n) = C_H \qquad (8.10)$$

$$A = \frac{C_C - C_H}{2\delta} \quad B = \frac{C_C + C_H}{2} \qquad (8.11)$$

where C_C = cooling capacity, maximum cooling heat extraction by cold air (W), C_H = heating capacity, maximum heating heat extraction by hot air (negative value) (W) and δ = one half of allowable room air temperature deviation range from the set point (°C).

Solving eqns. (8.8) and (8.9) for $H_{HE}(n)$ and $\theta_r(n)$, the following equations can be obtained, namely:

$$\theta_r(n) = \frac{1}{A - W_z(0) - K(n)} \left(H_{CL}(n) - B + \sum_{j=1}^{\infty} W_z(j) \cdot \theta_r(n-j) \right) \qquad (8.12)$$

$$H_{HE}(n) = \frac{A}{A - W_z(0) - K(n)}$$
$$\times \left(H_{CL}(n) - B + \sum_{j=1}^{\infty} W_z(j) \cdot \theta_r(n-j) \right) + B \qquad (8.13)$$

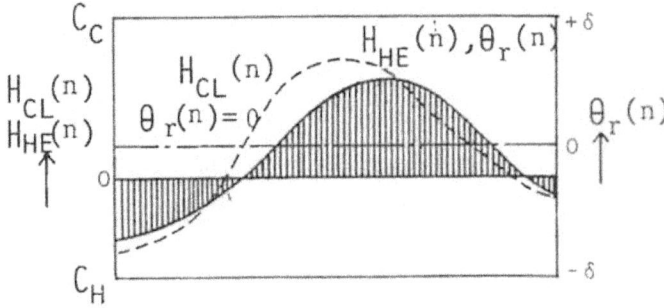

Fig. 8.7. Variation of room air temperature and heat extraction.

Since $H_{HE}(n)$ is always proportional to $\theta_r(n)$, they can be illustrated in the same graph as shown by the solid curve in Fig. 8.7. while the dotted curve indicates $H_{CL}(n)$ for $\theta_r(n) = 0$.

From eqns. (8.4), (8.5) and (8.13), sensible heat extraction is expressed by:

$$H_{\text{HES}}(n) = \frac{A}{A - W_z(0) - K(n)} \left(H_{\text{CLS}}(n) - B + \sum_{j=1}^{\infty} W_z(j)\theta_r(n-j) \right)$$
$$+ \frac{W_z(0) + K(n)}{A - W_z(0) - K(n)} H_{\text{CLL}} + B \qquad (8.14)$$

The following are the algorithms to obtain the performance data in the psychrometric process around the air conditioner connected with the dual duct system shown in Fig. 8.4.

Step 1. The conditions of outdoor air after precooling assuming sensible and latent precooling as $H_{3S}(n)$ and $H_{3L}(n)$ respectively so that:

$$\begin{aligned} H_3(n) &= H_{3S}(n) + H_{3L}(n) \\ \theta_3(n) &= \theta_1(n) - H_{3S}(n)/k_o(n) G C_p \\ x_3(n) &= x_1(n) - H_{3L}(n)/k_o(n) G \cdot r \end{aligned} \qquad (8.15)$$

Step 2. Mixed conditions of outside air and return air:

$$\begin{aligned} \theta_4(n) &= k_o(n)\theta_3(n) + [1 - k_o(n)]\theta_2(n) \\ x_4(n) &= k_o(n)x_3(n) + [1 - k_o(n)]x_2(n) \end{aligned} \qquad (8.16)$$

Step 3. Conditions of air after filter and fan:

$$\begin{aligned} \theta_5(n) &= \theta_4(n) + \Delta\theta_F \\ x_6(n) &= x_4(n) \end{aligned} \qquad (8.17)$$

Step 4. Discharge air temperature after mixing box:

$$\begin{aligned} \theta_7(n) &= k_c(n)\theta_5 + [1 - k_c(n)]\theta_6 \\ k_c(n) &= \frac{\theta_r(n)}{2\delta} + \frac{1}{2} \end{aligned} \qquad (8.18)$$

Step 5. Sensible heat extraction at cooling and heating coils:

$$\begin{aligned} H_{5S}(n) &= k_c(n)C_p G[\theta_4(n) - \theta_5] \\ H_{6S}(n) &= [1 - k_c(n)]C_p G[\theta_4(n) - \theta_6] \end{aligned} \qquad (8.19)$$

Step 6. Humidity ratio of hot air and cold air:

$$x_5(n) = f[x_4(n), \theta_5]$$
$$x_6(n) = x_4(n) \qquad (8.20)$$

Step 7. Discharge air humidity after mixing box:

$$x_{5L}(n) = k_c(n) \cdot x_5(n) + [1 - k_c(n)] \cdot x_6(n) \qquad (8.21)$$

Step 8. Latent heat extraction at cooling and heating coils:

$$H_{5L}(n) = k_c(n) \cdot G \cdot [x_4(n) - x_5(n)]$$
$$H_{6L}(n) = 0 \qquad (8.22)$$

where θ, x = temperature and humidity ratio of air respectively at various points in the system whose subscripts correspond to the numbers shown in Fig. 8.4 and Fig. 8.5(°C), (g kg^{-1}), $k_o(n)$ = ratio of outdoor air intake to total air flow rate (–), $k_c(n)$ = ratio of cold air flow rate to total air flow rate (–), G = total mass air flow rate (kg s^{-1}), C_p = specific heat of air (kJ kg^{-1} deg C^{-1}), r = latent heat of water vaporisation (kJ g^{-1}) and $\Delta\theta_F$ = temperature rise across the fan (°C).

It must be noted that system simulations in the psychrometric process throughout the duct loop are made on a steady state basis, whereas heat extraction is calculated on an unsteady state basis. This is because all the components have lighter mass, responding quickly to the change of temperature, and thus transient performance is neglected in the simulation.

8.3. AN EXAMPLE OF COMPONENT SIMULATION

An air conditioning system involves various kinds of components where the temperature and humidity of air vary or where the liquid temperature varies. A component that requires special consideration is the cooling coil. A cooling coil is a heat exchanger where air is cooled down while passing through chilled water coils; this causes water vapour within the air to condense on the surfaces of fins attached to the tubing as the surface temperature falls below the dew point of the air. In the case of a heating coil, the air temperature rises after passing through the coils, but the humidity ratio does not change. Condensation on the cooling coil makes the problem difficult. Approximation is usually employed instead of the rigorous determination of the heat and mass transfer processes. All the data needed for subsequent calculation are the temperature and humidity ratio of outlet air and the temperature of outlet water, from which the rate of heat exchange can be calculated.

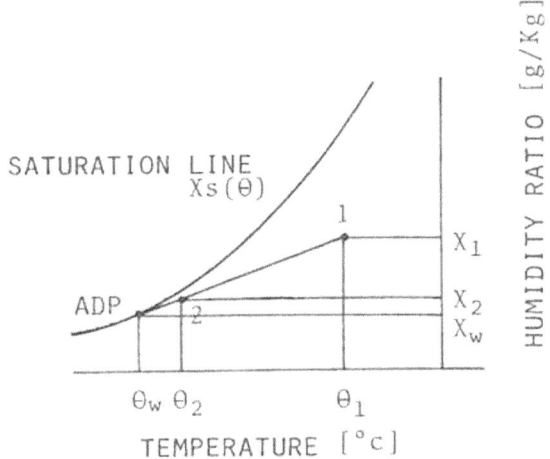

Fig. 8.8. Psychrometric process of cooling coil.

Referring to Fig. 8.8, a simple method of simulating the process across the cooling coil may be the one which uses a contact factor. A contact factor may be defined as the ratio of the flow rate of the air whose temperature reaches the apparatus dew point to the total flow rate of the air. The apparatus dew point can be considered nearly equal to the average of inlet and outlet temperature of chilled water in the coil. The rest of the air is considered to flow between the fins of the coil. This is an entirely hypothetical concept, but gives a very simple answer. Namely, giving the average water temperature in the coil θ_w and inlet air temperature θ_1, the outlet air temperature θ_2 can be expressed as:

$$\theta_2 = F_c \theta_w + (1 - F_c)\theta_1 \tag{8.23}$$

where F_c = contact factor.

For obtaining the humidity ratio of outlet air x_2, it is necessary to find the saturated humidity ratio against θ_w, which must be expressed in the form of a function:

$$x_w = x_s(\theta_w) \tag{8.24}$$

The function $x_s(\theta)$ can be derived from the Goff and Gratch equation that gives $f_s(\theta)$, the water vapour pressure balanced with water of θ (°C) in mmHg as follows:

$$\log f_s(\theta) = -7 \cdot 9028(\sigma - 1) + 5 \cdot 02808 \log \sigma$$
$$- 1 \cdot 3816 \times 10^{-7} [10^{11 \cdot 344(1 - 1/\sigma)} - 1]$$
$$+ 8 \cdot 1328 \times 10^{-3} [10^{-3 \cdot 49149(\sigma - 1)} - 1] + \log 1 \cdot 03323$$
$$\tag{8.25}$$

where $\sigma = 273 \cdot 16/(273 \cdot 16 + \theta)$.

Then $x_s(\theta)$ is given by:

$$x_s(\theta) = 622 \frac{f_s(\theta)}{f_a - f_s(\theta)} \quad (8.25a)$$

The function $x_s(\theta)$ may be approximately expressed in a polynomial such as:

$$x_s(\theta) = a_0 + a_1\theta + a_2\theta^2 + a_3\theta^3 + a_4\theta^4 \quad (8.26)$$

where $a_0 = 3.6066$, $a_1 = 0.27216$, $a_2 = 0.013314$, $a_3 = 0.11470 \times 10^{-3}$ and $a_4 = 0.80142 \times 10^{-5}$.

Then, the humidity ratio of outlet air x_2 is given by:

$$x_2 = F_C x_w + (1 - F_C) X_1 \quad (8.27)$$

where x_1 = humidity ratio of inlet air (g kg^{-1}), x_w = humidity ratio against θ_w(g kg^{-1}).

8.4. PART-LOAD PERFORMANCE OF AIR CONDITIONING COMPONENTS

Energy conversion equipment such as boilers, engines and refrigeration machines generally performs less efficiently when only a partial load is imposed on it than when it operates at full load. This is because equipment of this type is made so that it operates most efficiently at full load. The efficiency of energy conversion equipment is often expressed by the value of output energy to input energy, viz.,

$$\eta = \frac{E_o}{E_1} \quad (8.28)$$

where E_1 = energy supplied to the equipment over a given period (J), E_o = useful energy produced by the equipment over the same period (J). Thus:

$$E_o = \int_0^T H_o(t)\,dt \quad (8.29a)$$

$$E_1 = \int_0^T H_1(t)\,dt \quad (8.29b)$$

where t = time (s), $H_o(t)$ = heat output at time t (W), $H_1(t)$ = heat input at time t (W) and T = given period (s).

The heat required for the equipment is often called the heat load. The heat load on the equipment generally varies with time as described in the preceding chapter. The equipment then should operate to supply an equal amount of heat to the heat load. Namely:

$$H_o(t) = H_L(t) \tag{8.30}$$

where $H_L(t)$ = heat load at time t (W).

If the heat load at time t is less than the maximum probable heat demand $H_{L\max}$, the efficiency is usually less than in the case that $H_o(t) = H_{L\max}$.

The efficiency of the equipment at off-peak load is called the part-load efficiency and is a function of ratio of the load to full load, i.e.

$$\eta = f(p) \tag{8.31}$$

$$p = \frac{H_L(t)}{H_{L\max}} \tag{8.32}$$

Hence the heat input required for the equipment to yield the necessary amount of heat to be supplied to the main system at time t is:

$$H_1(t) = \frac{H_L(t)}{f(p)} \tag{8.33}$$

For example, if one uses a boiler showing such a performance as illustrated in Fig. 8.9, part load efficiency is expressed in a linear relationship to load factor as:

$$\eta = 0 \cdot 6 + 0 \cdot 2 \cdot p \tag{8.34}$$

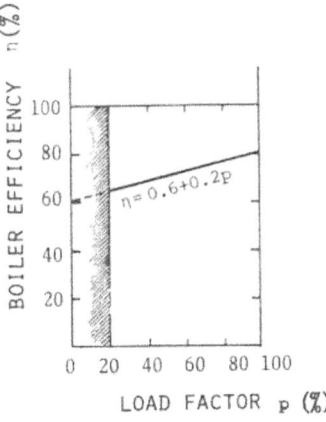

Fig. 8.9. Part-load efficiency of boiler (hypothetical).

When the main system calls for heat at time t at the rate of $H_L(t)$, which is 0·3 of full load for example, the efficiency at time t is:

$$\eta(t) = 0 \cdot 6 \times 0 \cdot 2 \times 0 \cdot 3 = 0 \cdot 66 \tag{8.35}$$

Then the heat input required for the boiler is:

$$H_1(t) = \frac{H_L(t)}{\eta(t)} = \frac{H_L(t)}{0 \cdot 66} \tag{8.36}$$

In the case of a centrifugal refrigeration machine, input energy is fed to the compressor in the form of electricity and the output is the rate of chilled water produced in the evaporator as a calorific quantity. The part-load performance is often expressed as a relationship between the heat rejection factor and the part-load factor as shown in Fig. 8.10. Heat rejection factor F_R is defined as:

$$F_R = \frac{\text{rate of heat exchange in condenser}}{\text{rate of heat exchange in evaporator}} \tag{8.37}$$

Load factor F_L is defined as:

$$F_L = \frac{\text{rate of heat load in chilled water } (H_c)}{\text{maximam rate of heat load in chilled water } (H_{c\max})} \tag{8.38}$$

Figure 8.10 shows only one curve, for example, for the case where the condensing temperature is 45°C and the evaporating temperature is 0°C and other curves are prepared for other conditions.

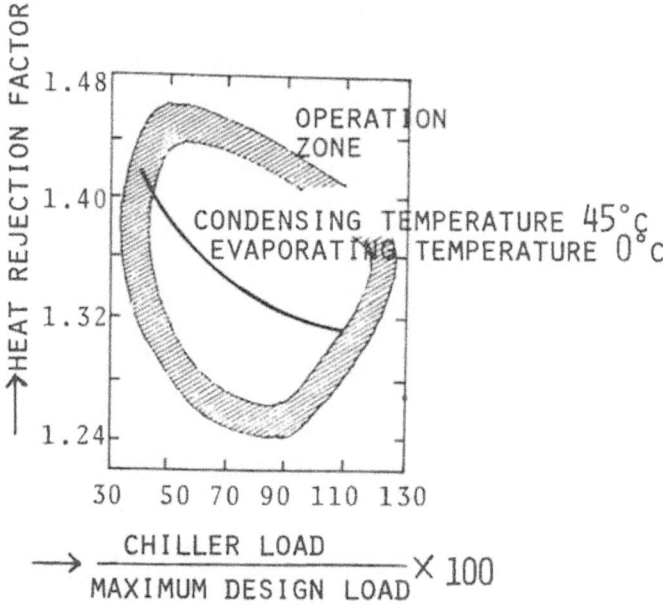

Fig. 8.10. Part-load performance of centrifugal refrigeration machine (generated from ASHRAE Guide and Data Book-Systems, 1970, p. 81).

It is necessary to use simulation to convert the curve into an equation to express F_R as a function of F_L:

$$F_R = f(F_L) \tag{8.39}$$

Polynomial fitting [8.2, 8.3] is often used to approximate the performance curve such as the one shown in Fig. 8.10. For example, if one uses the third order polynomial, eqn. (8.39) may be expressed as:

$$F_R = a_0 + a_1 F_L + a_2 F_L^2 + a_3 F_L^3 \tag{8.40}$$

where a_0, a_1, a_2 and a_3 are constants.

It is important to determine the range to which eqn. (8.40) is applied as shown in Fig. 8.10 where the operable zone is indicated.

It is also known that the efficiency of the refrigeration machine η_R can be expressed as a function of heat rejection factor in the form:

$$\eta_R = \frac{F_R}{F_R - 1} \tag{8.41}$$

On the other hand, the efficiency of the refrigeration machine η_R is the ratio of output cooling effect H_c to power input to compressor H_p viz.,

$$\eta_R = \frac{H_c}{H_p} \tag{8.42}$$

Of course, H_c may be equal to the cooling load on the cooling coil in air conditioner if the heat gain from pipes and pumps is neglected.

As all terms are variables with time, results of component simulation can be obtained from the following sequence:

Step 1. Calculate load factor at time t:

$$F_L(t) = H_c(t) / H_{c\,max} \tag{8.43}$$

Step 2. Calculate heat rejection factor at time t:

$$F_R(t) = f[F_L(t)] \tag{8.44}$$

Step 3. Calculate efficiency of refrigeration machine at time t:

$$\eta_R(t) = \frac{F_R(t)}{F_R(t) - 1} \tag{8.45}$$

Step 4. Calculate power input to compressor at time t:

$$H_p(t) = H_c(t) / \eta_R(t) \tag{8.46}$$

8.5. SIMULATION OF HEAT STORAGE SYSTEM

The heat storage system is one of the systems of air conditioning employed in large buildings and is unique to Japan. It is usually a water reservoir placed beneath the floor of the lowest basement by utilising the space between the foundation girders of the building as shown in Fig. 8.11. The purpose of heat storage in the water tank is to make the heat load variation during the day as even as possible. This can be achieved by operating the heat source components of smaller capacity during the night using off-peak electricity to store hot or cold water in the storage tank and then extracting the stored heat whenever room spaces

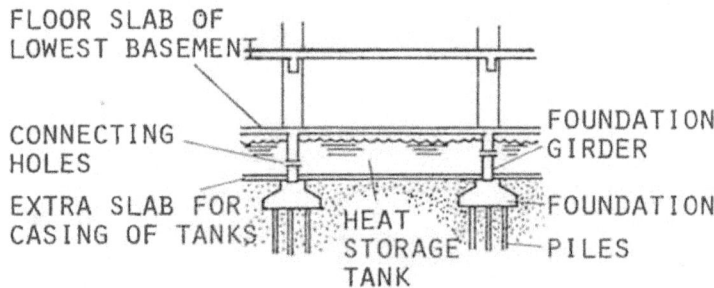

Fig. 8.11.   Configuration of heat storage tank beneath the basement.

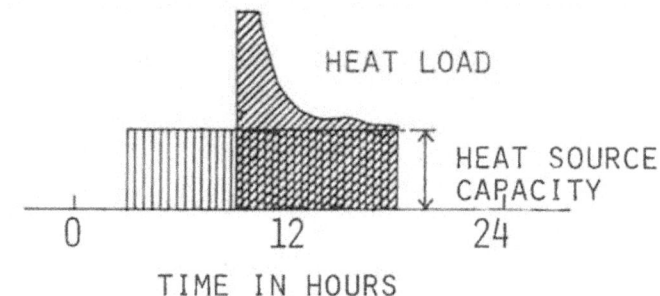

Fig. 8.12.   Profile of heat load and heat source operation with storage system.

call for heat. Without a heat storage system, a larger capacity of heat source equipment would be required for preconditioning prior to the time when occupancy starts in the morning as depicted in Fig. 8.12. The heat storage system is often coupled with a heat recovery system to remove a considerable amount of heat from lights and to store it in the storage tank for heating on the following day.

Basically, there are two loops around the heat storage tank of the air conditioning system as shown in Fig. 8.13. One is connected to the heat source and the other to the heat load.

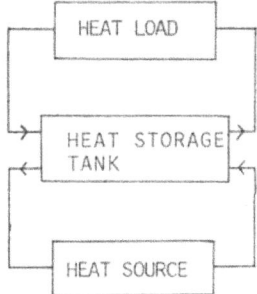

Fig. 8.13. Basic two loops around heat storage tank.

Two simple models of heat storage tank can be conceived. One is the perfect mixing type and the other is the piston flow type. The perfect mixing type of storage tank is the one in which the incoming water is perfectly mixed instantaneously so that there is no temperature distribution within the tank at any time. The piston flow type of storage tank is the one in which the incoming water is not mixed with the water in the tank but pushed forward so that the outgoing water temperature stays constant until a certain instant is reached when the incoming water flows out. If the temperature of the incoming water were constant, the temperature of the outgoing water of perfect mixing type would vary like line A in Fig. 8.14 (a) and that of piston flow type like line B. It is considered natural, however, that the temperature of outgoing water in general should vary like line C, which is somewhat between the above two types.

Figure 8.14 (b) shows the response of the outlet water temperature for constant temperature difference between inlet and outlet, which is useful for the actual convolution process to be described later.

In the water type of heat storage tank the incoming water is considered to be diffused within the tank and a temperature distribution builds up there at any time. It is necessary, therefore, to analyse the thermal performance of the heat storage tank as a system on an unsteady state basis.

Nakajima [8.4] introduced a theoretical model of heat storage system for air conditioning allowing for the diffusion process in the mixing mechanism of water in the tank.

For both loops around the tank as in Fig. 8.13 the fundamental response function of outlet water temperature for inlet water temperature can be expressed in the convolution form as

$$\Theta_2(t) = \int_0^t w_\Theta(\tau) \cdot \Theta_1(t-\tau) d\tau \qquad (8.47)$$

where $\Theta_1(t)$ = temperature difference between inlet and outlet (deg C), $\Theta_2(t)$ = outlet temperature in reference to the initial water temperature in the tank (deg C), $w_\Theta(\tau)$ = impulse response of outlet temperature for $\Theta_1(\tau)$.

To allow eqn. (8.47) to be expressed in dimensionless time Φ, the following conversion must be made, i.e.,

$$\Phi = \frac{t}{t_r} \quad t_r = \frac{V}{L} \tag{8.48}$$

where t_r = average staying period of water in the tank (s), V = volume of water tank (m³) and L = water flow rate (m³ s⁻¹).

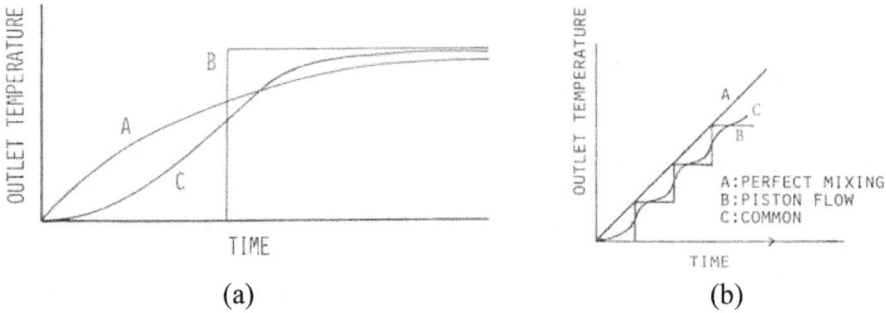

(a)   (b)

Fig. 8.14. Response of outlet temperature for inlet temperature when the temperature differential between inlet and outlet is constant [8.4].

Thus eqn. (8.47) may be converted into:

$$\Theta_2(\Phi) = \int_0^\Phi w(\zeta) \cdot \Theta_1(\Phi - \zeta) d\zeta \tag{8.49}$$

Assuming the diffusion process within the tank as a one-dimensional process in the direction of x, the temperature of water in the tank $\Theta(x, t)$ may be expressed by solving the following partial differential equation, namely:

$$\frac{\partial \Theta}{\partial \Phi} = E \frac{\partial^2 \Theta}{\partial x^2} - u \frac{\partial \Theta}{\partial x} \tag{8.50}$$

where E = diffusion coefficient (m² s⁻¹) and u = flow velocity of water (ms⁻¹).

When the inlet temperature is given in the form of a delta function, the solution of eqn. (8.50) for $\Theta_2(\Phi)$ is derived as

$$w(\Phi) = \sum_{n=1}^{\infty} \frac{2(-1)^{n+1} \mu_n^2 \exp(M)}{M^2 + 2M + \mu_n^2} \exp\left[-\left(\frac{M^2 + \mu_n^2}{2M}\right)\Phi\right] \tag{8.51}$$

where

μ_n = the nth positive root of the equation,

$$\cot \mu = \frac{1}{2}\left(\frac{\mu}{M} - \frac{M}{\mu}\right) \qquad (8.52)$$

$$M = \frac{ul}{2E} \qquad (8.53)$$

l = equivalent length of water storage tank (m)

$$l = ut_r \qquad (8.54)$$

M is a parameter characterising the mixing nature of the water in the storage tank; $M = 0$ for perfect mixing type and $M = \infty$ for piston flow type.

It is convenient for practical simulation purposes to state the response of outlet water temperature for the difference in heat flow in and out of the storage tank. Namely, the excitation function is given as

$$D(\Phi) = \frac{H_1(\Phi) - H_2(\Phi)}{C_p \gamma L} \qquad (8.55)$$

where $H_1(\Phi)$ = heat supplied to storage tank (W), $H_2(\Phi)$ = heat extracted from storage tank (W), $D(\Phi)$ = temperature decrease (deg C), C_p = specific heat of water (J kg^{-1} deg^{-1}), γ = specific weight of water (kg m^{-3}).

The outlet water temperature is obtained by solving the following integral equation:

$$\Theta_2(\Phi) - \int_0^\Phi w(\tau)\Theta_2(\Phi - \tau)d\tau = \int_0^\Phi w(\tau)D(\Phi - \tau)dt \qquad (8.56)$$

When $D(\Phi)$ is given in the form of unit function $U(\Phi)$, the solution function of eqn. (8.56), $A(\Phi)$, is given by Nakajima as in the following approximated equations depending on the parameter M [8.4]:

$M \le 7\cdot 5:$
$$A(\Phi) = \frac{1}{q}\left[1 - q + \left(\frac{q}{P}\Phi - b\right)U(\Phi - b)\right]$$

$M \le 12\cdot 5:$
$$A(\Phi) = \frac{1}{q}\left[1 - q + \frac{q}{P}\Phi - b - c_1 \exp\left(-\frac{q}{P}d_1\Phi\right)\sin 2\pi\left(\frac{q}{P}\Phi - b\right)\right.$$

$$\left. - c_2 \exp\left(-\frac{q}{P}d_2\Phi\right)\sin 2\pi\left(\frac{q}{P}\Phi - b\right)\right]\dots\dots\dots(8.57)$$

$$M = \infty: \qquad A(\Phi) = \sum_{r=1}^{\infty} U(\Phi - r)$$

where constants b, c_1, d_1, c_2 and d_2 are the values listed in Table 8.2, P = ratio of effective volume of storage tank taking account of dead zone (−) and q = ratio of effective flow taking account of short circuit flow in the tank (−).

Table 8.2
Constants for eqn. (8.57)

M	0	0·5	1·0	2·0	4·0	7·5	12·5	25·0	50·0	100
b	0	0·167	0·250	0·333	0·400	0·441	0·463	0·480	0·490	0·495
c_1							0·351	0·327	0·323	0·280
d_1							1·463	0·779	0·427	0·128
c_2									0·098	0·053
d_2									1·167	0·073

In order to combine the above equations with the heat load calculation routine for the overall simulation of an air conditioning system including heat storage tank, it is necessary to have eqns. (8.57) converted into the form expressed in time series by means of the procedure as explained in Chapter 2: the response for a unit function must be converted into the response for a triangular pulse.

8.6. SIMULATION OF HEAT RECOVERY SYSTEM

Heat recovery is essential in a modern air conditioning system in terms of energy conservation. There are two major items for heat recovery in air conditioning: one is to make use of heat of lights for space heating in winter time coupled with a heat storage tank and the other is to make use of waste heat from exhaust air to be exchanged with intaking outside air particularly in summer.

Quantitative assessments must be made at the design stage of the building and of the air conditioning system on the possible savings of annual energy consumption for heating and cooling using a heat recovery system compared with conventional air conditioning systems. An example of simulation study is introduced here on the preliminary analysis of annual energy consumption with different arrangements of an air conditioning system for a large office building in Tokyo. The hour by hour calculation was made by the engineering team of an architect's firm with the aid of a computer [8.5]. Table 8.3 shows the conditions of calculation for the building.

The cases compared with regard to outside air intake were the following:
Case 1. Rate of outside air intake is constant.
Case 2. Rate of outside air intake is variable depending on the occupancy.
Case 3. Total heat exchanger is used.
Case 4. Combination of Cases 2 and 3.

Table 8.3
Conditions for simulation

Floor area of a typical floor	2650 m^2
Effective rentable ratio	71 %
Lights	25 W m^{-2}
Occupants	1 person per 7 m^2
Rate of outside air intake	35 m^3 per person
Design room conditions:	
winter (December–March)	DB = 22 °C, RH = 50 %
spring and autumn	DB = 23·5 °C, RH = 50 %
summer (June–September)	DB = 25 °C, RH = 50 %
Hours of air conditioning operation	
weekdays 8 am–5 pm	
Saturdays 8 am–2 pm	
Sundays, holidays and new year's vacation 31 Dec.–3 Jan. no operation	

The results from hour by hour computation for 365 consecutive days using the standard weather data of Tokyo are shown in Fig. 8.15 and Table 8.4. Figure 8.15 represents monthly total energy consumption with the above four cases compared with monthly total heat extraction that does not include outside air load. It can be understood that the effect of the total heat exchanger is significant in summer months but rather poor in winter months. This is because the total heat exchange in winter partially offsets the cooling effect of the outside air at low temperature. Table 8.4 gives a summary of annual energy consumption expressed as a percentage relative to the Case 1

Table 8.4
Results of simulation—relative annual energy consumption for cooling and heating (%)

		Case 1	Case 2	Case 3	Case 4
Without control of outside air intake for cooling in winter	cooling	100	98	100	104
	heating	100	61	51	44
	total	100	85	82	82
With control of outside air intake for cooling in winter	cooling	100	87	81	77
	heating	100	61	51	44
	total	100	78	71	65

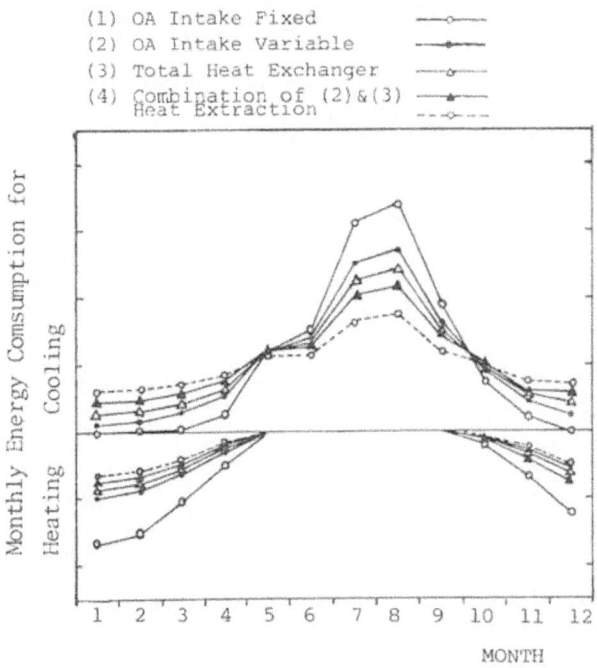

Fig. 8.15. Monthly energy consumption with different systems of outside air intake [8.5].

This shows that the energy saving in heating by variable outside air intake and by the use of a total heat exchanger is significant, whereas these would not contribute much to energy saving on an annual basis.
If another control were added to make use of the outside air intake for cooling in winter by eliminating the function of these two arrangements during the period, annual energy consumption for cooling would have been much reduced as shown by the figures in the bottom line of Table 8.4.

8.7. Simulation of Solar Heat Collector

The solar heat collector is the core component of the solar utilisation system. There are many different kinds of collectors. Here a flat plate, water flow type of collector is described as it is the most commonly used type. The fundamental section of the collector is shown in Fig. 8.16, where solar radiation is transmitted through the glass covering and absorbed by the collector plate, to be transferred to the water that flows within the pipe attached to the plate. Back insulation is used to prevent the solar heat from escaping to the rear side.

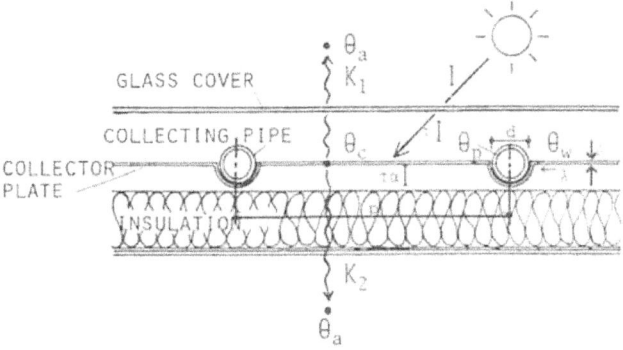

Fig. 8.16. Section of collector.

The amount of solar energy collected by the flat plate solar heat collector is given by a very simple formula known as the Hottel-Whillier-Bliss equation [8.6, 8.7] that states:

$$q_c = \tau\alpha I - K(\theta_c - \theta_a) = F_R[\tau\alpha I - K(\theta_{w1} - \alpha_a)] \tag{8.58}$$

where q_c = collection (W m^{-2}), F_R = heat removal efficiency, τ = solar transmissivity of glass covering, α = absorptivity of collector plate, K = thermal transmittance from collector plate to the ambient air (W m^{-2} deg C^{-1}), θ_c = plate temperature (°C), θ_{w1} = inlet water temperature (°C) and θ_a = ambient air temperature (°C).

Strictly speaking, all terms on the right-hand side or eqn. (8.58) are variables. For practical simulation purposes, therefore, one must decide how much approximation can be allowed for in respective cases. The following are the algorithms to obtain the outlet water temperature and the rate of collection from inlet water temperature, water flow rate and other data related to collector configuration.

Input
- $\tau\alpha$ = the product of transmissivity of sheet glass and absorptivity of collector plate including the effects of dirt and shadow cast by framing (–),
- $I(n)$ = total solar radiation upon collector surface at time n (W m^{-2}),
- K_1, K_2 = thermal transmittance from collector plate to ambient air through glass covering and through back insulation respectively (Wm^{-2} degC^{-1})
- $\theta_a(n)$ = ambient air temperature including the equivalent temperature differential due to long wavelength radiation exchange, at time n (°C),
- $\theta_{w1}(n)$ = inlet water temperature to the collector at time n (°C),
- d = diameter of collector pipe (m),
- p = pitch between collector pipes (m),
- δ = thickness of collector plate (m),
- λ = thermal conductivity of collector plate (Wm^{-1} degC^{-1}),

α_p = film coefficient along the inside surface of collecting pipe (Wm^{-2} deg C^{-1}),
λ_b = thermal conductivity of bond material (Wm^{-1} degC^{-1}),
g = thickness of bond material (m),
b = length of bond (m),
G = water flow rate per unit collector area (kg m^{-2} s^{-1}),
C_p = specific heat of fluid in the collecting pipe (J kg^{-1} degC^{-1}).

Output
$q_c(n)$ = rate or collection per unit collector area at time n (W m^{-2}),
$\theta_{w2}(n)$ = outlet water temperature of collector at time n(°C),
$\eta_c(n)$ = collector efficiency at time n.

Calculation sequence

Step 1. Combined thermal transmittance from collector plate to ambient air, K (W m^{-2} degC^{-1}):

$$K = K_1 + K_2 \tag{8.59}$$

If the rear side of collector faces an interior space with temperature θ_r:

$$K = K_1 + K_2 \frac{\theta_c(n) - \theta_r(n)}{\theta_c(n) - \theta_a(n)} \tag{8.60}$$

where θ_c is expected average collector plate temperature during collection and θ_a is expected average ambient air temperature during collection.

Step 2. Fin efficiency, Φ', Φ:

$$\Phi' = \frac{\tanh\left(\frac{p-d}{2}\sqrt{\frac{K}{\lambda\delta}}\right)}{\frac{p-d}{2}\sqrt{\frac{K}{\lambda\delta}}} \tag{8.61}$$

$$\Phi = \Phi' + \frac{d}{p}(1 - \Phi') \tag{8.62}$$

Step 3. Heat removal efficiency, F_R:

$$F_R = \frac{1 - \exp\left(-\frac{K}{GC_p}\right)}{\frac{K}{GC_p}} \cdot \frac{1}{\frac{1}{\Phi} + \frac{pK}{\pi d\alpha_p} + \frac{gpK}{\lambda_p b}} \tag{8.63}$$

Step 4. Rate of collection at time n, $q_c(n)$ (W m^{-2}):

$$q_c(n) = F_R\{\tau\alpha I(n) - K[\theta_{w1}(n) - \theta_a(n)]\} \qquad (8.64)$$

If $\tau\alpha I(n) - K[\theta_{w1}(n) - \theta_a(n)] < 0 \qquad q_c(n) = 0$

Step 5. Outlet water temperature of collector at time n, $\theta_{w2}(n)$ (°C):

$$\theta_{w2}(n) = \theta_{w1}(n) + \frac{q_c(n)}{GC_p} \qquad (8.65)$$

Step 6. Collector efficiency at time n, η_c:

$$\eta_c(n) = q_c(n) / I(n) \qquad (8.66)$$

For more strict simulation, the value of $\tau\alpha$ must be changed with solar incidence angle and corrected by taking account of multi-reflection between the glass and the collector plate. In the case where a selective surface is used for the collector plate, the value of K_1 must be modified. Otherwise radiation exchange between the glass and the collector plate should be incorporated in the sequence of the calculation by deriving the glass temperature as an unknown variable.

8.8. SIMULATION OF SOLAR HEATING SYSTEM

There are many kinds of solar space heating devices and systems. One of the simplest systems would be the one as shown in Fig. 8.17. The system consists of collector, storage tank, auxiliary heater, heating units, circulating pumps, three-way valve and control devices.

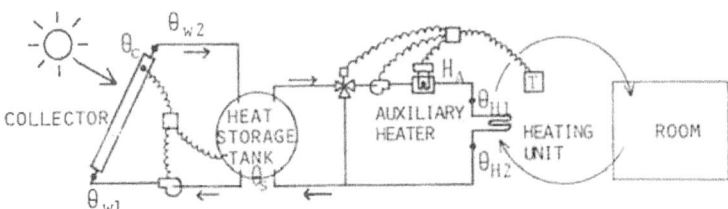

Fig. 8.17. Schematic diagram or solar heating system.

The collector pump is started when the collector plate temperature near the outlet gets higher than the water temperature in the storage tank by 3-5 degrees in practice and stops when this temperature difference is reduced to 0-1 degrees. Collection of solar energy is achieved while the collector pump is operating. Solar energy collected is stored in the solar tank and the water temperature in the tank gets gradually higher and higher until the pump stops in the late afternoon. Whenever the room space calls for heat, the circulation pump operates to withdraw hot water from the solar tank, to deliver it to the heating unit and to return the cooled water back to the tank.

The auxiliary heater is switched on when there is not enough heat left in the solar tank and the three-way valve controls the proportion of water flow from the solar tank.

The algorithm for the system simulation may be written as in the following, assuming a small tank that the water temperature in the tank would be uniform at any instant:

Input

$\tau\alpha$ = product of transmissivity of sheet glass and absorptivity of collector plate,
$I(n)$ = total solar radiation upon collector surface at time n (W m^{-2}),
K = combined thermal transmittance from collector plate to ambient air (W m^{-2} deg C^{-1}),
$\theta_a(n)$ = ambient air temperature at time n (°C),
A_c = collector area (m^2),
F_R = heat removal efficiency of collector (eqn. (8.63)),
$\theta_{w1}(n)$ = inlet water temperature collector at time n (°C),
G = mass flow rate of fluid through collector (m^3 s^{-1}),
C_p = specific heat of collecting fluid (J kg^{-1} deg C^{-1}),
V = volume of solar storage tank (m^3),
$\theta_s(n)$ = water temperature in the storage tank at time n (°C),
$\theta_{H1}(n)$ = inlet water temperature of heating units at time n (°C),
$\theta_{H2}(n)$ = outlet water temperature of heating units at time n (°C),
$H(n)$ = space heating load at time n (W),
$\theta_c(n)$ = collector plate temperature near the outlet at time n (°C),
γ = specific weight of fluid (kg m^{-3})
G_H = mass flow rate of fluid through heating unit (kg s^{-1}),
θ_{r0} = room air temperature set point (°C),
$\theta_r(n)$ = room air temperature at time n (°C)
θ_{r1} = room air temperature lower limit (°C),
$H_A(n)$ = rate of auxiliary heat supply at time n (W),
$W_z(j)$ = heating load weighting factors for room air temperature deviation (W deg C^{-1}).

Output

$H_c(n)$ = collected solar energy at time n (W),
$\theta_s(n)$ = water temperature in the solar heat storage tank at time n (°C),

$H_s(n)$ = rate of heat supply to the room by the heating unit at time n (W),
$\theta_r(n)$ = room air temperature at time n (°C).

Calculation sequence

Step 1. Collected solar energy at time at time n, $H_c(n)$, assuming $\theta_{w1}(n) = \theta_s(n-1)$ for the initial input:

$$H_c(n) = F_R\{\tau\alpha I(n) - K[\theta_{w1}(n) - \theta_a(n)]\}A_c \tag{8.67}$$

If $H_c(n) < 0$, it follows that $H_c(n) = 0$.

Step 2. Water temperature in the storage tank at time n, that is increased from the temperature at time $n-1$ owing to the collected solar energy $H_c(n)$ minus rate of heat supply to the heating unit $H_s(n)$, assuming $H_s(n) = H(n)$ for the initial input:

$$\theta_s(n) = \theta_s(n-1) + \frac{H_c(n) - H_s(n)}{C_p \gamma V} \tag{8.68}$$

Step 3. Outlet temperature of heating unit $\theta_{H2}(n)$ from the characteristics of heat exchange as a function of inlet temperature $\theta_{H1}(n)$ and room air temperature $\theta_r(n)$. This is simplified version of number of transfer (NTU) method [8.10]. assuming $\theta_{H1}(n) = \theta_s(n)$:

$$\theta_{H2}(n) = \theta_{H1}(n) + \varepsilon(\theta_{H1}(n) - \theta_r(n)) \tag{8.69}$$

Step 4. Rate of heat supply by the heating unit $H_s(n)$:

$$H_s(n) = C_p G_H[\theta_{H2}(n) - \theta_{H1}(n)] \tag{8.70}$$

Step 5. Iteration from Step 1 to Step 4, by letting:

$$\theta_{w1}(n) = \theta_s(n)$$

Step 6. Room air temperature at time n, $\theta_r(n)$:

$$\theta_r(n) = \theta_{r0} + \left(H_s(n) - H(n) - \sum_{j=1}^{\infty} W_z(j) \times [\theta_r(n-j) - \theta_{r0}]\right) \Big/ W_z(0) \tag{8.71}$$

Step 7. Check if $\theta_r(n)$ is within comfort range:

If $\theta_r(n) > \theta_{r1}$, go to Step 11

If $\theta_r(n) < \theta_{r1}$, $\theta_r(n) = \theta_{r1}$ and go to Step 8

Step 8. Heat required for maintaining comfort ($\theta_r(n) = \theta_{r1}$) at time n, $H_H(n)$:

$$H_H(n) = -H(n) + (\theta_{r1} - \theta_{r0})W_z \\ + \sum_{j=1}^{\infty} W_z(j) \times [\theta_r(n-j) - \theta_{r0}] \quad (8.72)$$

Step 9. Auxiliary heat required to supply $H_H(n)$ to the heating unit, $H_A(n)$:

$$H_A(n) = H_H(n) - H_s(n) \quad (8.73)$$

Step 10. Inlet water temperature to the heating unit at time n with auxiliary heat:

If $\theta_{H2}(n) < \theta_s(n)$

$$\theta_{H1}(n) = \theta_s(n) + \frac{H_A(n)}{C_p G_H}$$

If $\theta_{H2}(n) \geq \theta_s(n)$ \hfill (8.74)

$$\theta_{H1}(n) = \theta_{H2}(n) + \frac{H_A(n)}{C_p G_H}$$

Go to step 3.

Step 11. End of calculation for time n and step forward for time $n + 1$.

Problem:
Execute calculation sequence under the following conditions with the input data.

Input Data						Constants	
Time n	8	9	10	11	12	$A_c = 10$ m²	
$I(n)$ (W m⁻²)	-	200	300	400	500	$F_R = 0.85$	
$\theta_a(n)$ (°C)	-	6	8	12	20	$C_p = 1000$ J kg⁻¹ deg C⁻¹	
$H(n)$	-	3000	2600	2200	1800	$V = 1.2$ m³	
$\theta_r(n)$	18					$\gamma = 1.0$ kg m⁻³	
$H_s(n)$	1900					$G_H = 0.5$ kg s⁻¹	
$\theta_s(n)$	27					$\theta_{r0} = 20$ °C	
						$K = 6$ W m⁻² deg C⁻¹	
						$\theta_{r1} = 18$ °C	
						$W_z(0) = 0.9$ W deg C⁻¹	
						$W_z(1) = 0.05$ W deg C⁻¹	
						$\tau a = 0.9$	
						$\varepsilon = 0.7$	

Chapter 9

Computer Control of Air Conditioning

The purpose of computer control of an air conditioning system is to minimise energy consumption for air conditioning of occupied spaces within an appropriate comfort range, to achieve safe operation and to make an easier maintenance of air conditioning components with an economically justifiable installation. Compared with conventional automatic control, computer control brings higher reliability and versatility, makes it possible to predict future conditions for better control and keeps extensive records to expedite supervision of complicated systems.

It is important, however, to remember that the optimum design of an air conditioning system should be made in combination with the optimum control of system operation. In other words, the total system should be designed so that the comfortable environmental spaces can be realised by operating the smallest system at the highest efficiency with the lowest consumption of energy.

Instead of describing the hardware of a computer control system, this chapter refers briefly to the conceptual background of software used in the computer control of air conditioning.

9.1. A SYSTEM MODEL FOR COMPUTER CONTROL OF AIR CONDITIONING

In a general sense, the computer referred to is a digital computer. It is necessary for engineers to set up system models of air conditioning components and various circuits as discussed in Chapter 8 System Simulation of Air Conditioning. The system model for computer control is, however, naturally different from the system model for simulation. Whereas the system simulation requires the mathematical expression of characteristics of subsystems to be as accurate as possible, the computer used for control programs is generally of mini size for which simpler equations are considered more suitable.

Suppose that the control system for a cooling coil as shown in Fig. 9.1 has an electronic controller which controls the flow rate of the inlet water to the coil by regulating the motorised valve with a signal given by the thermostat located at the exit of coil. The system model for simulating the situation around the coil may be set up by attempting to express the relationships between the inlet and outlet air temperature, inlet and outlet water temperature and flow rates of water and air. Figure 9.2 represents the control system replaced by computer control, where the

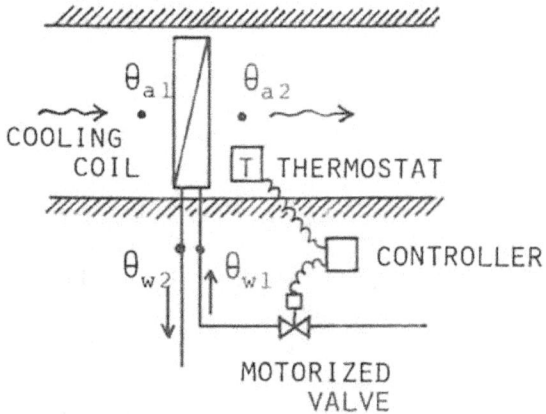

Fig. 9.1. Electronic control of flow rate of coil.

computer calculates the necessary water flow rate to the coil by a signal transmitted from the temperature sensor and delivers a command to the motorised valve so that the opening ratio can be adjusted to allow for the necessary water flow rate. This calculation routine must be simple, preferably expressed by a linear relationship. For example, suppose that the necessary water flow rate at time n, $L_w(n)$ (kgs^{-1}), may be expressed by the linear form as:

$$L_w(n) = a_1\theta_{a1}(n) + a_2\theta_{a2}(n) + b_1\theta_{w1}(n) + b_2\theta_{w2}(n) + cL_a(n) \qquad (9.1)$$

where $L_a(n)$ = air flow rate through coil (kgs^{-1}); $\theta_{a1}(n)$, $\theta_{a2}(n)$ = inlet and outlet air temperature respectively (°C); $\theta_{w1}(n)$, $\theta_{w2}(n)$ = inlet and outlet water temperature (°C) and a_1, a_2, b_1, b_2, c are constants.

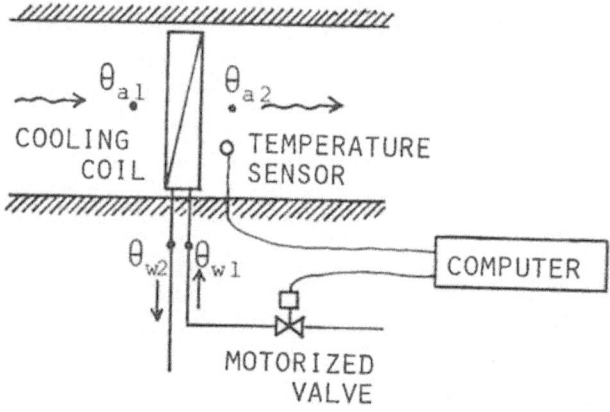

Fig. 9.2. Computer control of flow rate of coil.

The constants in eqn. (9.1) can be determined from the past operation data stored in the file of the computer. Then, the opening ratio of the motorised valve to give the necessary water flow rate can be computed with a predetermined relationship as:

$$p = f(L_w) \tag{9.2}$$

where p = the opening ratio of valve. The final operation to move the valve is made by converting a digital signal into an analog signal at the converter.

In general eqn. (9.2) is not linear. In the case of actual control, however, the incremental change in the opening ratio against the incremental change in the outlet air temperature is important. Then eqns. (9.1) and (9.2) may be combined to give:

$$p(n+1) - p(n) = a_2[\theta_{a2}(n+1) - \theta_{a2}(n)] \tag{9.3}$$

When θ_{w1}, θ_{w2}, θ_{a1}, L_a do not change from time n to $n + 1$, the linear relationship as expressed by eqn. (9.3) may be valid with reasonable accuracy.

Receiving a command to set outlet air temperature $\theta_{a2}(n + 1)$ from elsewhere, the computer only ought to be executed to calculate eqn. (9.3) for regulating the water flow rate.

9.2. METHOD OF OPTIMISATION IN THE CONTROL

For optimisation in the control of an air conditioning system one must define the evaluation functions which ensure optimisation. The evaluation functions may be expressed as:

$$E_i = f_i(x_1, x_2, \ldots) \tag{9.4}$$

where E_i = variables of evaluation, $x_1, x_2,\ldots$ = parameters to be optimised. Then to achieve optimisation, it is necessary to find out the values of $x_1, x_2,\ldots$ for optimising the value of E_i.

For example, E_1 may be taken as energy consumption for a day, E_2 room air temperature at any time of occupancy and so on. Since there are several variables to be evaluated overall, it is not so easy to find out the values of parameters to be optimised.

There are also many constraints which confine the parameters to be varied within a certain range. In this sense the parameters themselves may be considered as evaluation variables of higher priority in terms of the computation algorithm.

Nakahara et al. [9.1] stated that to minimise energy consumption was a primary variable of evaluation and the effective temperature of room air was a primary constraint in their design of an air conditioning system with computer control. It may be understood that the effective temperature of a space resulted from the control can be considered as a variable for evaluation of higher priority than minimisation of energy consumption. It is always important to define the evaluation functions for planning effective computer control of air conditioning systems.

9.3. CONTROL OF START AND STOP OF AIR CONDITIONING COMPONENTS

If the perimeter zone of the room space is heated or cooled by fan-coil units, the question arises as to when the fan-coil units must be started prior to the time of

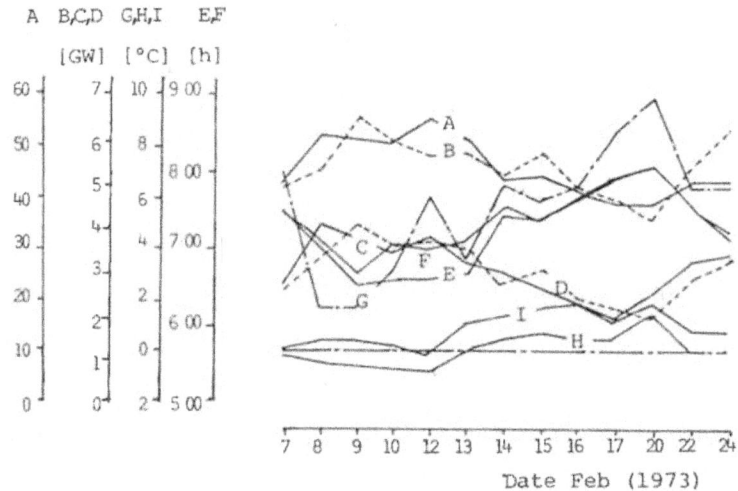

Remarks;
Respective curve indicates characteristic value of the symbol described in Fig.9.3

(A) : average Z of a day
(B) : average C* of a day
(C) : Lq heating load, actual
(D) : Lq* heating load, predicted
(E) : opT(North system) optimum start-up time
(F) : opT(South system) optimum start-up time
(G) : average outdoor temperature
       (8:00 p.m. 7:00 a.m.)
(H) : deviation of controlled room temperature at
       8:55 a.m. (North system)
(I) : deviation of controlled room temperature at
       8:55 a.m. (South system)

Fig. 9.3. The performance characteristics of fan-coil start-up optimisation for pre-heating [9.1].

occupancy. This is an especially important problem in the control of air conditioning on intermittent operation if energy consumption is to be minimised.

Nakahara et al. used the following equation to determine the optimum starting time t_s of fan-coil units:

$$t_s = t_0 - [k_L E(j) + P(j-1)] \qquad (9.5)$$

where t_0 = time when occupancy starts, $E(j)$ = predicted heat load from t_c to 11a.m., $P(j-1)$ = penalty function, parameter j identifies the day in question and $(j-1)$ the previous day, k_L = constant.

$$E(j) = \sum_{n=t_c}^{11} C(j,n)\{k_1[30-\theta_a(n)] + k_2[30-\theta_r(n)] + k_2[30-\theta_F(n)]$$

(9.6)

where t_c = starting time of recording the trend of outside air temperature $\theta_a(n)$, room air temperature $\theta_r(n)$ and floor slab temperature $\theta_F(n)$, $C(j, n)$ = coefficient determined from the learning process based on the past data associated with the difference between predicted and real heat load of the previous day, k_1, k_2, k_3 = constants determined from learning process. The so-called learning process may be defined as the process by which the computer acquires data, uses the data for prediction, modifies the data if the data used was inadequate and finds the correct data for control.

Essentially it is a repetition of iteration and generally refers to finding the constant values in hypothetical formulas.

An example of the performance data taken at the Osaka Obayashi Building is shown in Fig. 9.3.

9.4. CONTROL OF OUTSIDE AIR INTAKE

Since heating and cooling loads associated with outside air intake are so great in air conditioning it is well worthwhile attempting to control the amount of outside air intake on a reasonable basis. Introduced here is a very effective example of controlling outside air intake achieved by Nakahara et al. [9.1] in a large office building as cited previously. There are two different criteria to be considered in controlling outside air intake; one is to let in outside air as a heat source when the room requires cooling in winter or intermediate seasons and the other is to reduce the rate of outside air intake as much as possible to the limit that CO_2 concentration in the room would not exceed the threshold value. The former is rather easy to do and the latter is quite unique and interesting.

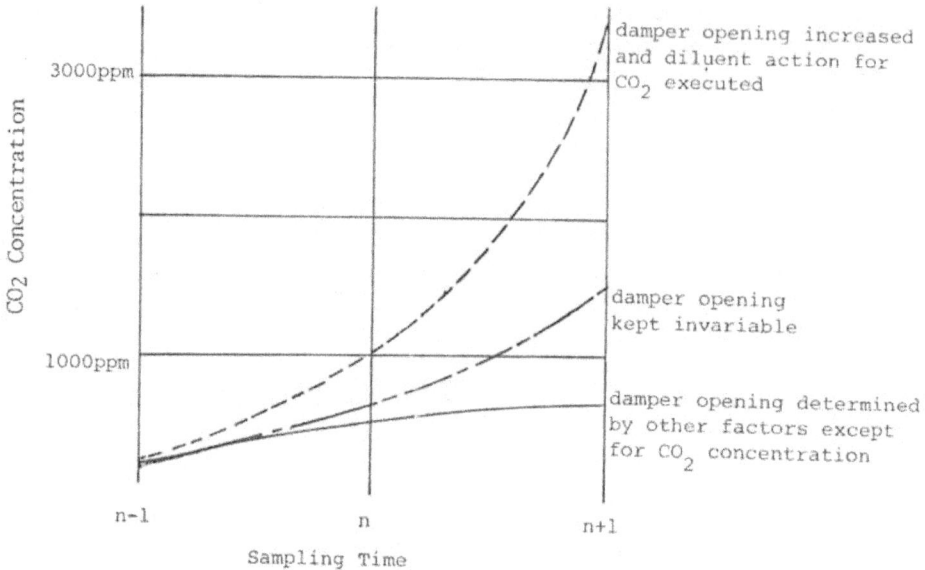

Fig. 9.4. Prediction of carbon dioxide gas concentration and outside air damper action at sampling time *n* [9.1].

The equation for predicting the CO_2 concentration of room air is given as:

$$C(n) = C_a(n) + \left[1 - \exp\left(-\frac{Q(n-1)}{V}\Delta t\right)\right]\frac{k(n)}{Q(n-1)}$$

$$+ \exp\left(-\frac{Q(n-1)}{V}\Delta t\right)[C(n-1) - C_a(n-1)] \quad (9.7)$$

where $C(n)$, $C_a(n)$ = CO_2 concentration of room air and outside air respectively at time n (ppm), $Q(n-1)$ = rate of outside air intake (m³h⁻¹), V = air volume in the interior space (m³), $k(n)$ = generation rate of CO_2 within the building (cm³h⁻¹) and Δt = sampling time interval (= 5min).

Control of outside air intake is made in such a way that when CO_2 concentration is lower than 1000 ppm (warning value), the outside air (OA) damper is set at the position corresponding to the predicted $C(n)$ from eqn. (9.7) and when the predicted $C(n)$ might exceed 3000 ppm (threshold value), the OA damper is wide open immediately to dilute the room air. The characteristics of the OA damper opening are shown in Fig. 9.4.

9.5. PREDICTION CONTROL

Prediction control of air conditioning is different from real-time control. In real-time control used in the field of process industries, the computer acquires the process data in real time, processes the data using the predefined procedures, issues various kinds of commands to the object process and then controls it. For example, the target of maintaining a constant temperature of a space may be realised by a control command to make rise or fall of the temperature continuously given in real time to the object process when the actual temperature is going down or up to the target temperature.

This concept, so-called feedback control or real-time control, is often used in computer control of air conditioning systems. There are, however, those cases where a satisfactory control command for a future point of time may not be obtained only with the information at the concurrent time. In other words, it is likely to occur when the control command of real-time control fails to act fast enough for satisfactory operation, or where real-time control requires large-scale devices if it is to act in time. It may be called prediction control when the heat load of tomorrow is predicted and control is simultaneously made by using various data obtained today. As the state of the process in the future is generally unknown at the time of control, it must be predicted by executing some calculations and then issuing a control command on line based on the prediction. For using computerised prediction control, the following factors must be predetermined [9.2].

1. What is to be predicted? ... Object of prediction.
2. How far in future to be predicted? ... Range of prediction.
3. When is it to be predicted? ... Time of prediction.
4. What data can be used? ... Inputs for prediction.
5. For what control is the prediction to be made? ... Control target.
6. What accuracy is required? ... Accuracy of prediction.
7. To what degree does an operator take part in control? ... Control level.

In addition, the learning process is important for prediction control. The deeper the operation experience, the clearer the operation characteristics of various devices and the thermal response characteristics of building structure will become. These characteristics can be theoretically analysed to some degree, but theoretical strictness tends to make complication of models. It may be considered more practical, therefore, to have some appropriate constants substituted into certain simplified equations for setting up control models. The learning process mainly aims at obtaining these appropriate constants during the period of trial operation.

Besides these data and algorithms directly required for actual control, some fundamental studies for the above must be made and always referred to as off-line information. Figures 9.5 and 9.6 show the points of the above description.

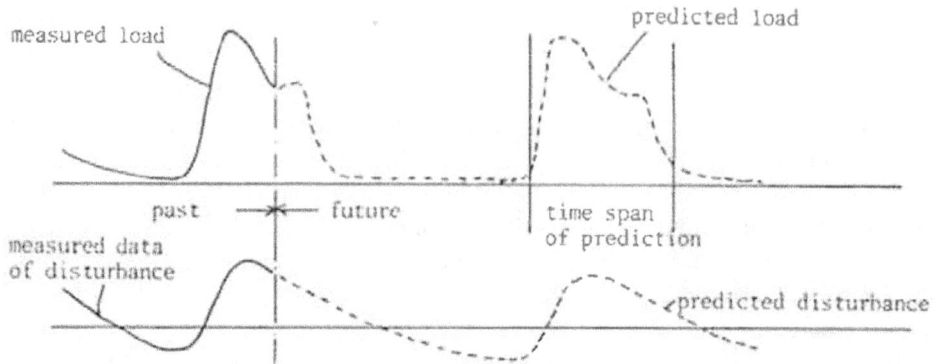

Fig. 9.5. Profiles of load and disturbance [9.2]

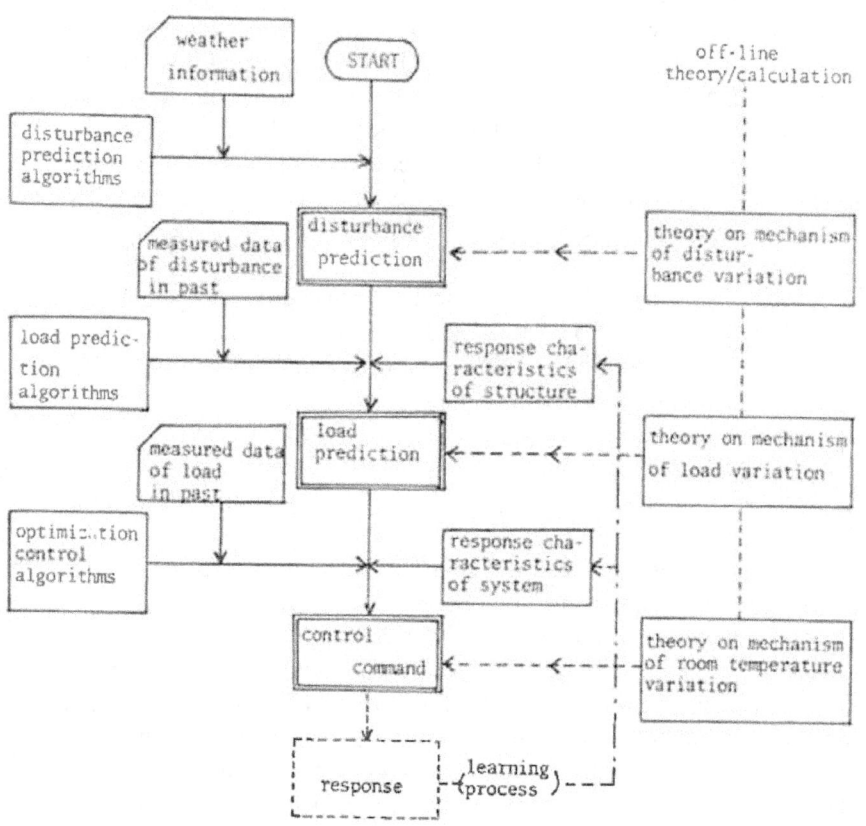

Fig. 9.6. General flow chart of prediction control [9.2].

Prediction control is considered effective in minimising energy consumption in a heat recovery system combined with a heat storage tank. Especially in winter, it is necessary to predict the future heating load profile of 24 or 48 hours in advance and to store the optimum amount of heat within the storage tanks. If this predicted amount of heat storage is equal to the shaded area as shown in Fig. 9.7, this amount is considered optimum. There are several computation methods for load prediction and a regression model is suggested in this scheme. Briefly, this method is such that the heating and cooling loads are regressively analysed with parameters of inside and outside conditions to be specified in the preceding period and then a prediction model for heating and cooling loads can be made.

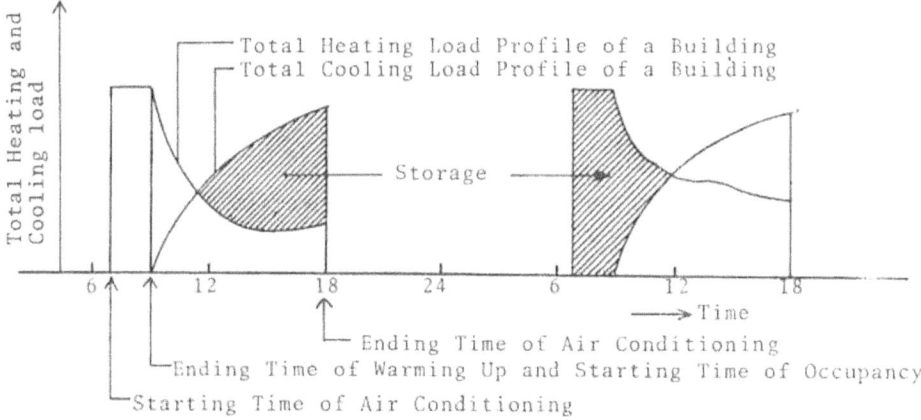

Fig. 9.7. Total heating and cooling loads in winter [9.2]. Time in day hours.

The measurable variables for this model are defined as follows: $y(n)$ = hourly mean value of heating load from time $t = (n - 1) \Delta t$ to $n \Delta t$, $x_1(n)$, $x_2(n)$, $x_3(n)$,... = hourly mean values of outside air temperature, outside air humidity, solar radiation, electric power consumption by illumination, electric power consumption by business machines and heat generated by occupant persons per unit area and other parameters from time $t = (n-1) \Delta t$ to $n \Delta t$ respectively.

Here, new variables as hourly increments of the above variables are introduced, viz.:

$$Y(n) = y(n) - y(n-1)$$
$$X_k(n) = x_k(n) - x_k(n-1) \qquad \text{for } k = 1, 2, 3, \ldots \qquad (9.8)$$

An unmeasurable variable β_0 must be defined to express the amount of stored energy in the building structure.

Incremental heating load $Y(n)$ may be considered linear in relation to the variables, $X_k(n)$ and β_0, to be expressed as:

$$Y(n) = \beta_0 + \beta_1 X_1(n) + \beta_2 X_2(n) + \beta_3 X_3(n) + \cdots + e(n) \qquad (9.9)$$

where $\beta_1, \beta_2, \beta_3,...$ are regression coefficients.

A variable $e(n)$ means an error term to be added because the objective variable $Y(n)$ cannot be explained exactly by the measured variables $X_1(n), X_2(n),...$. The values of these variables measured every hour from the beginning to the end of the air-conditioning period are substituted into eqn. (9.9) and then the following relations are obtained:

$$\begin{aligned}
Y(n) &= \beta_0 + \beta_1 X_1(n) + \beta_2 X_2(n) + \beta_3 X_3(n) + \cdots + e(n) \\
Y(n-1) &= \beta_0 + \beta_1 X_1(n-1) + \beta_2 X_2(n-1) + \beta_3 X_3(n-1) + \cdots + e(n-1) \\
Y(n-2) &= \beta_0 + \beta_1 X_1(n-2) + \beta_2 X_2(n-2) + \beta_3 X_3(n-2) + \cdots + e(n-2) \\
&\vdots \\
Y(n-j) &= \beta_0 + \beta_1 X_1(n-j) + \beta_2 X_2(n-j) + \beta_3 X_3(n-j) + \cdots + e(n-j)
\end{aligned} \qquad (9.10)$$

Equation (9.10) can be rewritten with vector matrix notation as follows:

$$\mathbf{Y} = \mathbf{X}.\boldsymbol{\beta} + \mathbf{e} \qquad (9.11)$$

Where

$$\mathbf{Y} = \begin{bmatrix} Y(n) \\ Y(n-1) \\ Y(n-2) \\ \vdots \\ Y(n-j) \end{bmatrix} \qquad \mathbf{X} = \begin{bmatrix} Y(n) & X_1(n) & X_2(n) & \cdots \\ Y(n-1) & X_1(n-1) & X_2(n-1) & \cdots \\ Y(n-2) & X_1(n-2) & X_2(n-2) & \cdots \\ \vdots & & & \\ Y(n-j) & X_1(n-j) & X_2(n-j) & \cdots \end{bmatrix}$$

$$\boldsymbol{\beta} = \begin{bmatrix} \beta_0 \\ \beta_1 \\ \beta_2 \\ \vdots \\ \beta_j \end{bmatrix} \qquad \mathbf{e} = \begin{bmatrix} e(n) \\ e(n-1) \\ e(n-2) \\ \vdots \\ e(n-j) \end{bmatrix}$$

The square error matrix $\mathbf{e}^t \cdot \mathbf{e}$ can be derived from eqn. (9.11) as:

$$\begin{aligned}
\mathbf{e}^t.\mathbf{e} &= [\mathbf{Y} - \mathbf{X}.\boldsymbol{\beta}]^t .[\mathbf{XY} - \mathbf{X}.\boldsymbol{\beta}] \\
&= \mathbf{Y}.\mathbf{Y} - \mathbf{Y}^t \mathbf{X}\boldsymbol{\beta} - 2\boldsymbol{\beta}^t \mathbf{X}^t \mathbf{Y} + \boldsymbol{\beta}^t \mathbf{X}^t.\mathbf{X}.\boldsymbol{\beta}
\end{aligned} \qquad (9.12)$$

Differentiating eqn. (9.12) with respect to the matrix [$\boldsymbol{\beta}$] and equating it to zero, the optimum coefficient [$\hat{\boldsymbol{\beta}}$] of the prediction model can be obtained as:

$$\hat{\beta} = [\mathbf{X}^t . \mathbf{X}]^{-1} . [\mathbf{X}^t . \mathbf{Y}] \qquad (9.13)$$

Substituting eqn. (9.13) into eqn. (9.9), the following prediction model is established:

$$Y(n) = \hat{\beta}_0 + \hat{\beta}_1 X_1(n) + \hat{\beta}_2 X_2(n) + \cdots \qquad (9.14)$$

Substituting the incremental values of predicted weather data and the present data of inside conditions into eqn. (9.14), the incremental values of heating and cooling loads can be obtained. Then the load profile for the next day can be predicted on line for making control commands. The optimal coefficients may vary among four seasons and they must be frequently reviewed and updated.

Appendix

Solution of the problem in page 208.

Calculation Sequence for n=8

Total step	Calc Sequence	θ_r (n)	θ_{w1} (n)	H_c (n)	H_s (n)	θ_s (n)	θ_{H1} (n)	θ_{H2} (n)	H_H (n)	H_A (n)
1	Initial guess	18.0	27.0		1,900					0
2	Step 1 eq.(8.67)	18.0	27.0	459	1,900					0
3	Step 2 eq.(8.68)	18.0	27.0	459	1,900	25.8				0
4	Assumption: $\theta_{H1}(n) = \theta_s(n)$	18.0	27.0	459	1,900	25.8	25.8			0
5	Step 3 eq.(8.69)	18.0	27.0	459	1,900	25.8	25.8	20.3		0
6	Step 4 eq.(8.70)	18.0	27.0	459	1,092	25.8	25.8	20.3		0
7	Step 5 Iteration	18.0	25.8		1,092					0
8~18	iterate the calculation until $\theta_{w1}(n)$ converges									
19	Step 5 converged ($\theta_{w1}(n) \approx \theta_s(n)$)	18.0	26.4	483	1,177	26.4	26.4	20.5		0
20	Step 6 eq.(8.71)	16.4	26.4	483	1,177	26.4	26.4	20.5		0
21	Step 8 Use auxiliary heater eq.(8.72)	16.4	26.4	483	1,177	26.4	26.4	20.5	1,960	0
22	Step 9 eq.(8.73)	16.4	26.4	483	1,177	26.4	26.4	20.5	1,960	783
23	Step 10 eq.(8.74)	16.4	26.4	483	1,177	26.4	30.3	20.5	1,960	783
24	Step 3 eq.(8.69)	16.4	26.4	483	1,177	26.4	30.3	20.6	1,960	783
25	Step 4 eq.(8.70)	16.4	26.4	483	1,944	26.4	30.3	20.6	1,960	783
26	Step 6 eq.(8.71)	18.0	26.4	483	1,944	26.4	30.3	20.6	1,960	783
27~49	iterate the calculation until $\theta_r(n)$ converges									
50	Step 6 eq.(8.71)	18.0	26.4	483	1,956	26.4	31.9	22.1	1,960	1,088

Summary of Otput Data

n	θ_r (n)	θ_{w1} (n)	H_c (n)	H_s (n)	θ_s (n)	θ_{H1} (n)	θ_{H2} (n)	H_H (n)	H_A (n)
8	18.0	-	-	1,900	27.0	-	-	-	-
9	18.0	26.4	483	1,956	26.4	31.9	22.1	1,960	1,088
10	18.3	26.1	1,368	1,706	26.1	26.1	20.4	1,560	0
11	18.1	27.0	2,303	1,224	27.0	27.0	20.9	1,166	0
12	19.4	28.6	3,387	1,473	28.6	28.6	21.3	762	0

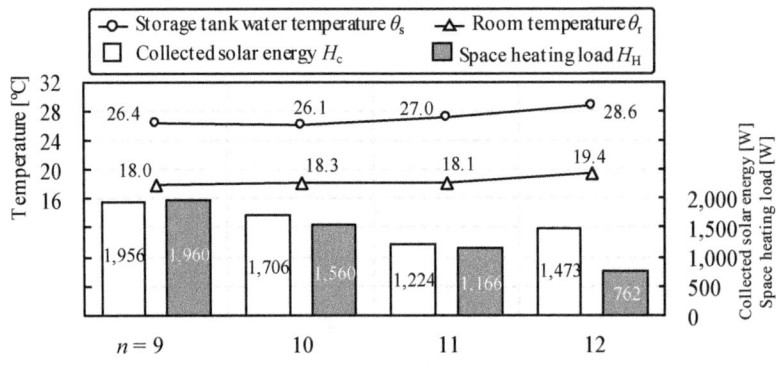

220

References

Chapter 1

1.1. THEKAEKARA, M. P. (Sept.–Oct. 1970). Proposed standard values or the solar constant and the solar spectrum, *J. Environmental Science*, 13(4), 6-9.
1.2. BERLACE, H. (May 1928). Zur Theorie der Beleuchtung einer horizontalen Flache durch Tageslicht, *Meteorologische Zeitschrift*.
1.3. STEPHENSON, D. G. (1965). Equations for solar heat gain through windows, *Solar Energy*, 9(2).
1.4. NEHRINC, G. (1962). Uber den Warmefluss durch Aussenwande und Dacher in Klimatisierte Raume infolge der periodischen Tagesgange der bestimmenden Meteorologischen Elemente, *Gesundheits-Ingenieur*, 83(8).
1.5. NAGATA, T. (Oct.1975). Questions against Berlage's formula on diffuse sky radiation, *Transactions AIJ*, p. 381 (Japanese).
1.6. PARMELEE, G. V. (1954). Irradiation of vertical and horizontal surfaces by diffuse solar radiation from cloudless skies, *ASHVE Transactions*, 60.
1.7. LIU, B. Y. H. AND JORDAN, R. C. (1960). The interrelationship and characteristic distribution of direct, diffuse and total solar radiation, *Solar Energy*, 4(3).
1.8. KIMURA, K. AND STEPHENSON, D. C. (1969). Solar radiation on cloudy days, *ASHRAE Transactions*, 75, Part 1.
1.9. UDAGAWA, M. AND KIMURA, K. (March, 1972). 'Deduction of Direct and Diffuse Solar Radiation on Cloudy Conditions from Cloud Amount,' 2nd Symposium on City, Architecture and Meteorology, Tokyo (Japanese).
1.10. ROBINSON, N. (Ed.) (1966). *Solar Radiation*, Elsevier Publishing Co., Amsterdam.
1.11. THRELKELD, J. C. (1962). *Thermal Environmental Engineering*, Prentice-Hall, Inc., Englewood Cliffs, N.J.
1.12. GIVONI, B. (1969). *Man, Climate and Architecture*, Elsevier Publishing Co., Amsterdam.
1.13. GEIGER, R. (1966). *The Climate near the Ground*, Harvard Univ. Press, Cambridge, Mass.
1.14. KIMURA, K. (1970). *Fundamental Theories of Building Services*, Gakkensha, Chapter 23 (Japanese)

Chapter 2

2.1. MAEDA, T. (1969). *Theories of Heat Transfer (Dennetsu-gaku)*, Architecture and Building Science Series (Kenchiku-gaku Taikei), Vol. 8, 2nd Edn, Shokokusha, Tokyo (Japanese).
2.2. CARSLAW, H. S. AND JAEGER, J. C. (1959). *Conduction of Heat in Solids*, 2nd Edn, Oxford University Press.
2.3. CHURCHILL, R. V. (1958). *Operational Mathematics*, McGraw-Hill Book Co., New York.
2.4. PIPES, L. A. (Mar.1957). Matrix analysis of heat transfer problems, J. Franklin Institute.

2.5. MITALAS, G. P. AND STEPHENSON, D. C. (1967). Room thermal response factors, *ASHRAE Transactions*, 73, Part 1.
2.6. MITALAS, G. P. AND ARSENEAULT, J. G. (June, 1967). Computer Program No. 26 of the Division of Building Research Ottawa. Also Fortran IV Program to Calculate Heat Flux Response Factors for a Multi-Layer Slab.
2.7. MATSUO, Y. (1970). Calculation of method of solar heat gain, *Air Conditioning and Refrigeration*, 10(3) (Japanese).
2.8. KIMURA, K. AND ISHINO, H. (Nov. 1971). 'An Approximate Calculation Method of Convolution in Time-series,' Abstract Proceedings of the Technical Meeting of Architectural Institute of Japan (Japanese).
2.9. STEPHENSON, D. G. AND MITALAS, G. P. (1971). Calculation of heat conduction transfer functions for multilayer slabs, *ASHRAE Transactions*, Part 1.
2.10. MITALAS, G. P. AND ARSENEAULT, J. G. (1970). 'Fortran IV Program to Calculate Z-Transfer Functions for the Calculation of Transient Heat Transfer through walls and Roofs,' First Symposium on the Use of Computers for Environmental Engineering Related to Buildings, Gaithersburg, Maryland, USA, Nov. 30-Dec. 2. Also (Oct., 1971) NBS Building Science Series 39 published by USGPO.
2.11. DOETSCH, G. (1961). *Anleitung zum Praktischen Gebrauch der Laplace Transformation*, 2nd Edn, R. Oldenbourg Verlag, Munchen.
2.12. 'Proposed Procedures for Determining Heating and Cooling Loads for Energy Calculations,' ASHRAE Task Group on Energy Requirements for Heating and Cooling, 1968.
2.13. 'Procedures for Determining Heating and Cooling Loads for Computerised Energy Calculations,' ASHRAE Task Group on Energy Requirements for Heating and Cooing, 1971.
2.14. KIMURA, K. (1970). *Fundamentals of Building Services*, Gakkensha, Chapters 16, 17 and 22 (Japanese).

Chapter 3

3.1. YAMAMOTO, G. (1954). *Taiki-Fukusha-Gaku* (*Theory of Atmospheric Radiation*), Iwanami Pub. Co. (Japanese).
3.2. PHILIPPS, H. (1940). Zur Theorie der Warmestrahlung im Bodennahe, *Grerl. Beitr. Z. Geophys.*, 56, 229.
3.3. SATO, A., ITO, N., KIMURA, K., OKA, J. *et al.* (Jan. 1972). Research on the wind variation in the urban area and its effects in environmental engineering No. 7 and No. 8—study on the convective heat transfer on exterior surface of buildings, *Transactions of Architectural Institute of Japan*, No. 191 (Japanese).
3.4. ITO, N., KIMURA, K. AND OKA, J. (1972). A field experiment study on the convective heat transfer coefficient on exterior surface of a building, *ASHRAE Transactions*, 78, Part 1.
3.5. KIMURA, K. (1970). *Fundamental Theories of Building Services*, Gakkensha, Chapter 24 (Japanese).
3.6. MCADAMS, W. H. (1954). *Heat Transmission*, 3rd Edn, McGraw-Hill Book Co., New York.
3.7. JACOB, M., *Heat Transfer*, John Wiley & Sons, Vol. 1 (1950) and Vol. 2 (1957).
3.8. HOTTEL, H. C. AND SAROFIM, A.F. (1969). *Radiative Transfer*, McGraw-Hill Book

Co., New York.
3.9. ECKERT, E. R. G. (1950). *Introduction to the Transfer of Heat and Mass*, McGraw-Hill Book Co., New York.

Chapter 4

4.1. *SHASE Handbook of Heating, Air-Conditioning and Sanitary Engineering*, Vol. 11, Chapter 2, 1975 (Japanese).
4.2. CARRIER AIR CONDITIONING COMPANY (1965). *Handbook of Air Conditioning System Design*, McGraw-Hill.
4.3. KIMURA, K. (April, 1964). Heat storage and solar radiation transmitted through a glass window, *SHASE J.*, 38(4) (Japanese).
4.4. INOUE, U., KIMURA, K. AND TANAKA, T. (July, 1967). Heat load characteristics of revolving air conditioning test room, *SHASE J.*, 41(7) (Japanese).
4.5. KIMURA, K., TANAKA, T. AND MIYAGAWA, Y. (July, 1970). Experimental study on the heat load variation from glass window with revolving air conditioning test room, *SHASE J.*, 44(7) (Japanese).
4.6. ISHINO, H. AND KIMURA, K. (April, 1973). Study On the determination of weighting factors in time series in the calculation method of air conditioning load, *Transaction of Architectural Institute of Japan*, No. 206 (Japanese).
4.7. PARMELEE, G. V. AND AUBELE, W. W. (1952). The shading of sunlit glass—an analysis of the effect uniformly spaced flat opaque stats, *ASHVE Transactions*.
4.8. PARMELEE, G. V. AND VILD, D.J. (1953). Design data for stat type sun shade for use in load estimating, *ASHVE Transactions*.
4.9. KIMURA, K. (May, 1964). 'Experiments on the Shading Performance of Venetian Blind with Aluminium Slats,' The 39th Technical Meeting of Kanto Branch of AIJ (Japanese).
4.10. KIMURA, K. (1970). 'Optimum Shape of External Shade for the window to Minimise Annual Solar Heat Gain and to Maximise View Factor,' Paper presented to the First Symposium on the Use of Computers for Environmental Engineering Related to Building, Washington DC, Nov. 30th-Dec. 2nd.
4.11. OLGYAY, V. (1963). *Design with Climate*, Princeton Univ. Press, NJ.
4.12. ARONIN, J. E. (1953). *Climate and Architecture*, Reinhold Pub. Co.
4.13. *ASHRAE Guide: Handbook of Fundamentals*, ASHRAE, New York, 1967.
4.14. ARCHITECTURAL INSTITUTE OF JAPAN, 'Data Manual for Architectural Design,' Vol. 2, Marusen, Tokyo, 1960 (Japanese).
4.15. KIMURA, K. (1971). 'Cooling Load Caused by Solar Radiation from Glass Windows,' Memoirs of School of Science and Engineering, Waseda University, No.35.
4.16. KIMURA, K. (1970). *Fundamentals of Building Services*, Gakkensha, Chapter 7 (Japanese)

Chapter 5

5.1. HOPKINSON, R. G. AND LONGMORE, J. (1959). The permanent supplementary artificial lighting of interiors, *Transactions IES*, 24, 121-148.
5.2. KIMURA, K. AND STEPHENSON, D. G. (1968). Cooling load caused by lights,

ASHRAE Transactions, 74, Part 11.

5.3. ISHINO, H. AND KIMURA, K. (April, 1973). Study on the determination o time series weighting factors in air conditioning load calculation, *Transactions oj the Architectural Institute of Japan*, No. 206 (Japanese).

5.4. SHASE, Air Conditioning Standardisation Committee (1972). Computerisec calculation method of annual energy requirements for air conditioning, *SHASE Journal*, 46(3) (Japanese).

5.5. KIMURA, K., MAEKAWA, K., ISHIKAWA, K., TANAKA, Y. AND MURAO, M. (1969) Experimental study on the heat removal from lighting through troffers witl intake of air conditioning (3rd Report), *Transactions of SHASE, Japan*, (Japanese).

5.6. ILLUMINATION ENGINEERING SOCIETY, *IES Lighting Handbook* (4th Edn), New York, 1966.

5.7. FLYNN, J. E. AND MILLS, S. M. (1962). *Architectural Lighting Graphics* Reinhold Pub. Corp., New York.

5.8. HEWITT, H. AND VAUSE, A. S. (1966). *Lamps and Lighting*, Arnold Pub., London

5.9. HOPKINSON, R. D., 'Architectural Physics-Lighting,' BRS Dept. of Scientific and Industrial Research, HMSO, 1963.

5.10. CARRIER AIR CONDITIONING COMPANY (1965). *Handbook of Air Conditioning System Design*, McGraw-Hill.

5.11. INOUE, U. (Ed.) (1964). *Planning of Building Services for High Rise Buildings* Shokokusha, Tokyo (Japanese).

5.12. MITALAS, G. P. (1973-74). Cooling load caused by lights, *Transactions CSME* 2(3).

Chapter 6

6.1. TAMURA, G. T. AND WILSON, A. G. (1967). Pressure differences caused by chimney effect in three high buildings, *ASHRAE Transactions*, 73, Part II.

6.2. TAMURA, G. T. AND WILSON, A. G. (1968). Pressure differences caused by win on two tall buildings, *ASHRAE Transactions*, 74, Part I.

6.3. KIMURA, K. (1970). *Fundamental Theories of Building Services*, Gakkensha Chapters 25 and 26 (Japanese).

Chapter 7

7.1. *ASHRAE Guide*: *Handbook of Fundamentals*, ASHRAE, New York, 1967.

7.2. INSTITUTION OF HEATING AND VENTILATING ENGINEERS, *IHVE Guide*, 1965.

7.3. LOKMANHEKIM, M. (Ed.) (1971). Procedure for Determining Heating and Cooling Loads for Computerised Energy Calculations, ASHRAE, New York.

7.4. 'Dynamic Air Conditioning Load Calculation Method by Computer,' Interim Report by the Heat Load Calculation Subcommittee of the Air Conditioning Standardisation Committee of SHASE, SHASE Journal, 46(3), Mar. 1972 (Japanese).

7.5. KIMURA, K. (1970). *Fundamental Theories of Building Services*, Gakkensha Tokyo, Chapters 29 and 30 (Japanes).

7.6. SAITO, H. AND KIMURA, K. (1974). 'Computerised Calculation Procedures o Dynamic Air Conditioning Load Developed by SHASE of Japan,' Second

Symposium on the Use of Computers for Environmental Engineering Related to Buildings, Paris.

7.7. KIMURA, K. (1972). Simulation of Cooling and heating loads under intermittent operation of air conditioning, ASHRAE Transactions, 76, Part I.

Chapter 8

8.1. *ASHRAE Guide: Handbook of Fundamentals*, ASHRAE, New York, 1967.
8.2. STOECKER, W. F. (1971). *Design of Thermal System*, McGraw-Hill.
8.3. STOECKER, W. F. (Ed.) (1969). Proposed *Procedures for Simulating the Performance of Components and Systems for Energy Calculation*, ASHRAE, New York.
8.4. NAKAJIMA, Y. (Oct. 1972). Studies on thermal weight of thermal storage tanks (Part I)—Theoretical analysis, *Transactions of the Architectural Institute of Japan*, No. 200 (Japanese).
8.5. NAKAMURA, A., MAKI, E., KATO, A. AND INOOKA, T. (Oct. 1974). 'An Analysis on the Effect Energy Conservation Techniques in Air Conditioning Design,' Proceedings of the Annual Meeting of the Architectural Institute of Japan (Japanese).
8.6. HOTTEL, H. C. AND WOERTZ, B. B. (1942). Performance of flat-plate solar heat collectors, *ASME Transactions*, 64.
8.7. WHILLIER, A. (1967). 'Design Factors Influencing Collector Performance,' in *Low Temperature Engineering Applications of Solar Energy*, ASHRAE, New York.
8.8. GORDON, G. (1969). *System Simulation*, Prentice-Hall, Inc., Englewood Cliffs, NJ.
8.9. *ASHRAE Guide and Data Book-Systems* (1970), p. 81.
8.10. Kays, W. M. and London, A.L. (1964), Compact Heat Exchangers, 2nd ed., McGraw-Hill, New York

Chapter 9

9.1. NAKAHARA, N. NAD HACHISUKA, S. (June, 1974). 'Air conditioning Facilities of Osaka Ohbayashi Building and its On-Line Computer Operating Systems of Optimization and Prediction Features,' Second Symposium on the Use of Computers for Environmental Engineering Related to Buildings, Paris.
9.2. KIMURA, K., ISHINO, H., TAKAHASHI, T. AND KOIZUMI, S. (June 1974). 'Weather Information Telecommunication System for Computer Control of Air Conditioning,' Second Symposium on the Use of Computers for Environmental Engineering Related to Buildings, Paris.
9.3. SHERRATT, A. F. C. (1969). *Air Conditioning System Design for Buildings*, Elsevier Publishing Co.

Index

Absorptance, 102
Absorption coefficient, 85, 86
Absorptivity, 87-88, 168
Air flow, 105, 125
    velocity, 76, 77, 80
Air intake control, 213
Air mass, 10
Albedo, 17
Appliances, cooling load associated with, 166
Atmospheric radiation, 68-70
Atmospheric transmissivity, 10, 11

Berlage's formula, 12, 15, 18
Black body constant, 64
Boiler performance, 193
Bouguer's formula, 11, 12
Brise-soleil, 112, 119
Brunt's formula, 69
Building services and environment,
    interaction, 2

Ceiling panel, 126, 135, 141
Ceiling plenum, 126, 134, 141, 146
Ceiling space, 135, 138
CO_2 concentration, 213
Common ratio, 55, 100, 141, 143
Component simulation, 190
Computer calculation, 29, 80
Computer control, 209
    optimisation, 211
    system model, 209
Computers, 182
Condensation, 190
Contact factor, 191
Convective heat transfer, 61
    inside room, 82-83
Convective heat transfer coefficient,
    66-68, 71, 75-82, 98, 107, 109, 134
Convolution, 37, 44, 163, 197
Cooling coil, 190, 191
    control system, 209
Cooling load, 159, 180, 186, 195
    algorithm for calculating, 164
    associated by solar heat gain, 167
    caused by lights, 132-140
    classification, 163
    components of, 162
    types of, 162
    weighting factors, 98, 118, 140-145
Cracks, air leakage characteristics, 147

Delta function, 37, 38, 42
Differential equations, 40
Diffusion coefficient, 198
Dimensional analysis, 66
Dimensionless numbers, 68

Double glazing, 89
Dual duct system, 185, 189
Duhamel's integral, 38

Effective radiation, 64
Effective radiation constant, 64
Egg-crate louvre, 113
Emissivity, 64, 68, 71, 76, 82
Energy
    conservation, 200
Energy—contd.
    consumption, 200, 201, 209, 211
    conversion equipment, 192
Environmental and building
    services, interaction, 2
Environmental space system, 181
Eppley pyrheliometer, 95
Excitation function, 31, 35, 199
Exfiltration, 147-158
Explicit procedure, 29
Extinction coefficient, 10
    hypothetical, 12

Fan-coil units, 212, 213
Feedback control, 215
Film coefficient, 61-63, 73
    inside, 81
    outside, 61-63
Film conductance, inside, 62
Finite difference method, 27-30
Flow chart, 180
Fluid temperature, 34, 47
Fluorescent lamps, 122, 125
Form factor, 64, 167
Fourier series, 30
Frequency response, 30, 32, 33
Fresnel's equation, 85
Furniture, heat absorption by, 173

Gay-Lussac's law, 151
Glass temperature, 112
Graetz number, 68
Grashof number, 68
Greenhouse effect, 87

Heat-absorbing glass, 107
Heat
    balance
        at floor surface, 82
        at inside surface of exterior wall, 82
        at outside surfaces of buildings, 70-75
Heat—contd.
    balance—contd.
        equations, 70, 72, 74, 75, 128, 135
        for room air, 83
    capacity, 25

conduction
   periodic steady, 30-35
   unsteady state; see Unsteady state
exchanger, shell and tube type, 183-185
extraction, 84, 95, 138, 162, 170-180, 187, 201
flow, 25, 44-49, 56, 60, 72, 75, 81, 84, 93, 109, 171
gain, 25, 36, 47, 61, 73, 85, 90, 99, 102, 156, 164
input, 193, 194
load, 159-180, 193, 194
   calculation, 61
   components of, 163
   definition, 132
   types of, 132
loss, 61, 62, 72
recovery system, 200-202
rejection factor, 194-195
storage
   load, 170
   system, 196-200
   tank, 177, 196, 200, 206
transfer, 61, 81-84
   coefficient, 204
      combined surface, 61
      convective, 61-84, 98, 107, 109, 115, 134
      inside surface, 81
      overall, 61, 72
      radiative, 63-66
transmission
   across exterior walls and roofs, 167
   across glass windows, 167
Heaviside's expansion theorem, 51
Hottel-Whillier-Bliss equation, 203
Human body, heat generated by, 165
Humidity ratio, 169, 189

Illumination level, 121, 122
Implicit method, 29
Impulse response, 37-40, 42, 49, 72, 197
Incandescent lamps, 122
Indicial response, 35, 42
Infiltration, 147-158, 162, 168, 187
   by stack effect, 156-158
   by wind, 149
Inlet temperature, 198
Input energy, 192, 194
Input Function, 58
Input items in system simulation, 182
Iteration, 72, 207

Kirchhoff's Law, 64

Lamps, energy distribution of, 124
Laplace transform, 40-44, 50
Learning process, 213, 215
Lighting, integrated system, 125-128
Lights
   cooling load caused by, 132-140
   cooling load weighting factors
      for power input to, 140-146
   heat from, 121-146, 164, 176, 196

Load factor, 194
Load prediction, 217
Luminaires, 124, 132
Luminous efficiency, 122, 125

Natural ventilation, 156
Newton-Raphson method, 52
Nocturnal radiation, 68
Nusselt number, 68

Occupants, heat From, 164
Openings, air leakage characteristics, 147
Optimum coefficient, 218
Output
   energy, 192
   function, 58
   items in system simulation, 183
Outside surfaces of buildings, heat balance at, 70-74

Parmelee's equation, 18
Part-load
   efficiency, 193
   performance, 192-195
Periodic steady heat conduction, 30-35
Plenum
   air temperature, 126
   space, thermal system model, 141
   ventilation, 139
Polynomial fitting, 195
Power input, 195
Prandtl number, 68
Preconditioning load, 170, 173-180
Preconditioning period, 199, 173-180
Prediction control, 215-219
Prediction model, 217, 218
Pressure difference, 149-152, 169
Pressure loss, 147
Profile angle, 13, 102, 118
Psychrometric chart, 186
Psychrometric process, performance data, 189

Radiation exchange at inside surface, 84
Radiative heat transfer, 63
   inside room, 81-84
Radiative heat transfer coefficient, 63-66
Ramp functions, 50
Real-time control, 215
Reflectivity, 88
Refrigeration machine, 194
Regression
   coefficients, 218
   model, 217
Re-radiation from external shading, 112-117
Response factors, 72, 84, 118, 133, 141, 171
   definition and usage, 47-49
   derivation of, 50-55
   examples of, 52-55
   practical application of, 56-57
   types of, 48-49
Response function, 197

Reverse transformation, 41, 43
Revolving air conditioning test room, 95
Reynolds number, 68
Room air temperature, 169-173, 176-180

Shading coefficients, 93
Simulation, see System simulation
Slabs, unsteady state heat conduction,
   see Unsteady state heat
   conduction
Snell's law, 89
Sol-air temperature, 61, 74, 118
Solar altitude, 8, 10, 19, 23
Solar azimuth, 8, 13
Solar constant, 4
   hypothetical, 12
Solar energy, 205
Solar heat
   collector, 202-205
Solar heat—contd.
   gain, 116, 167
      cooling load associated with, 93-98
      cooling load weighting factors for, 98-101
      from glass windows, 85-120
         of different orientation, 90-93
         with external shading, 117-120
         with inside venetian blinds, 102-107
   standard, 91, 100
Solar heating system, 205-208
Solar position, 8
Solar radiation, 4-24, 61, 71, 74, 175, 202
   angle of incidence of, 91
   absorption, rejection and transmission for sheet
      glass, 85-90
   cloudy days, 20-24
   direct and diffuse components, 24
   declination angle, 8, 9
   diffuse, 14-17, 18, 20, 91, 117, 166
   direct, 12-13, 91, 117, 166
   direct normal, 10, 12, 15, 18
   extraterrestrial, 5, 7
   global, breaking down into direct and diffuse
      components, 17-20
   hour angle, 8
   incident, 112, 117
   intensity of, 4, 5, 9
   relationship generalized for cloudy conditions, 24
   through glass windows, 85, 162, 166
   heat gain from, 143
   total, 112
   total horizontal, 18, 19, 20, 23
   transmissivity of sheet glass, 86, 90
Solar spectral irradiance curve, 5
Solar spectrum, 5
   wavelength bands, 87
Solar time, 9
Solution function, 199
Square error matrix, 218
Stack effect, 152
   combination of wind and, 156-158

infiltration by, 152-156
Starting time control, 212-213
Stefan-Boltzmann's Law, 63
Storage load factor, 93-95, 100, 138
Sun-shade, 102, 112, 115, 117
Superposition principle, 161, 175
Surface film, 47
Surface heat flow, 34, 38, 72, 171
   matrix expression of, 44-49
Surface reflectance, 85
Surface temperature, 25, 34, 35, 39, 83
   excitation, 39, 42, 48, 49
   matrix expression of, 44-49
Suspended ceiling, 132
System model, 182-185
   for computer control, 209-211
System simulation, 181-208
   object of, 181
   use of, 181

Temperature
   difference, 197
   distribution, 104, 183, 197
   excitation, 47
   gradient, 25-30
Thermal systems, 181
Tilt angle, 13
Transfer function, 42, 45
Transfer matrix, 45, 46, 47
Transmissivity, 86, 88-90, 103
Troffers, performance of, 129-131

Unit function, 35, 50, 199
Unit triangle pulse, 48
Unsteady state heat conduction, 35
   factors contributing to, 25
   fundamental equation of, 26
   in flat wall, 39
   one-dimensional, 27
   partial differential equation, 27, 35
   through walls and slabs, 25-60
Urban environment, 1
Useful energy, 192

Venetian blinds, 107-112, 121
   absorptivity and transmissivity of, 103
   painted in light colour, 108
   thermal characteristics, 107-111

Wall
   as thermal system, 29
   unsteady state heat conduction through,
      see Unsteady state heat conduction
Waste heat, 200
Water vapour pressure, 68, 191
Weber-Fechner's law, 121
Weighting factors
   cooling load, 96-102, 140-146, 140, 160
   heat extraction, 170, 177, 187
   relating incident solar radiation into shade assembly

to heat discharged from shade surface, 118
    room air temperature, 174, 175
Weighting function, 37
Wind
  infiltration by, 149
  effects, combination of stack and, 156-158
  pressure, 149, 168
    coefficient, 149, 168
  speed, 61, 75, 77, 80
  velocity, 157, 169
Windows
  solar heat gain from, 85-120
  solar radiation through, 143, 160

Z-transfer factors, 59
Z-transfer function, 59
Z-transform, 57-60

About the author

Ken-ichi Kimura

Born in 1933, Professor Kimura graduated Waseda University in Tokyo with B. Arch., M. Sc. and D. Eng. He has taught architectural environment at Department of Architecture, Waseda University for 43 years and retired in 1999 to become Professor Emeritus. His work covers from fundamental theories in architectural environment, vernacular architecture to basic issues on building services such as thermal comfort, indoor air quality and visual comfort. He joined in the solar energy project at Massachusetts Institute of Technology 1960-62 and Division of Building Research, National Research Council in Ottawa 1967-69. Professor Kimura was President of Society of Heating, Air Conditioning and Sanitary Engineering of Japan 1994-96 and President of Japan Solar Energy Society 1984-86. He has been active in various domestic and international academic societies. Besides Fellow and Life Member of ASHRAE, he has honoured to receive F. Daniels Award of International Solar Energy Society, PLEA Award and technical paper awards from Architectural Institute of Japan .and SHASE. As an environmental architect, Kimura designed Kimura Solar house and several solar houses as well as a design consultant for several solar building projects. He wrote numerous research papers and books on architectural environment and building services.

Scientific Basis of Air Conditioning
Author: Ken-ichi Kimura

First Edition: 1977; ISBN 0 85334 732 8
Publisher: Applied Science Publishers, London

Revised Edition: 2010
Publisher: Building Research Institute, Tsukuba, Ibaraki, Japan

Second Edition: 2016; ISBN 978-4-9907042-3-0
Publisher: International Research Institute on Human Environment,
13-21 Enoki-cho, Tokorozawa, Saitama 359-1104 Japan
Downloadable: http://www.irihe.org or http://www.f.waseda.jp/kkimura/

© Ken-ichi Kimura
Printed in Japan

www.ingramcontent.com/pod-product-compliance
Lightning Source LLC
Chambersburg PA
CBHW080548230426
43663CB00015B/2752